THE MIDAS FLESH VOLUME TWO

This Book Belongs To:

BOOM! BOX

THE MIDAS FLESH Volume Two, June 2015. Published by BOOM!
Box, a division of Boom Entertainment, Inc. The Midas Flesh is ™ & © 2015
Ryan North. Originally published in single magazine form as THE MIDAS
FLESH No. 5-8. ™ & © 2014 Ryan North. All rights reserved. BOOM! Box™
and the BOOM! Box logo are trademarks of Boom Entertainment, Inc.,
registered in various countries and categories. All characters, events, and
institutions depicted herein are fictional. Any similarity between any of the
names, characters, persons, events, and/or institutions in this publication to
actual names, characters, and persons, whether living or dead, events, and/
or institutions is unintended and purely coincidental. BOOM! Studios does not
read or accept unsolicited submissions of ideas, stories, or artwork.

A catalog record of this book is available from OCLC and from the BOOM!
Studios website, www.boom-studios.com, on the Librarians Page.

BOOM! Studios, 5670 Wilshire Boulevard, Suite 450, Los Angeles, CA
90036-5679. Printed in China. First Printing.

ISBN: 978-1-60886-727-1 , eISBN: 978-1-61398-398-0

BOOM! BOX™

"I THINK I'D LIKE EVERYTHING I TOUCH TO TURN TO GOLD."

CREATED & WRITTEN BY
RYAN NORTH

ILLUSTRATED BY
**SHELLI PAROLINE
& BRADEN LAMB**

LETTERED BY **STEVE WANDS**
COVER BY **SAM BOSMA**

DESIGNER **SCOTT NEWMAN**
ASSOCIATE EDITOR **JASMINE AMIRI**
EDITOR **SHANNON WATTERS**

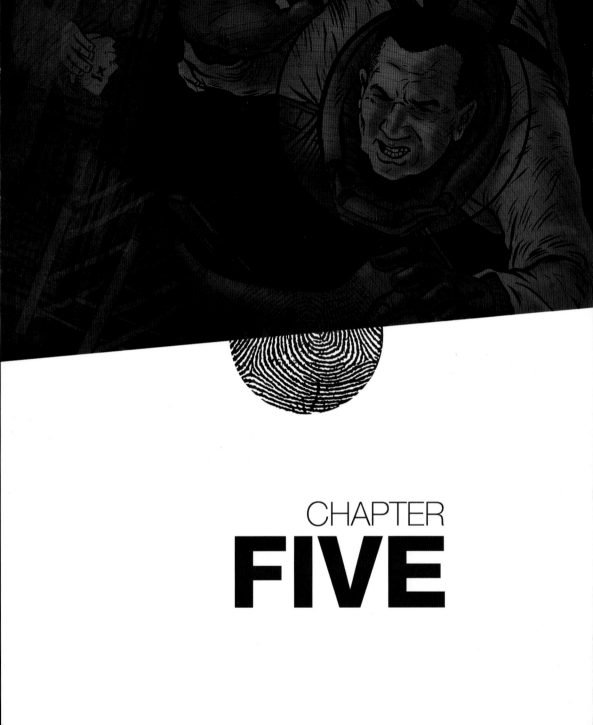

CHAPTER
FIVE

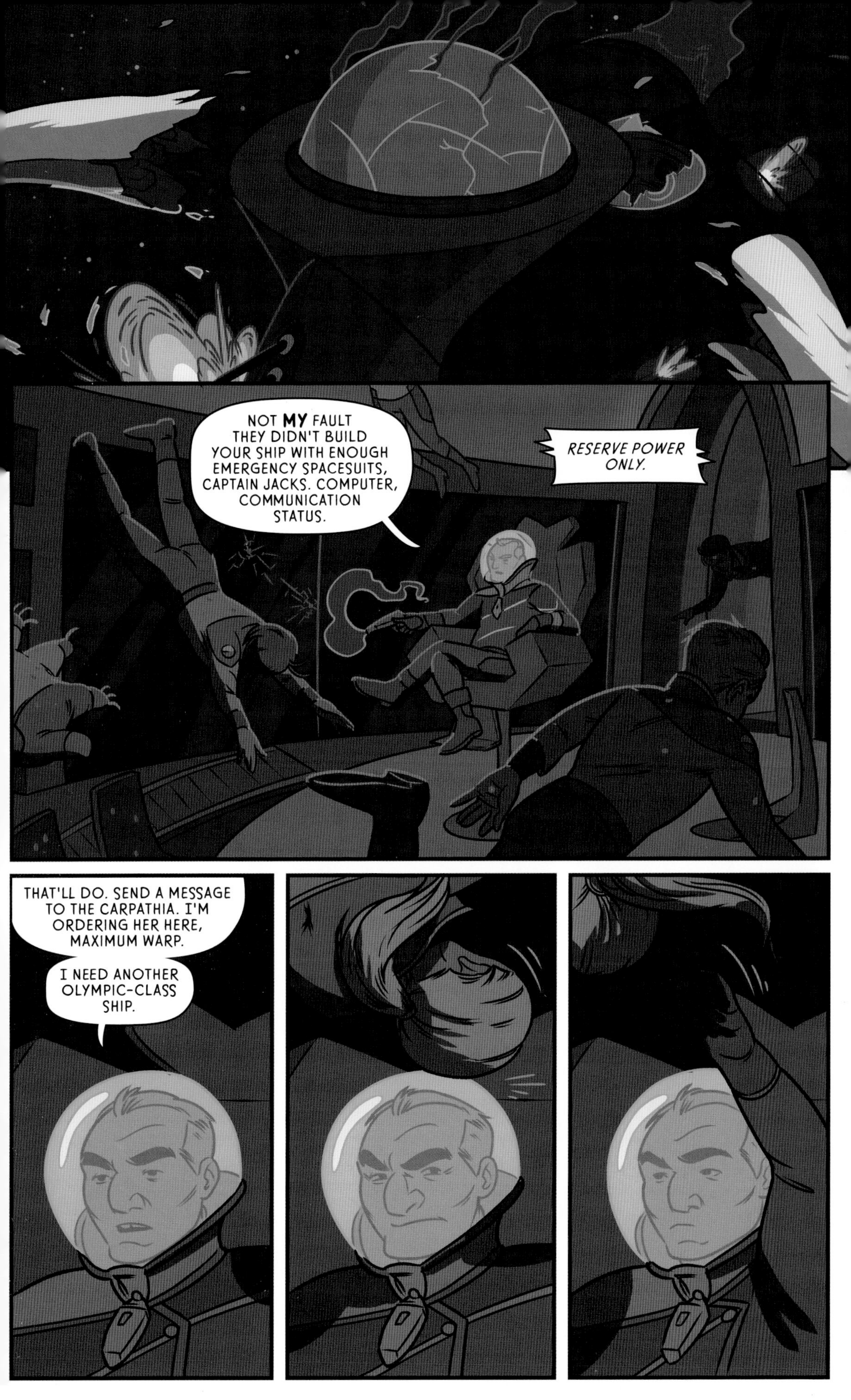
NOT MY FAULT THEY DIDN'T BUILD YOUR SHIP WITH ENOUGH EMERGENCY SPACESUITS, CAPTAIN JACKS. COMPUTER, COMMUNICATION STATUS.
RESERVE POWER ONLY.
THAT'LL DO. SEND A MESSAGE TO THE CARPATHIA. I'M ORDERING HER HERE, MAXIMUM WARP.
I NEED ANOTHER OLYMPIC-CLASS SHIP.

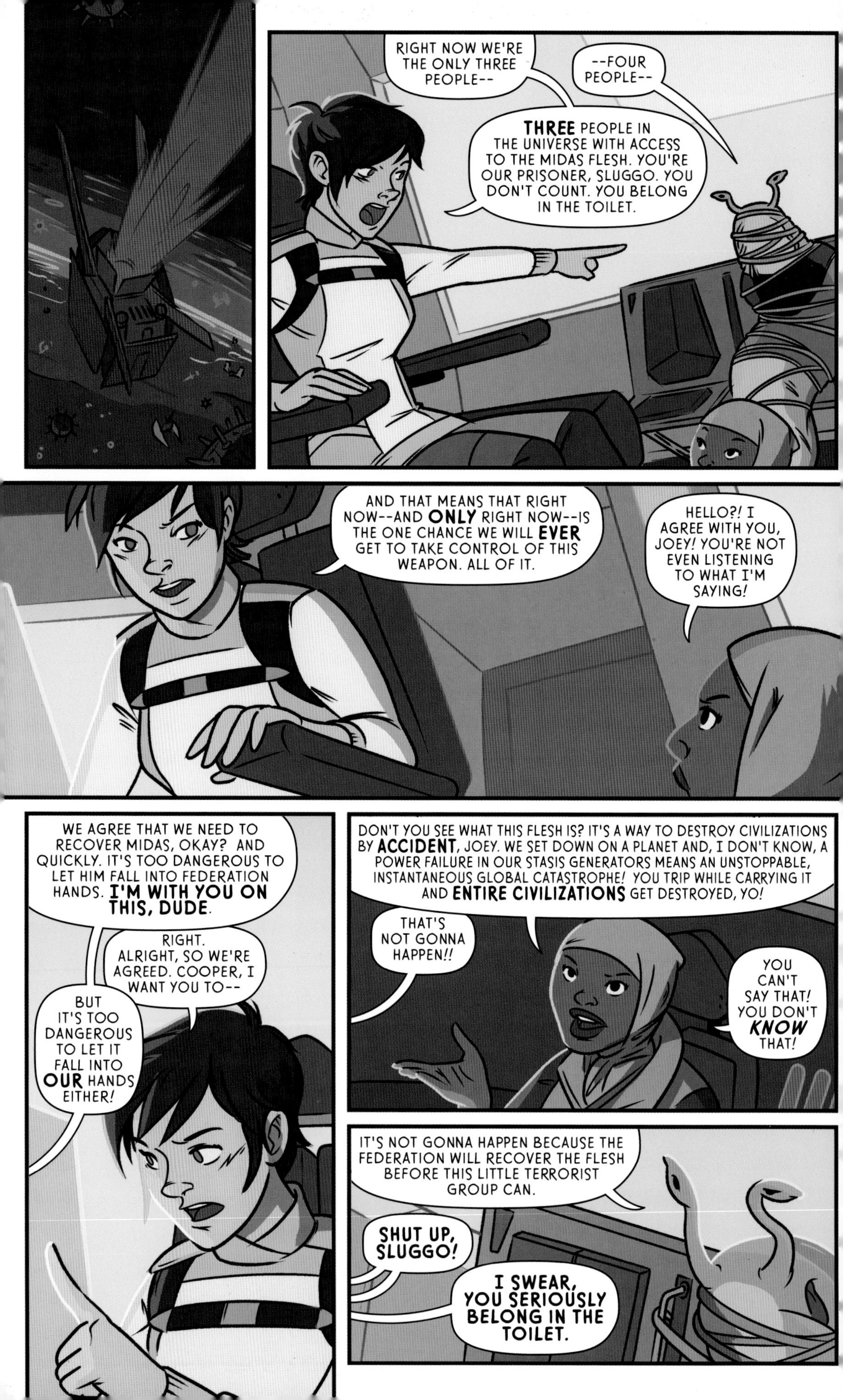

RIGHT NOW WE'RE THE ONLY THREE PEOPLE--
--FOUR PEOPLE--
THREE PEOPLE IN THE UNIVERSE WITH ACCESS TO THE MIDAS FLESH. YOU'RE OUR PRISONER, SLUGGO. YOU DON'T COUNT. YOU BELONG IN THE TOILET.
AND THAT MEANS THAT RIGHT NOW--AND **ONLY** RIGHT NOW--IS THE ONE CHANCE WE WILL **EVER** GET TO TAKE CONTROL OF THIS WEAPON. ALL OF IT.
HELLO?! I AGREE WITH YOU, JOEY! YOU'RE NOT EVEN LISTENING TO WHAT I'M SAYING!
WE AGREE THAT WE NEED TO RECOVER MIDAS, OKAY? AND QUICKLY. IT'S TOO DANGEROUS TO LET HIM FALL INTO FEDERATION HANDS. **I'M WITH YOU ON THIS, DUDE**.
RIGHT. ALRIGHT, SO WE'RE AGREED. COOPER, I WANT YOU TO--
BUT IT'S TOO DANGEROUS TO LET IT FALL INTO **OUR** HANDS EITHER!
DON'T YOU SEE WHAT THIS FLESH IS? IT'S A WAY TO DESTROY CIVILIZATIONS BY **ACCIDENT**, JOEY. WE SET DOWN ON A PLANET AND, I DON'T KNOW, A POWER FAILURE IN OUR STASIS GENERATORS MEANS AN UNSTOPPABLE, INSTANTANEOUS GLOBAL CATASTROPHE! YOU TRIP WHILE CARRYING IT AND **ENTIRE CIVILIZATIONS** GET DESTROYED, YO!
THAT'S NOT GONNA HAPPEN!!
YOU CAN'T SAY THAT! YOU DON'T ***KNOW*** THAT!
IT'S NOT GONNA HAPPEN BECAUSE THE FEDERATION WILL RECOVER THE FLESH BEFORE THIS LITTLE TERRORIST GROUP CAN.
SHUT UP, SLUGGO!
I SWEAR, YOU SERIOUSLY BELONG IN THE TOILET.

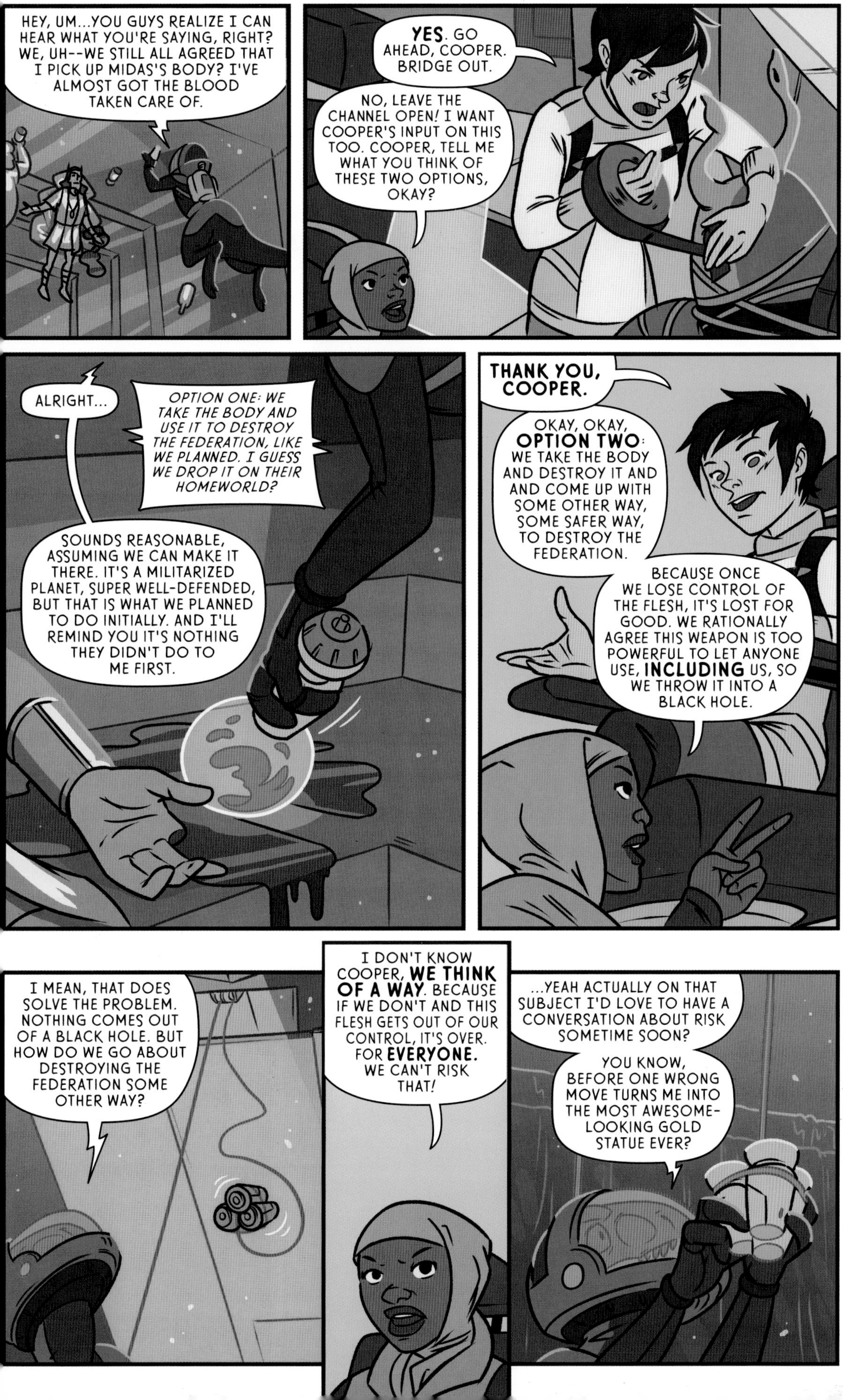
HEY, UM...YOU GUYS REALIZE I CAN HEAR WHAT YOU'RE SAYING, RIGHT? WE, UH--WE STILL ALL AGREED THAT I PICK UP MIDAS'S BODY? I'VE ALMOST GOT THE BLOOD TAKEN CARE OF.
YES. GO AHEAD, COOPER. BRIDGE OUT.
NO, LEAVE THE CHANNEL OPEN! I WANT COOPER'S INPUT ON THIS TOO. COOPER, TELL ME WHAT YOU THINK OF THESE TWO OPTIONS, OKAY?
ALRIGHT...
OPTION ONE: WE TAKE THE BODY AND USE IT TO DESTROY THE FEDERATION, LIKE WE PLANNED. I GUESS WE DROP IT ON THEIR HOMEWORLD?
SOUNDS REASONABLE, ASSUMING WE CAN MAKE IT THERE. IT'S A MILITARIZED PLANET, SUPER WELL-DEFENDED, BUT THAT IS WHAT WE PLANNED TO DO INITIALLY. AND I'LL REMIND YOU IT'S NOTHING THEY DIDN'T DO TO ME FIRST.
THANK YOU, COOPER.
OKAY, OKAY, OPTION TWO: WE TAKE THE BODY AND DESTROY IT AND AND COME UP WITH SOME OTHER WAY, SOME SAFER WAY, TO DESTROY THE FEDERATION.
BECAUSE ONCE WE LOSE CONTROL OF THE FLESH, IT'S LOST FOR GOOD. WE RATIONALLY AGREE THIS WEAPON IS TOO POWERFUL TO LET ANYONE USE, INCLUDING US, SO WE THROW IT INTO A BLACK HOLE.
I MEAN, THAT DOES SOLVE THE PROBLEM. NOTHING COMES OUT OF A BLACK HOLE. BUT HOW DO WE GO ABOUT DESTROYING THE FEDERATION SOME OTHER WAY?
I DON'T KNOW COOPER, WE THINK OF A WAY. BECAUSE IF WE DON'T AND THIS FLESH GETS OUT OF OUR CONTROL, IT'S OVER. FOR EVERYONE. WE CAN'T RISK THAT!
...YEAH ACTUALLY ON THAT SUBJECT I'D LOVE TO HAVE A CONVERSATION ABOUT RISK SOMETIME SOON?
YOU KNOW, BEFORE ONE WRONG MOVE TURNS ME INTO THE MOST AWESOME-LOOKING GOLD STATUE EVER?

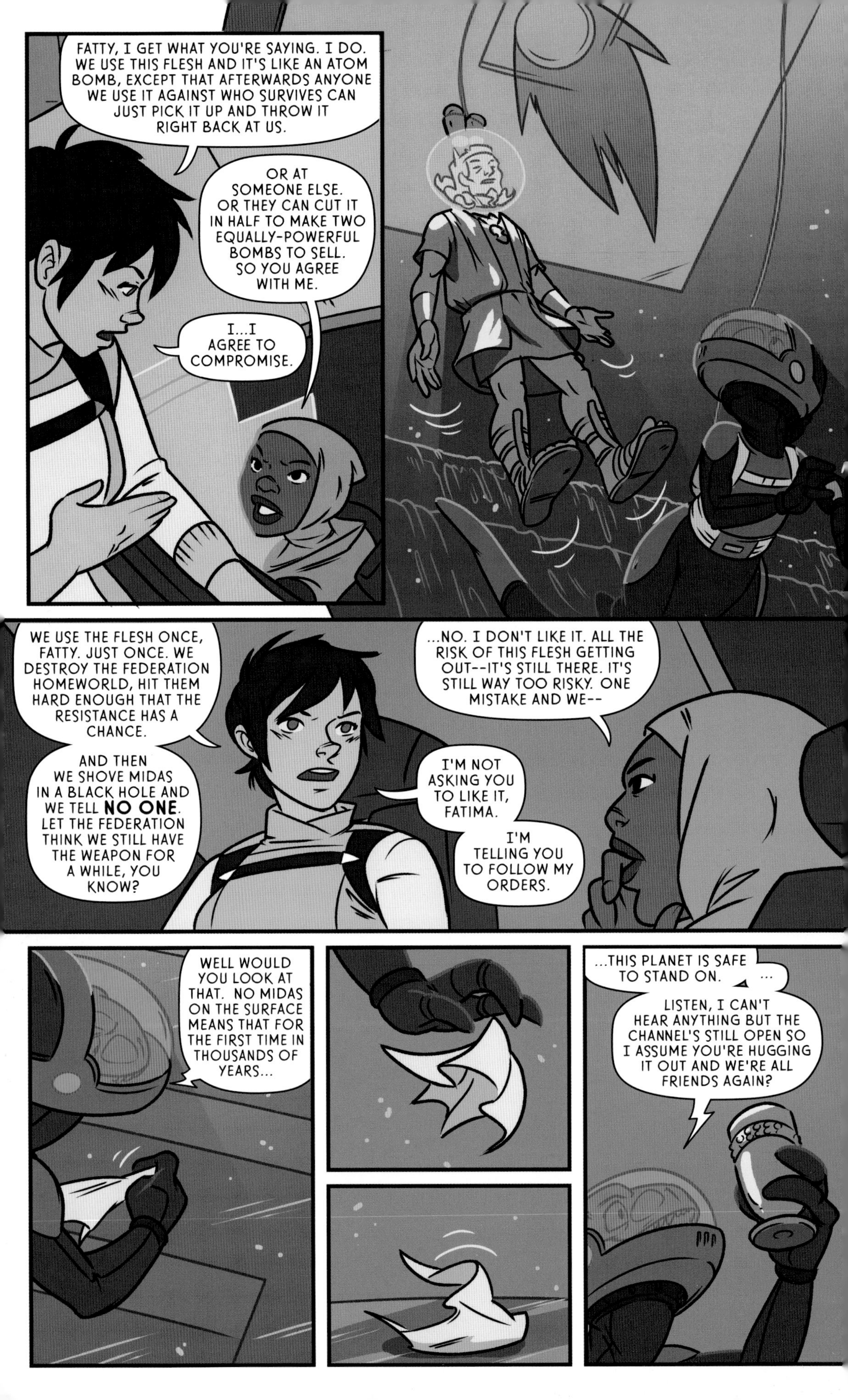
FATTY, I GET WHAT YOU'RE SAYING. I DO. WE USE THIS FLESH AND IT'S LIKE AN ATOM BOMB, EXCEPT THAT AFTERWARDS ANYONE WE USE IT AGAINST WHO SURVIVES CAN JUST PICK IT UP AND THROW IT RIGHT BACK AT US.
OR AT SOMEONE ELSE. OR THEY CAN CUT IT IN HALF TO MAKE TWO EQUALLY-POWERFUL BOMBS TO SELL. SO YOU AGREE WITH ME.
I...I AGREE TO COMPROMISE.
WE USE THE FLESH ONCE, FATTY. JUST ONCE. WE DESTROY THE FEDERATION HOMEWORLD, HIT THEM HARD ENOUGH THAT THE RESISTANCE HAS A CHANCE.
AND THEN WE SHOVE MIDAS IN A BLACK HOLE AND WE TELL **NO ONE**. LET THE FEDERATION THINK WE STILL HAVE THE WEAPON FOR A WHILE, YOU KNOW?
...NO. I DON'T LIKE IT. ALL THE RISK OF THIS FLESH GETTING OUT--IT'S STILL THERE. IT'S STILL WAY TOO RISKY. ONE MISTAKE AND WE--
I'M NOT ASKING YOU TO LIKE IT, FATIMA.
I'M TELLING YOU TO FOLLOW MY ORDERS.
WELL WOULD YOU LOOK AT THAT. NO MIDAS ON THE SURFACE MEANS THAT FOR THE FIRST TIME IN THOUSANDS OF YEARS...
...THIS PLANET IS SAFE TO STAND ON.
...
LISTEN, I CAN'T HEAR ANYTHING BUT THE CHANNEL'S STILL OPEN SO I ASSUME YOU'RE HUGGING IT OUT AND WE'RE ALL FRIENDS AGAIN?

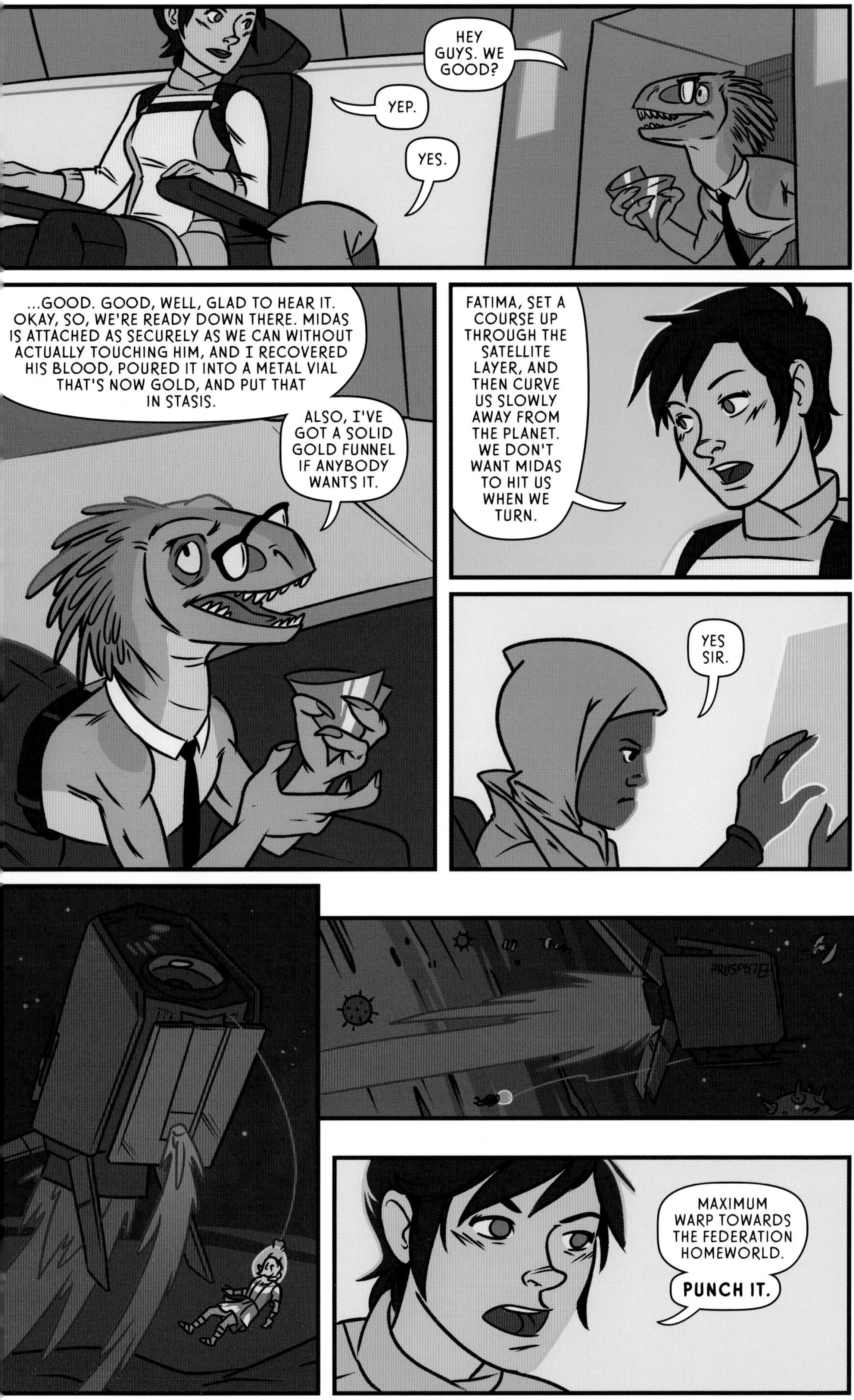
HEY GUYS. WE GOOD?
YEP.
YES.
...GOOD. GOOD, WELL, GLAD TO HEAR IT. OKAY, SO, WE'RE READY DOWN THERE. MIDAS IS ATTACHED AS SECURELY AS WE CAN WITHOUT ACTUALLY TOUCHING HIM, AND I RECOVERED HIS BLOOD, POURED IT INTO A METAL VIAL THAT'S NOW GOLD, AND PUT THAT IN STASIS.
ALSO, I'VE GOT A SOLID GOLD FUNNEL IF ANYBODY WANTS IT.
FATIMA, SET A COURSE UP THROUGH THE SATELLITE LAYER, AND THEN CURVE US SLOWLY AWAY FROM THE PLANET. WE DON'T WANT MIDAS TO HIT US WHEN WE TURN.
YES SIR.
MAXIMUM WARP TOWARDS THE FEDERATION HOMEWORLD.
PUNCH IT.

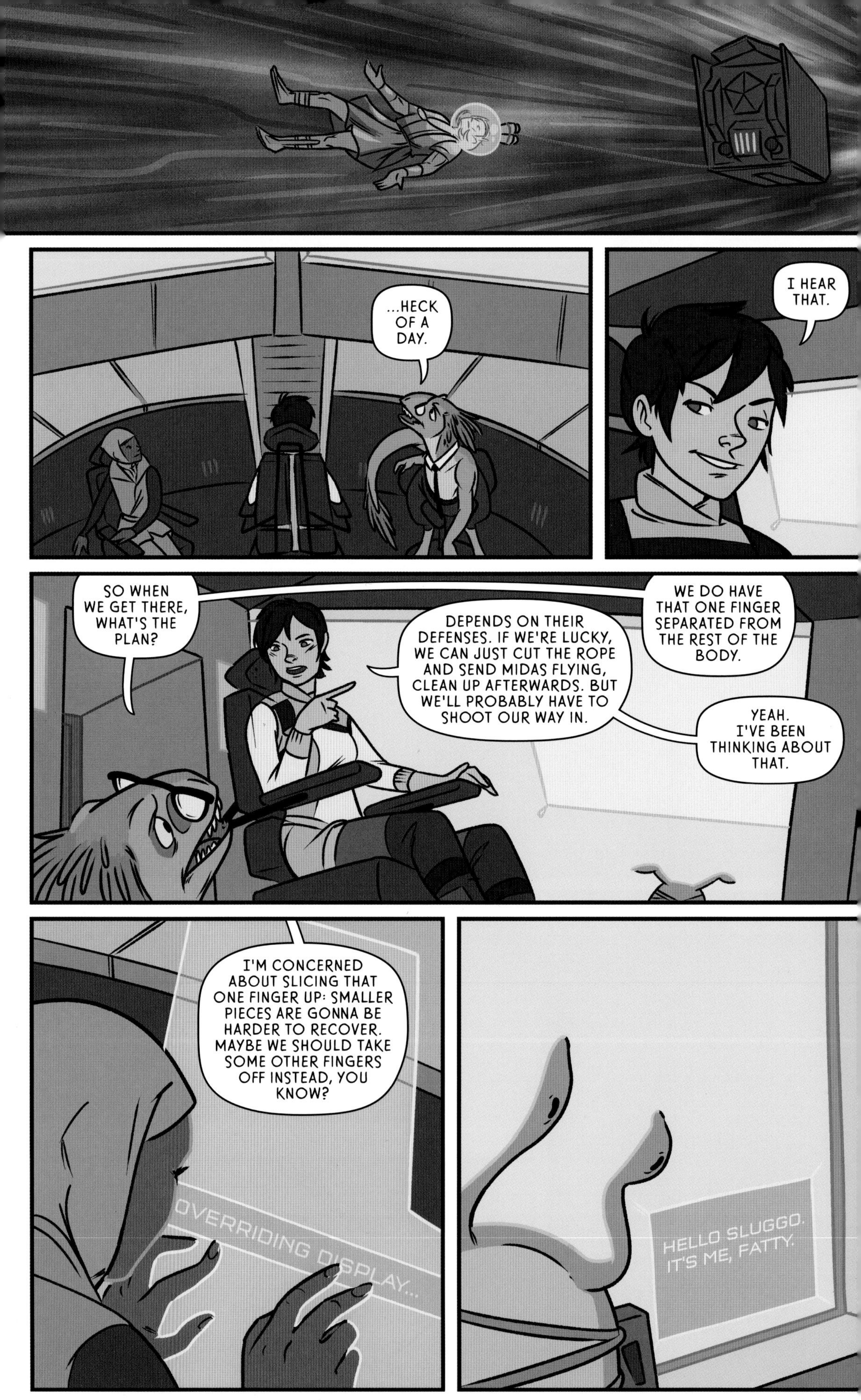
...HECK OF A DAY.
I HEAR THAT.
SO WHEN WE GET THERE, WHAT'S THE PLAN?
DEPENDS ON THEIR DEFENSES. IF WE'RE LUCKY, WE CAN JUST CUT THE ROPE AND SEND MIDAS FLYING, CLEAN UP AFTERWARDS. BUT WE'LL PROBABLY HAVE TO SHOOT OUR WAY IN.
WE DO HAVE THAT ONE FINGER SEPARATED FROM THE REST OF THE BODY.
YEAH. I'VE BEEN THINKING ABOUT THAT.
I'M CONCERNED ABOUT SLICING THAT ONE FINGER UP: SMALLER PIECES ARE GONNA BE HARDER TO RECOVER. MAYBE WE SHOULD TAKE SOME OTHER FINGERS OFF INSTEAD, YOU KNOW?
OVERRIDING DISPLAY...
HELLO SLUGGO. IT'S ME, FATTY.

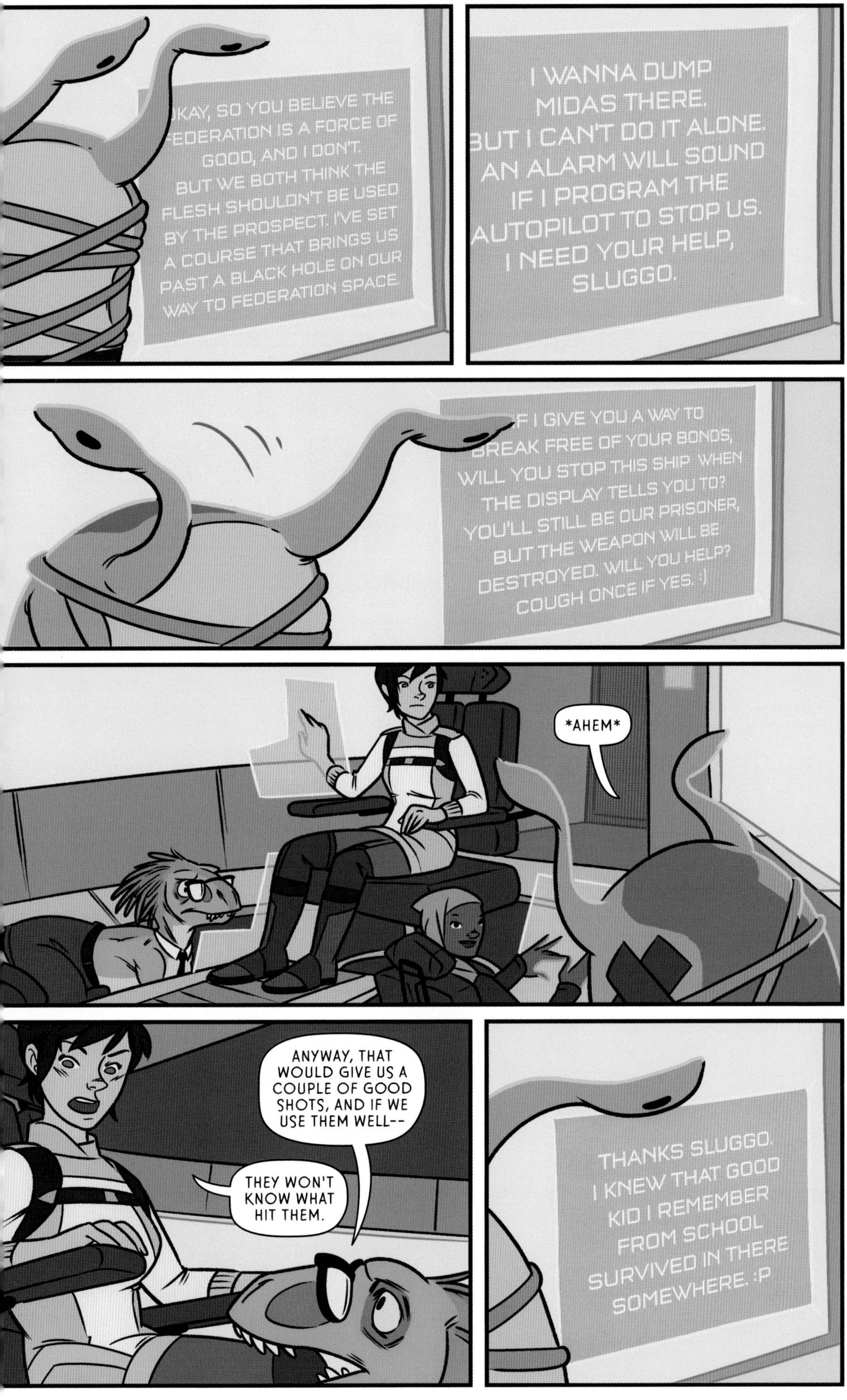
OKAY, SO YOU BELIEVE THE FEDERATION IS A FORCE OF GOOD, AND I DON'T. BUT WE BOTH THINK THE FLESH SHOULDN'T BE USED BY THE PROSPECT. I'VE SET A COURSE THAT BRINGS US PAST A BLACK HOLE ON OUR WAY TO FEDERATION SPACE.
I WANNA DUMP MIDAS THERE. BUT I CAN'T DO IT ALONE. AN ALARM WILL SOUND IF I PROGRAM THE AUTOPILOT TO STOP US. I NEED YOUR HELP, SLUGGO.
IF I GIVE YOU A WAY TO BREAK FREE OF YOUR BONDS, WILL YOU STOP THIS SHIP WHEN THE DISPLAY TELLS YOU TO? YOU'LL STILL BE OUR PRISONER, BUT THE WEAPON WILL BE DESTROYED. WILL YOU HELP? COUGH ONCE IF YES. :)
AHEM
ANYWAY, THAT WOULD GIVE US A COUPLE OF GOOD SHOTS, AND IF WE USE THEM WELL--
THEY WON'T KNOW WHAT HIT THEM.
THANKS SLUGGO. I KNEW THAT GOOD KID I REMEMBER FROM SCHOOL SURVIVED IN THERE SOMEWHERE. :P

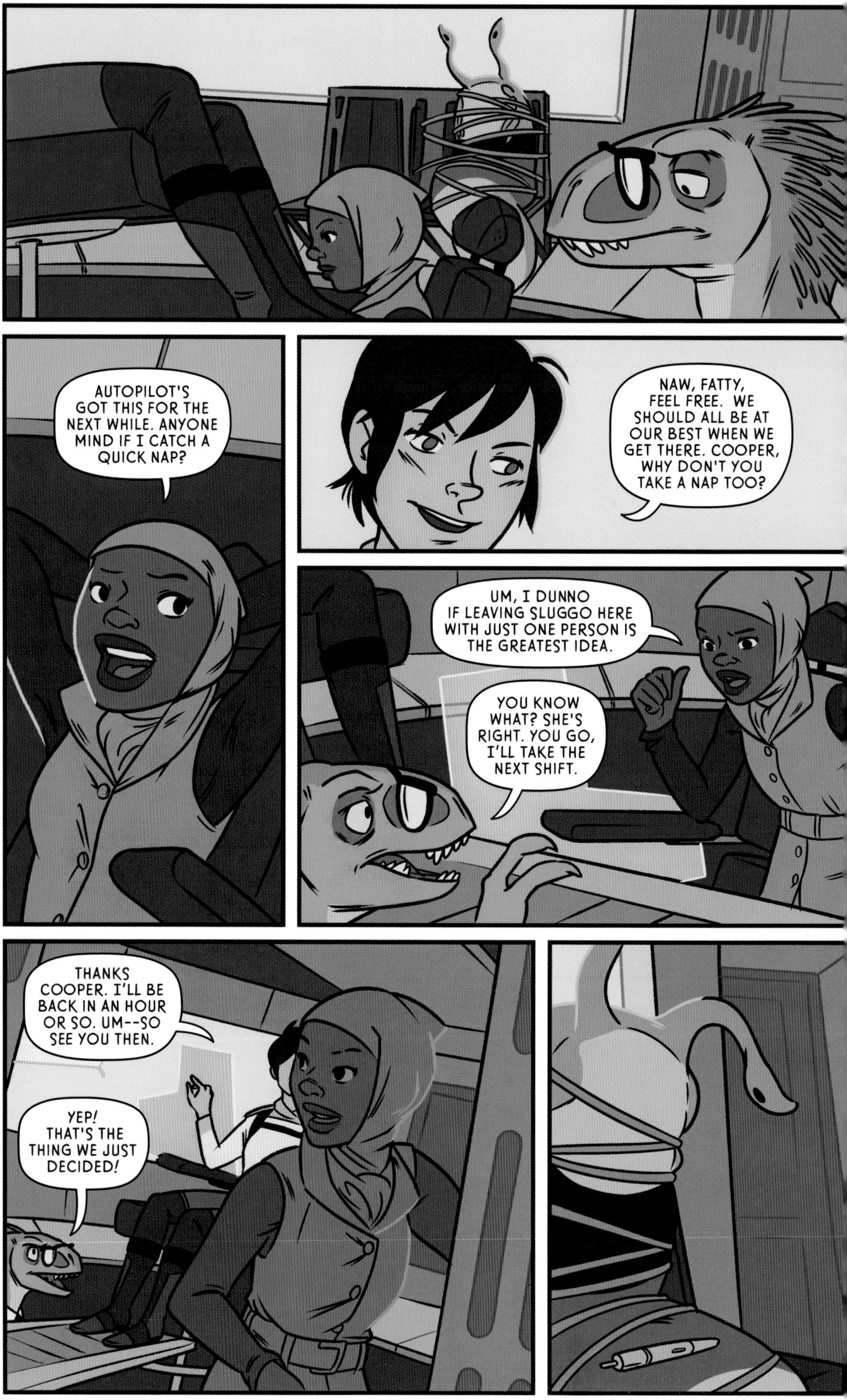
AUTOPILOT'S GOT THIS FOR THE NEXT WHILE. ANYONE MIND IF I CATCH A QUICK NAP?
NAW, FATTY, FEEL FREE. WE SHOULD ALL BE AT OUR BEST WHEN WE GET THERE. COOPER, WHY DON'T YOU TAKE A NAP TOO?
UM, I DUNNO IF LEAVING SLUGGO HERE WITH JUST ONE PERSON IS THE GREATEST IDEA.
YOU KNOW WHAT? SHE'S RIGHT. YOU GO, I'LL TAKE THE NEXT SHIFT.
THANKS COOPER. I'LL BE BACK IN AN HOUR OR SO. UM--SO SEE YOU THEN.
YEP! THAT'S THE THING WE JUST DECIDED!

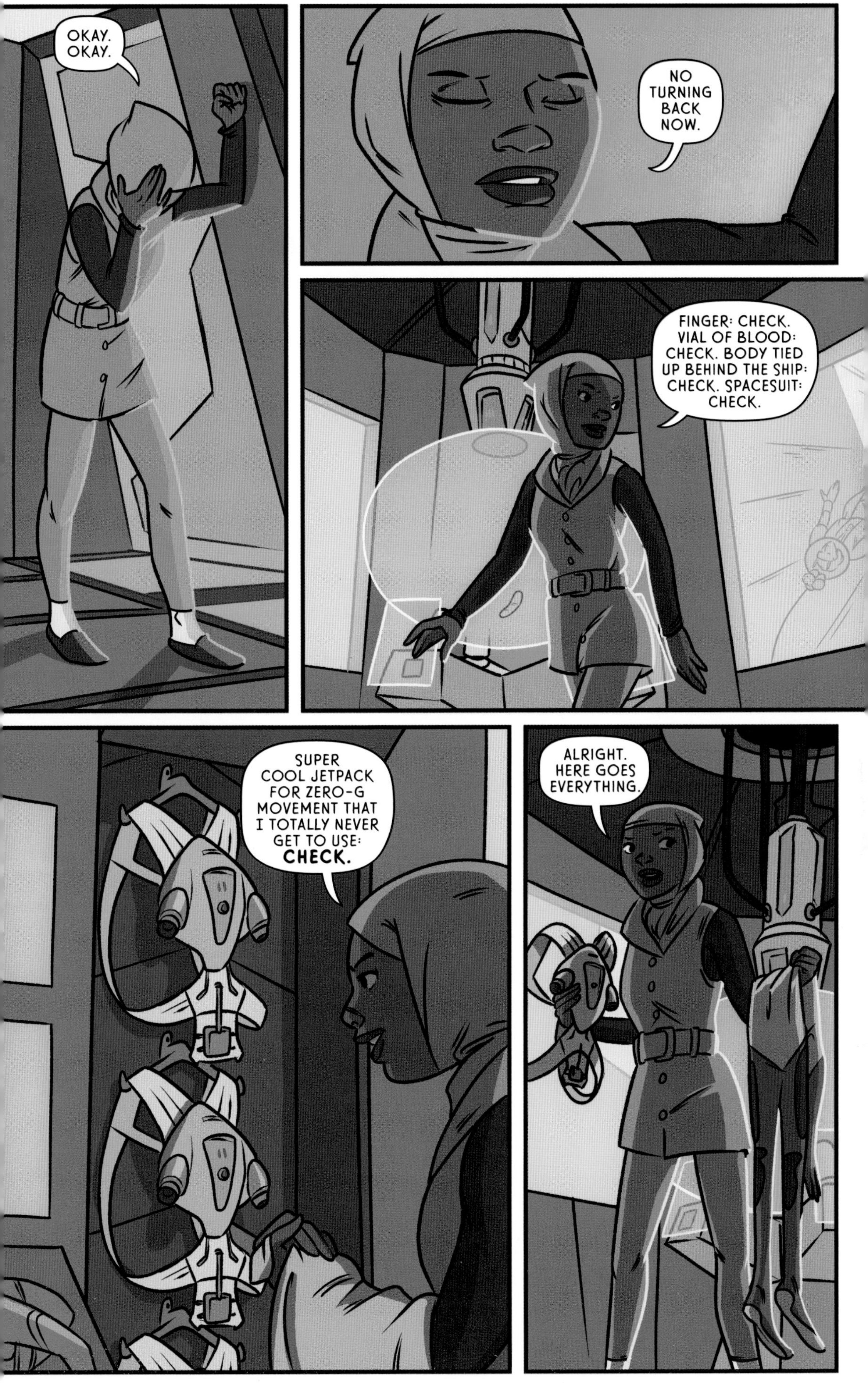
OKAY. OKAY.
NO TURNING BACK NOW.
FINGER: CHECK. VIAL OF BLOOD: CHECK. BODY TIED UP BEHIND THE SHIP: CHECK. SPACESUIT: CHECK.
SUPER COOL JETPACK FOR ZERO-G MOVEMENT THAT I TOTALLY NEVER GET TO USE: **CHECK.**
ALRIGHT. HERE GOES EVERYTHING.

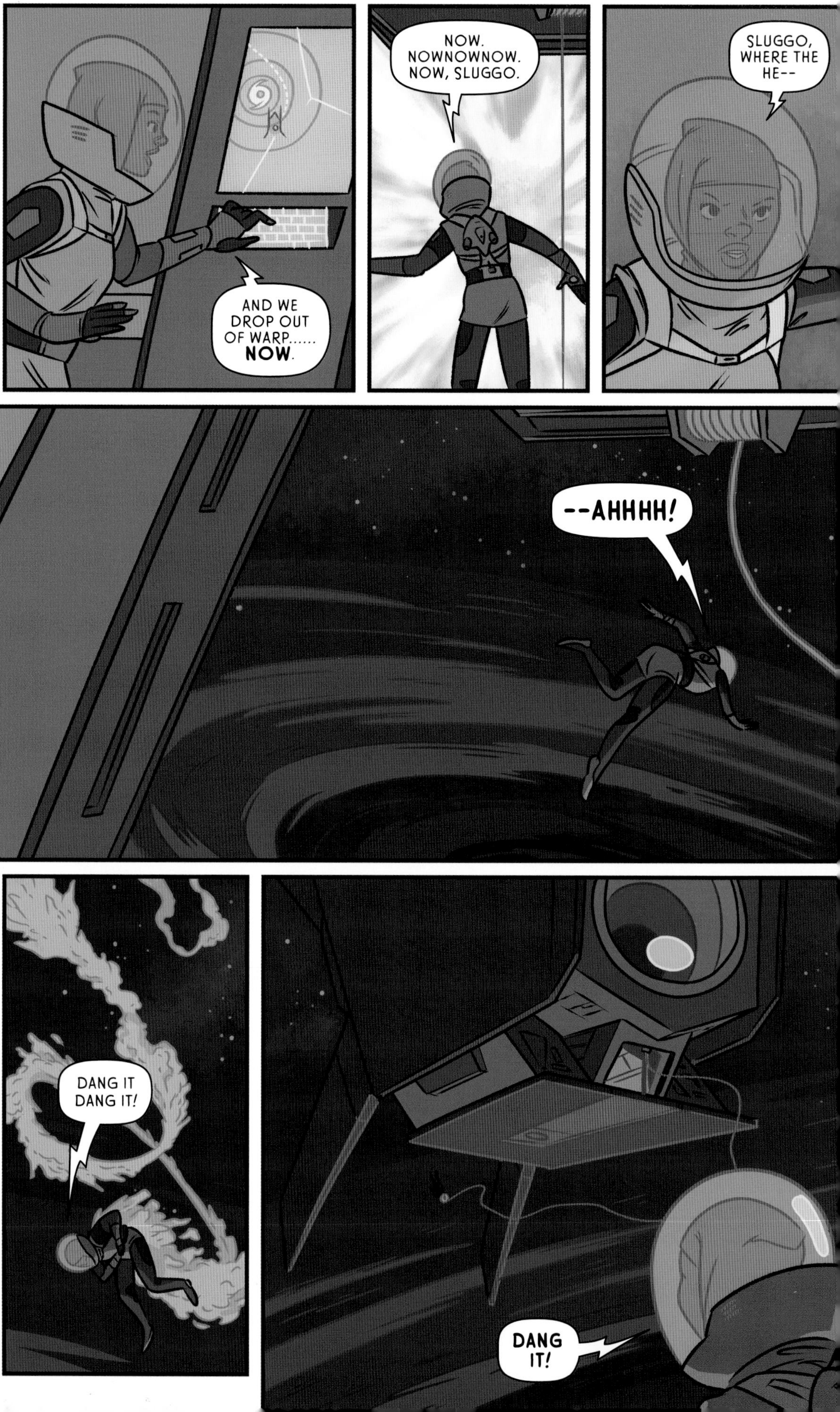
AND WE DROP OUT OF WARP...... **NOW**.
NOW. NOWNOWNOW. NOW, SLUGGO.
SLUGGO, WHERE THE HE--
--AHHHH!
DANG IT DANG IT!
DANG IT!

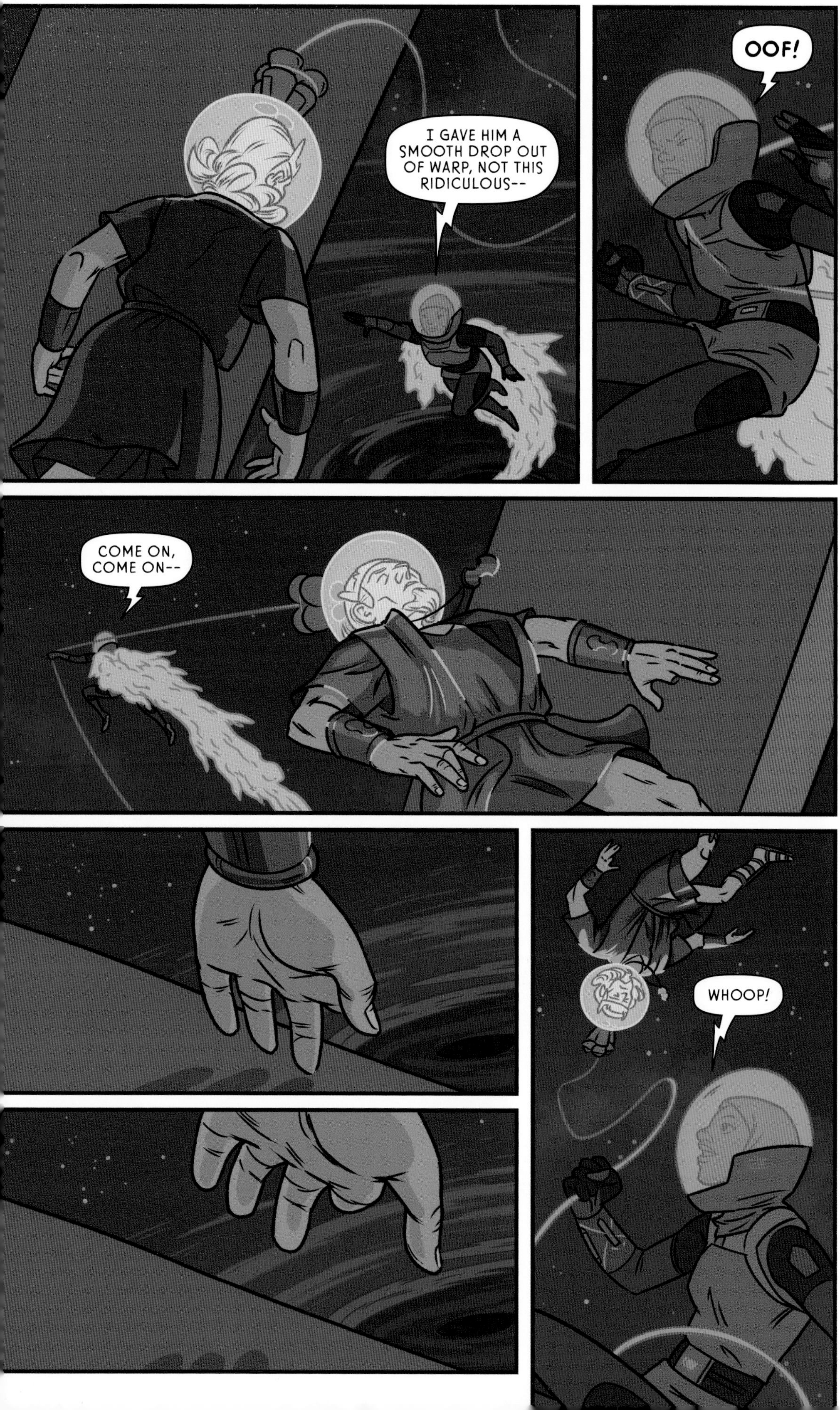
I GAVE HIM A SMOOTH DROP OUT OF WARP, NOT THIS RIDICULOUS--
OOF!
COME ON, COME ON--
WHOOP!

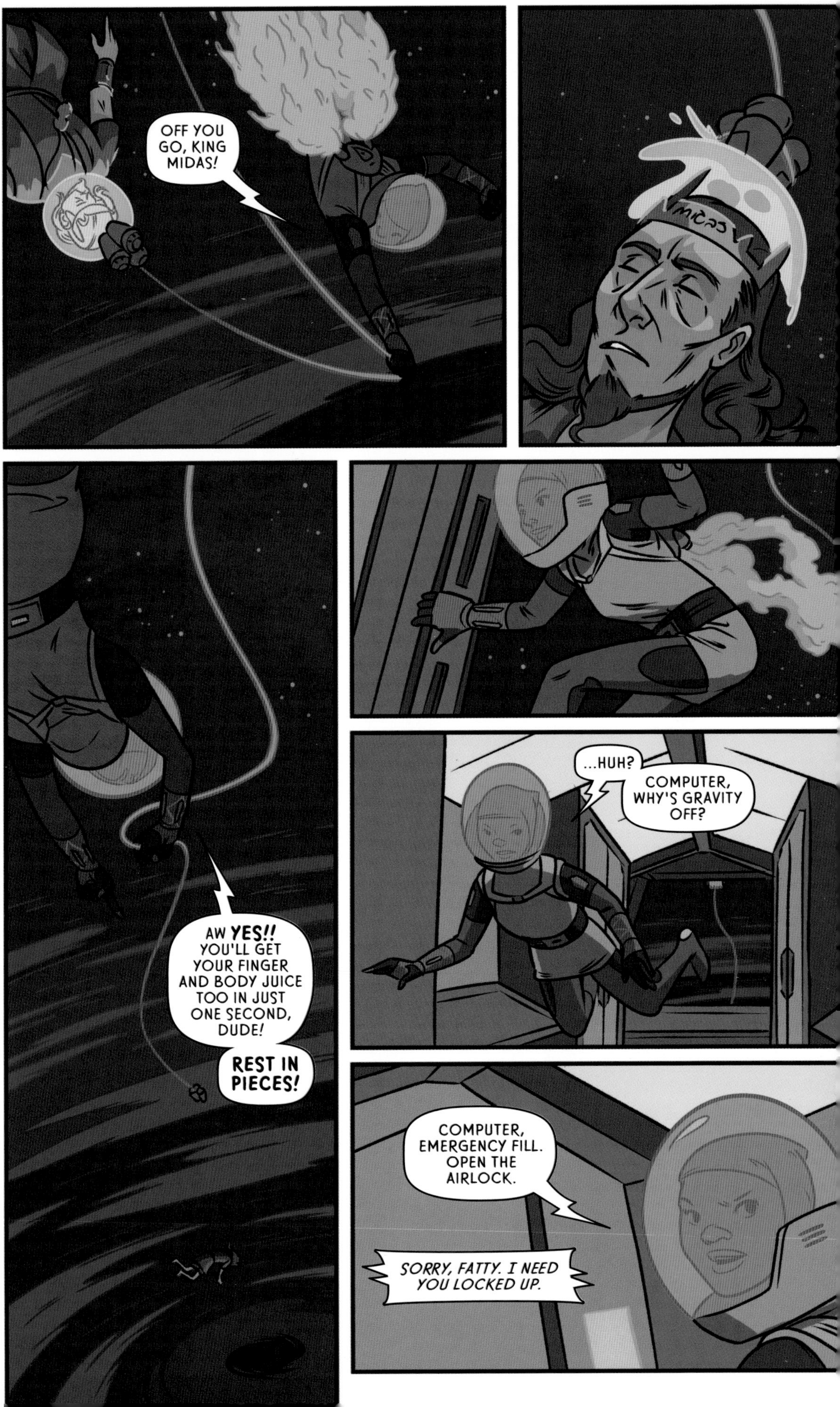
OFF YOU GO, KING MIDAS!
MIDAS
AW YES!! YOU'LL GET YOUR FINGER AND BODY JUICE TOO IN JUST ONE SECOND, DUDE!
REST IN PIECES!
...HUH?
COMPUTER, WHY'S GRAVITY OFF?
COMPUTER, EMERGENCY FILL. OPEN THE AIRLOCK.
SORRY, FATTY. I NEED YOU LOCKED UP.

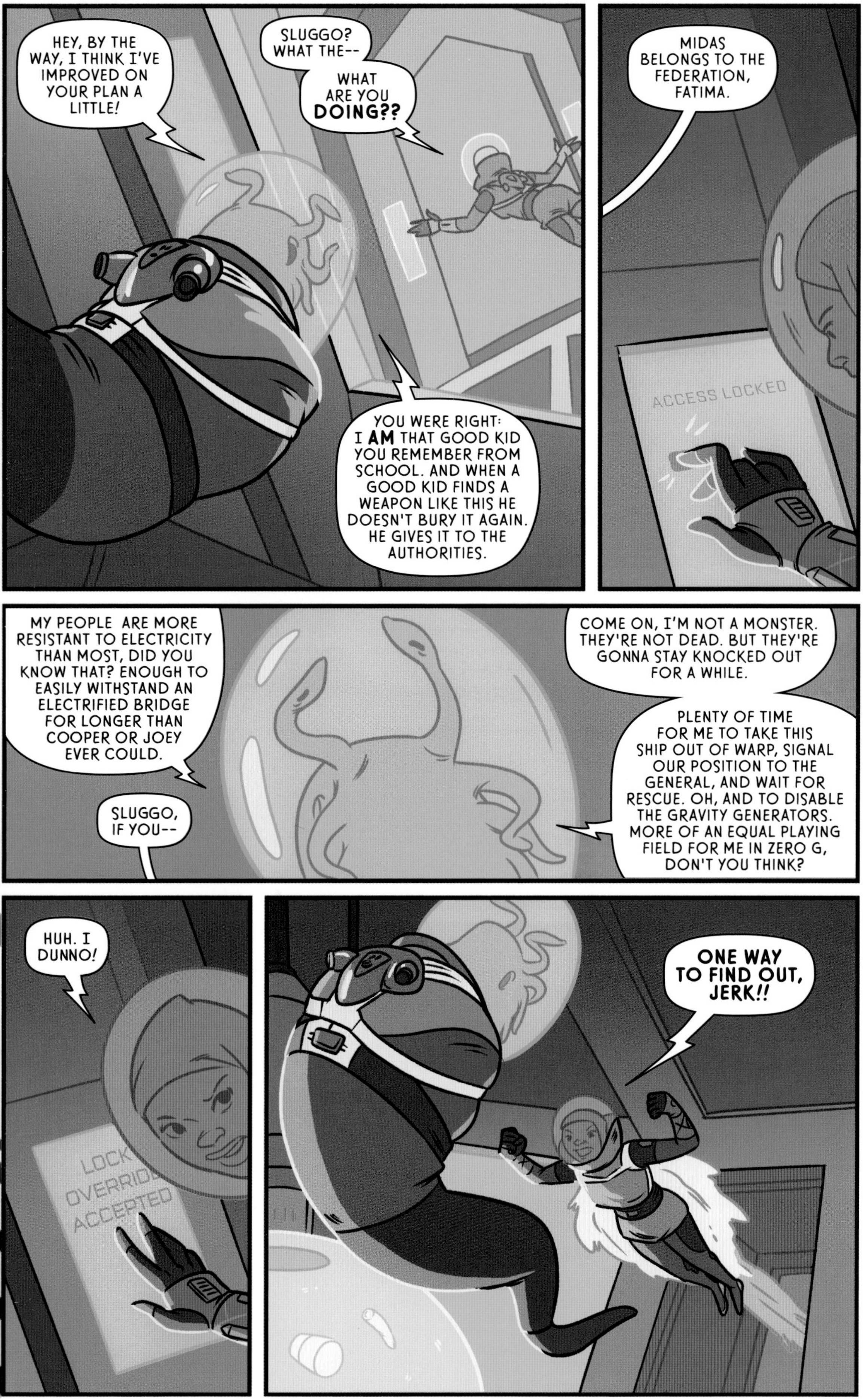
HEY, BY THE WAY, I THINK I'VE IMPROVED ON YOUR PLAN A LITTLE!
SLUGGO? WHAT THE--
WHAT ARE YOU **DOING??**
YOU WERE RIGHT: I **AM** THAT GOOD KID YOU REMEMBER FROM SCHOOL. AND WHEN A GOOD KID FINDS A WEAPON LIKE THIS HE DOESN'T BURY IT AGAIN. HE GIVES IT TO THE AUTHORITIES.
MIDAS BELONGS TO THE FEDERATION, FATIMA.
ACCESS LOCKED
MY PEOPLE ARE MORE RESISTANT TO ELECTRICITY THAN MOST, DID YOU KNOW THAT? ENOUGH TO EASILY WITHSTAND AN ELECTRIFIED BRIDGE FOR LONGER THAN COOPER OR JOEY EVER COULD.
SLUGGO, IF YOU--
COME ON, I'M NOT A MONSTER. THEY'RE NOT DEAD. BUT THEY'RE GONNA STAY KNOCKED OUT FOR A WHILE.
PLENTY OF TIME FOR ME TO TAKE THIS SHIP OUT OF WARP, SIGNAL OUR POSITION TO THE GENERAL, AND WAIT FOR RESCUE. OH, AND TO DISABLE THE GRAVITY GENERATORS. MORE OF AN EQUAL PLAYING FIELD FOR ME IN ZERO G, DON'T YOU THINK?
HUH. I DUNNO!
ONE WAY TO FIND OUT, JERK!!

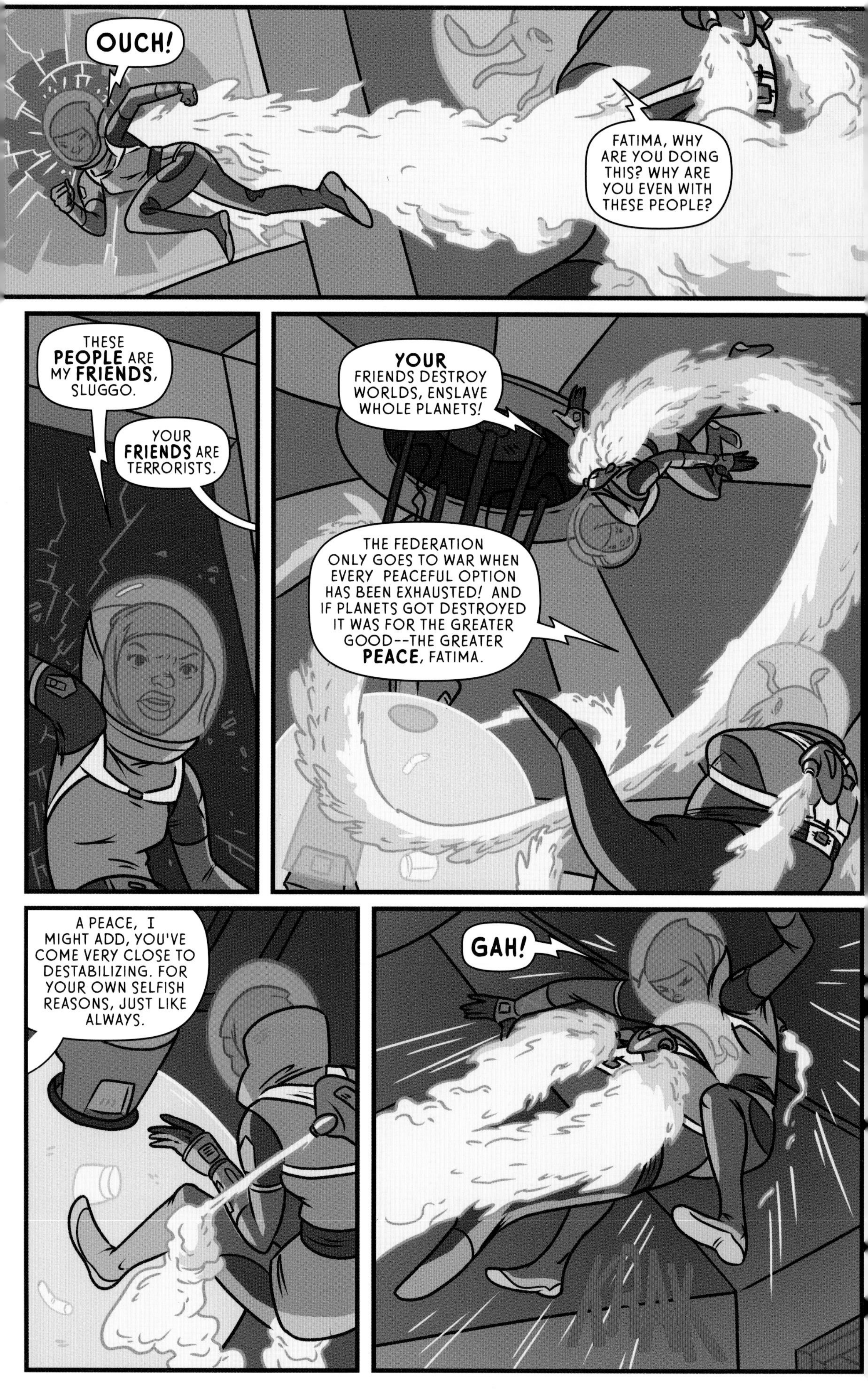
OUCH!
FATIMA, WHY ARE YOU DOING THIS? WHY ARE YOU EVEN WITH THESE PEOPLE?
THESE **PEOPLE** ARE MY **FRIENDS**, SLUGGO.
YOUR **FRIENDS** ARE TERRORISTS.
YOUR FRIENDS DESTROY WORLDS, ENSLAVE WHOLE PLANETS!
THE FEDERATION ONLY GOES TO WAR WHEN EVERY PEACEFUL OPTION HAS BEEN EXHAUSTED! AND IF PLANETS GOT DESTROYED IT WAS FOR THE GREATER GOOD--THE GREATER **PEACE**, FATIMA.
A PEACE, I MIGHT ADD, YOU'VE COME VERY CLOSE TO DESTABILIZING. FOR YOUR OWN SELFISH REASONS, JUST LIKE ALWAYS.
GAH!

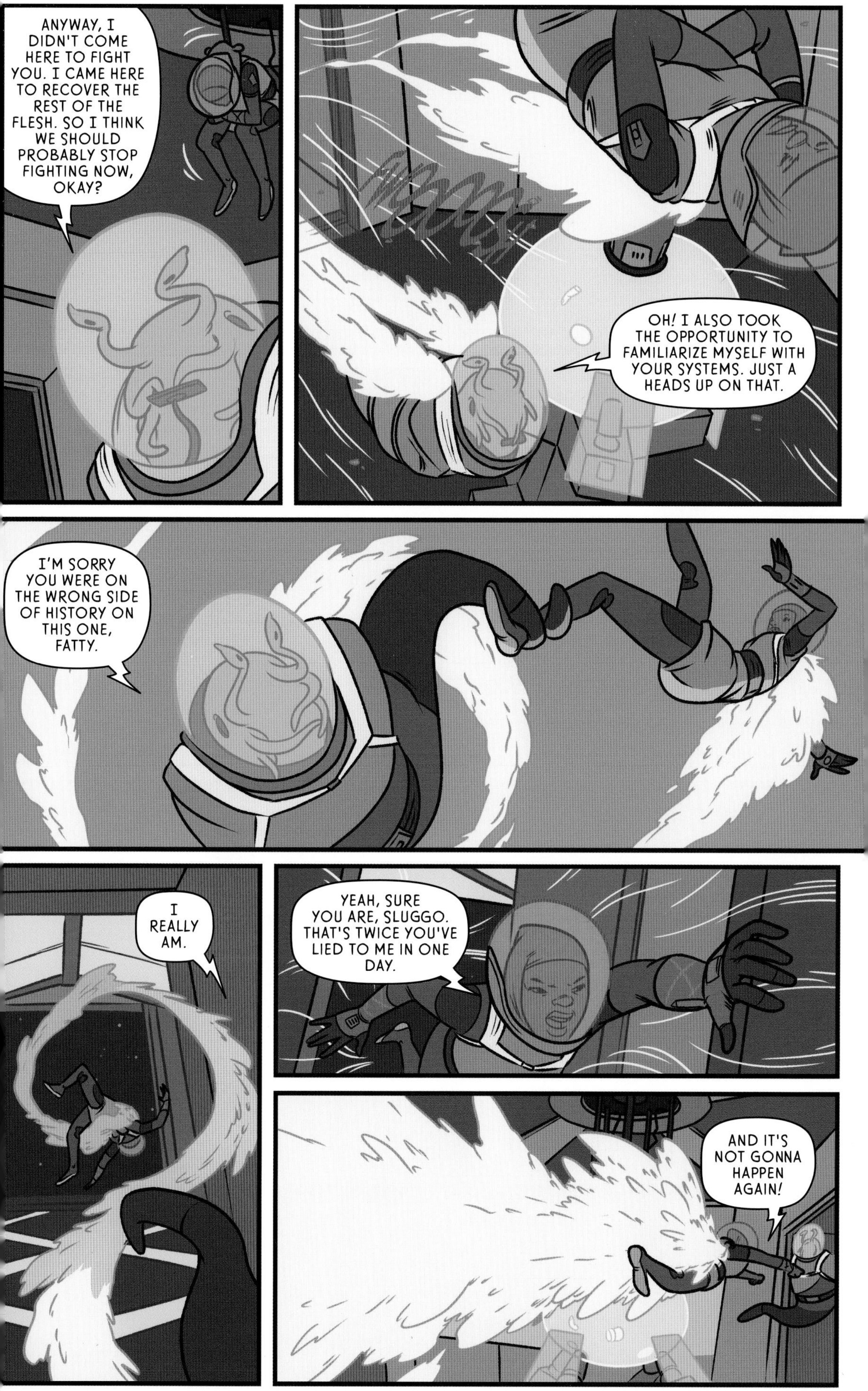
ANYWAY, I DIDN'T COME HERE TO FIGHT YOU. I CAME HERE TO RECOVER THE REST OF THE FLESH. SO I THINK WE SHOULD PROBABLY STOP FIGHTING NOW, OKAY?
OH! I ALSO TOOK THE OPPORTUNITY TO FAMILIARIZE MYSELF WITH YOUR SYSTEMS. JUST A HEADS UP ON THAT.
I'M SORRY YOU WERE ON THE WRONG SIDE OF HISTORY ON THIS ONE, FATTY.
I REALLY AM.
YEAH, SURE YOU ARE, SLUGGO. THAT'S TWICE YOU'VE LIED TO ME IN ONE DAY.
AND IT'S NOT GONNA HAPPEN AGAIN!

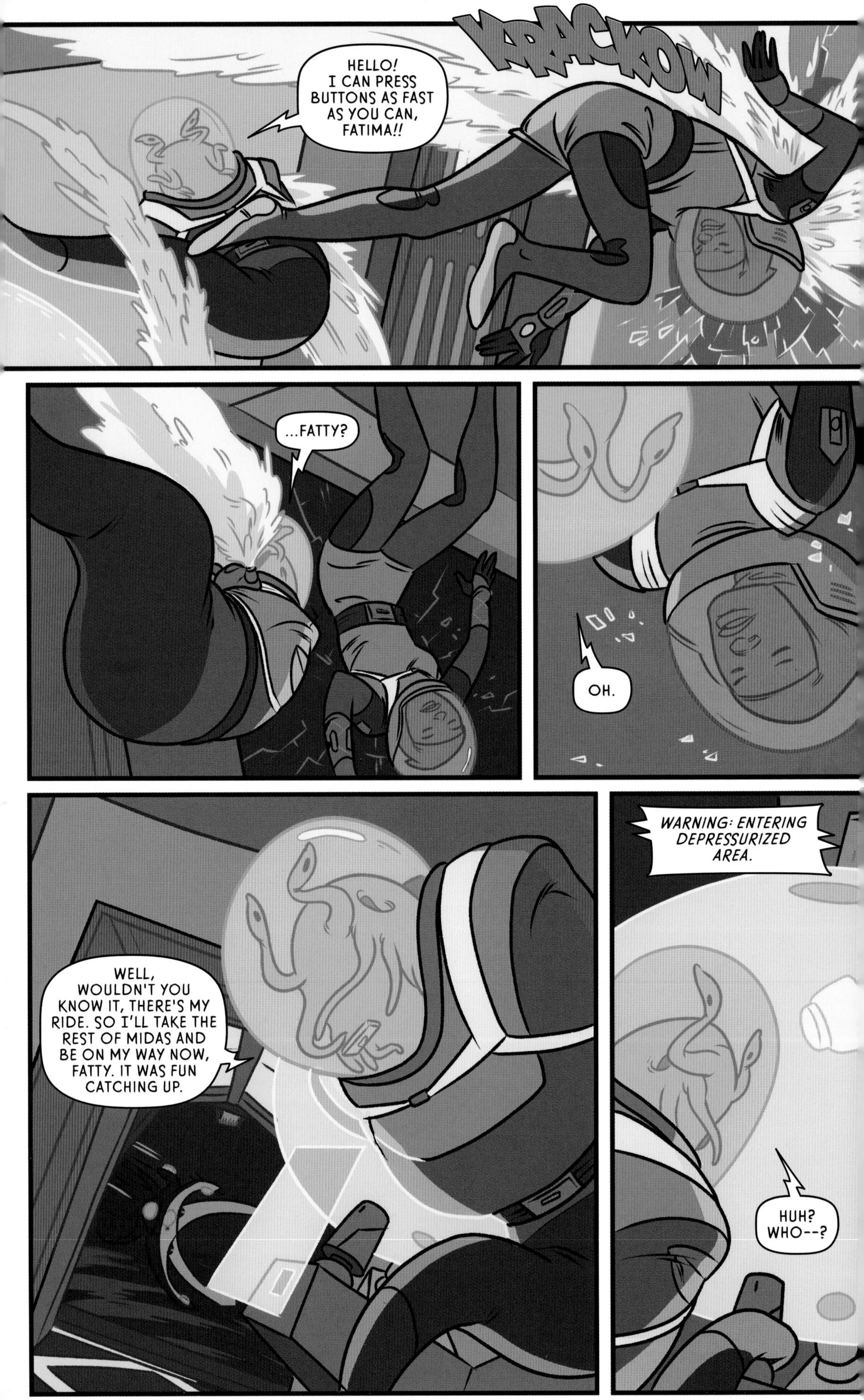
KRACKOW
HELLO! I CAN PRESS BUTTONS AS FAST AS YOU CAN, FATIMA!!
...FATTY?
OH.
WELL, WOULDN'T YOU KNOW IT, THERE'S MY RIDE. SO I'LL TAKE THE REST OF MIDAS AND BE ON MY WAY NOW, FATTY. IT WAS FUN CATCHING UP.
WARNING: ENTERING DEPRESSURIZED AREA.
HUH? WHO--?

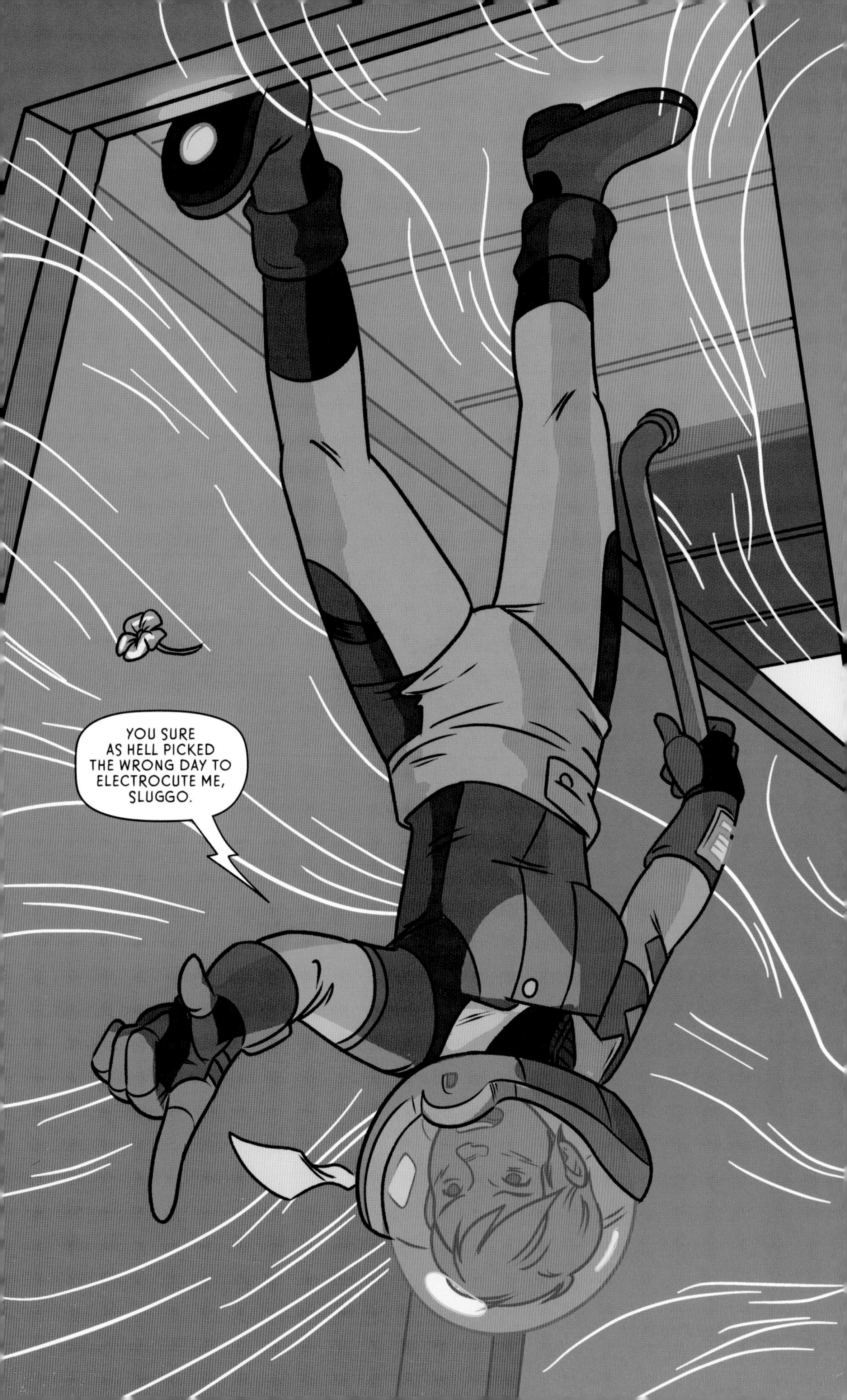
YOU SURE AS HELL PICKED THE WRONG DAY TO ELECTROCUTE ME, SLUGGO.

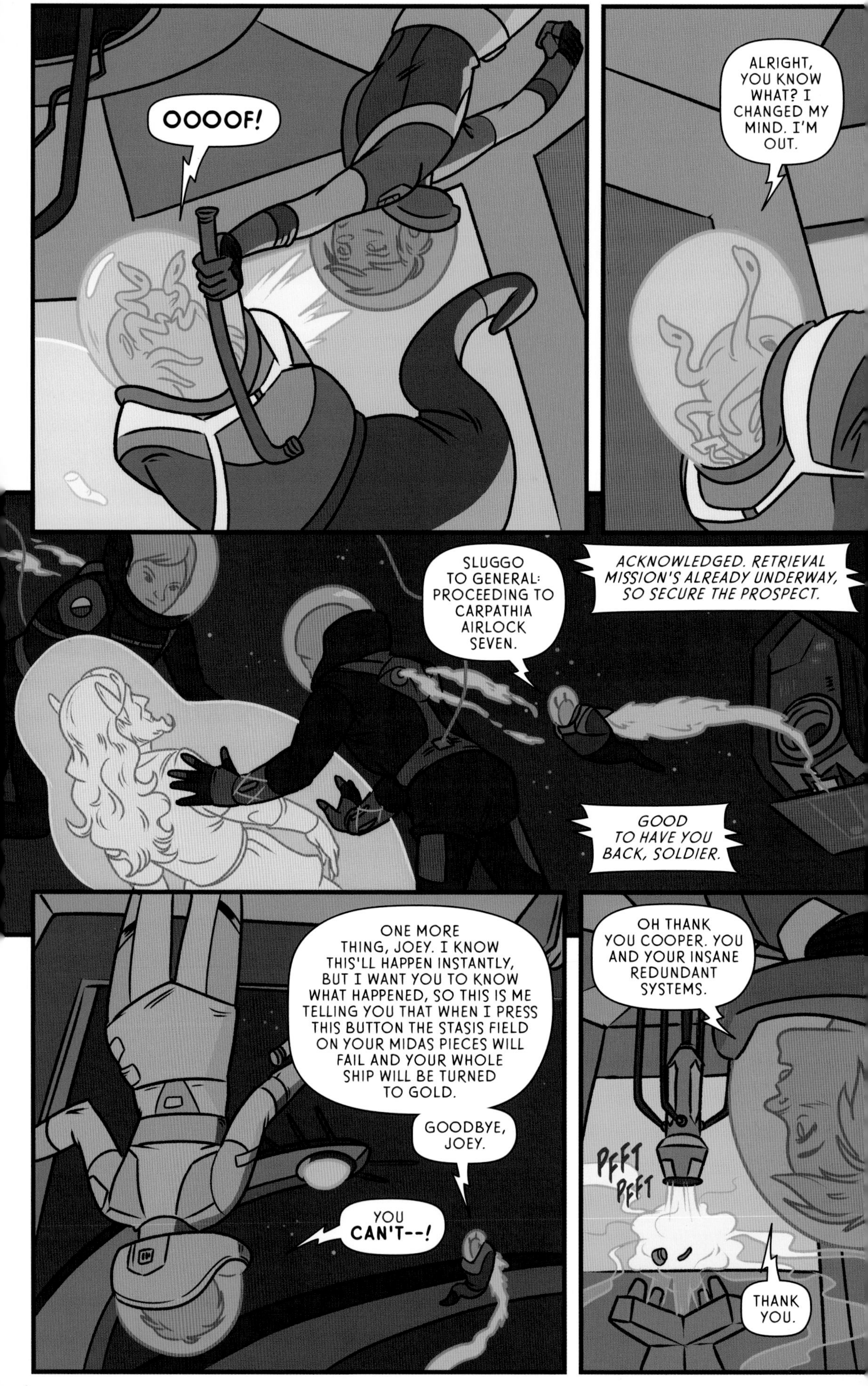

OOOOF!
ALRIGHT, YOU KNOW WHAT? I CHANGED MY MIND. I'M OUT.
SLUGGO TO GENERAL: PROCEEDING TO CARPATHIA AIRLOCK SEVEN.
ACKNOWLEDGED. RETRIEVAL MISSION'S ALREADY UNDERWAY, SO SECURE THE PROSPECT.
GOOD TO HAVE YOU BACK, SOLDIER.
ONE MORE THING, JOEY. I KNOW THIS'LL HAPPEN INSTANTLY, BUT I WANT YOU TO KNOW WHAT HAPPENED, SO THIS IS ME TELLING YOU THAT WHEN I PRESS THIS BUTTON THE STASIS FIELD ON YOUR MIDAS PIECES WILL FAIL AND YOUR WHOLE SHIP WILL BE TURNED TO GOLD.
GOODBYE, JOEY.
YOU CAN'T--!
OH THANK YOU COOPER. YOU AND YOUR INSANE REDUNDANT SYSTEMS.
PFFT PFFT
THANK YOU.

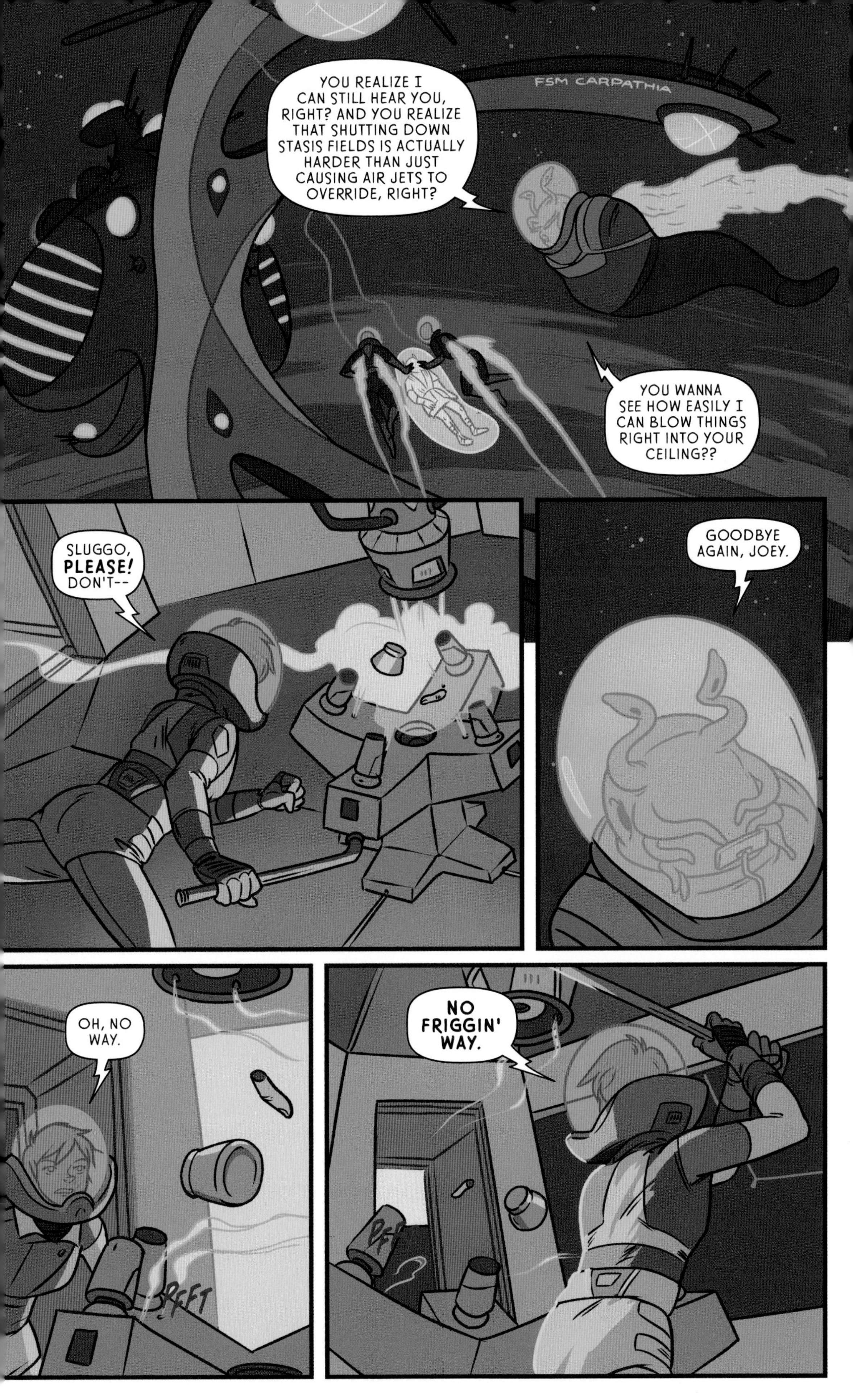
FSM CARPATHIA
YOU REALIZE I CAN STILL HEAR YOU, RIGHT? AND YOU REALIZE THAT SHUTTING DOWN STASIS FIELDS IS ACTUALLY HARDER THAN JUST CAUSING AIR JETS TO OVERRIDE, RIGHT?
YOU WANNA SEE HOW EASILY I CAN BLOW THINGS RIGHT INTO YOUR CEILING??
SLUGGO, PLEASE! DON'T--
GOODBYE AGAIN, JOEY.
OH, NO WAY.
PFFT
NO FRIGGIN' WAY.

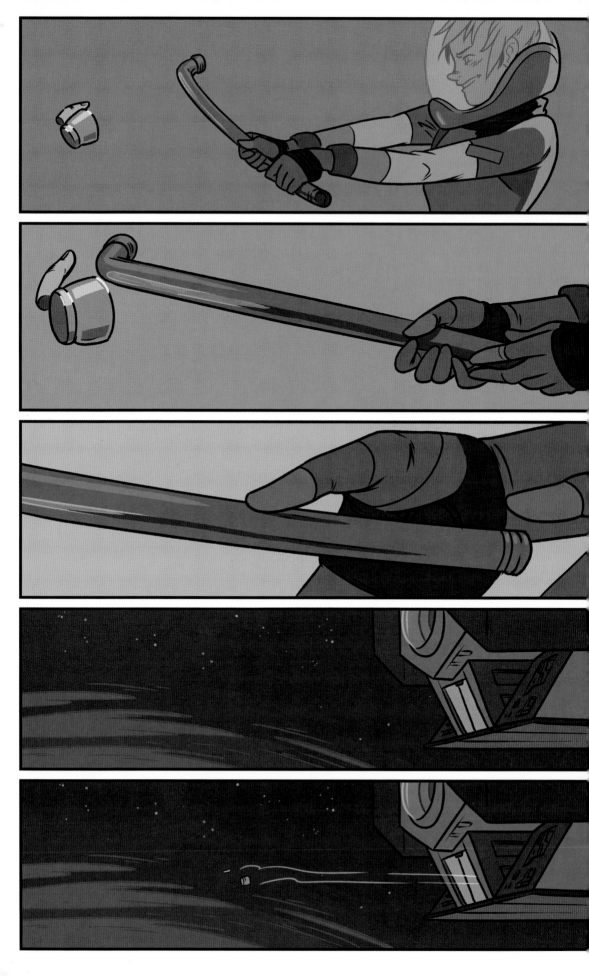

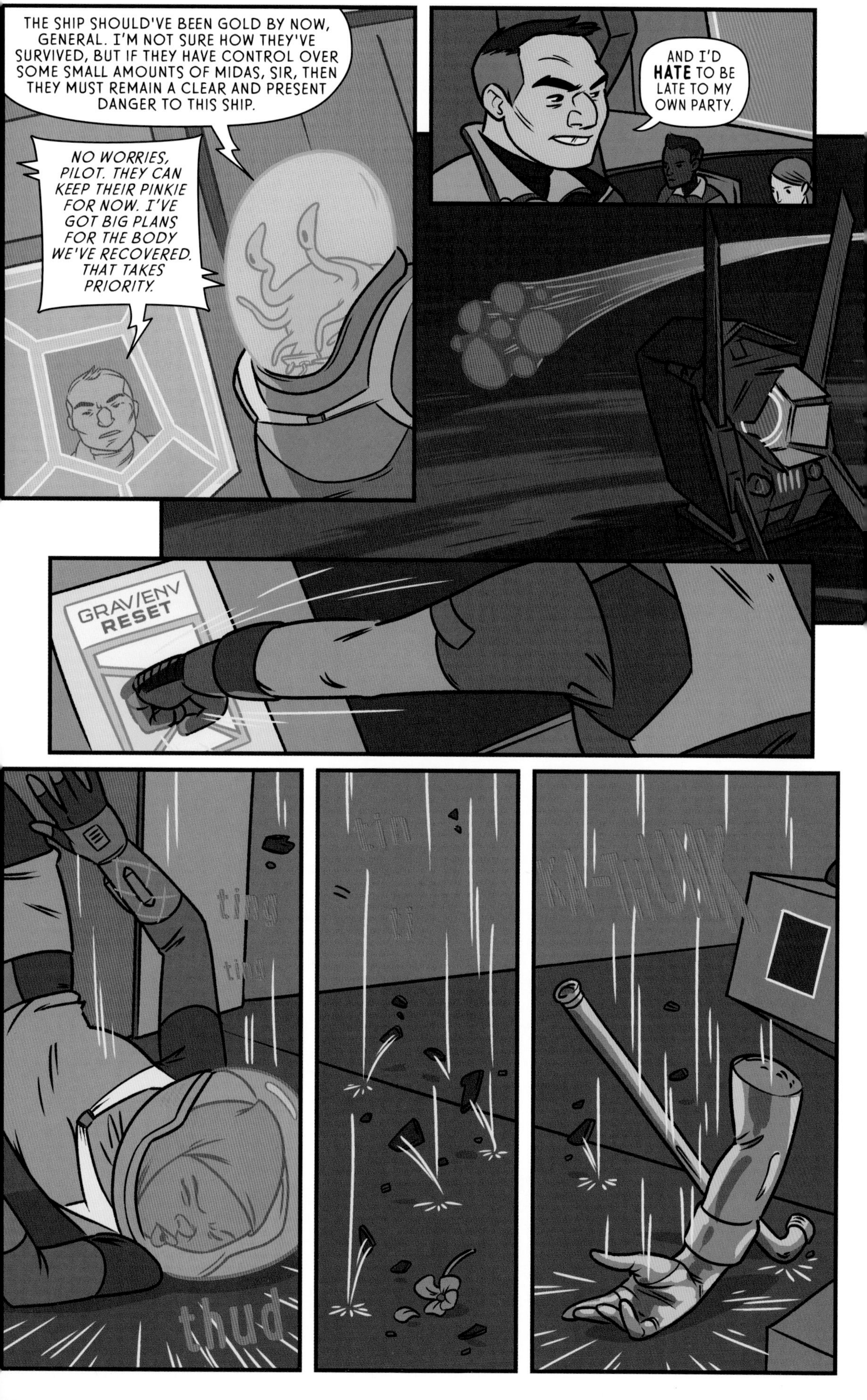
THE SHIP SHOULD'VE BEEN GOLD BY NOW, GENERAL. I'M NOT SURE HOW THEY'VE SURVIVED, BUT IF THEY HAVE CONTROL OVER SOME SMALL AMOUNTS OF MIDAS, SIR, THEN THEY MUST REMAIN A CLEAR AND PRESENT DANGER TO THIS SHIP.
NO WORRIES, PILOT. THEY CAN KEEP THEIR PINKIE FOR NOW. I'VE GOT BIG PLANS FOR THE BODY WE'VE RECOVERED. THAT TAKES PRIORITY.
AND I'D **HATE** TO BE LATE TO MY OWN PARTY.
GRAV/ENV
RESET
ting
ting
thud
tin
ti
KA-THUNK

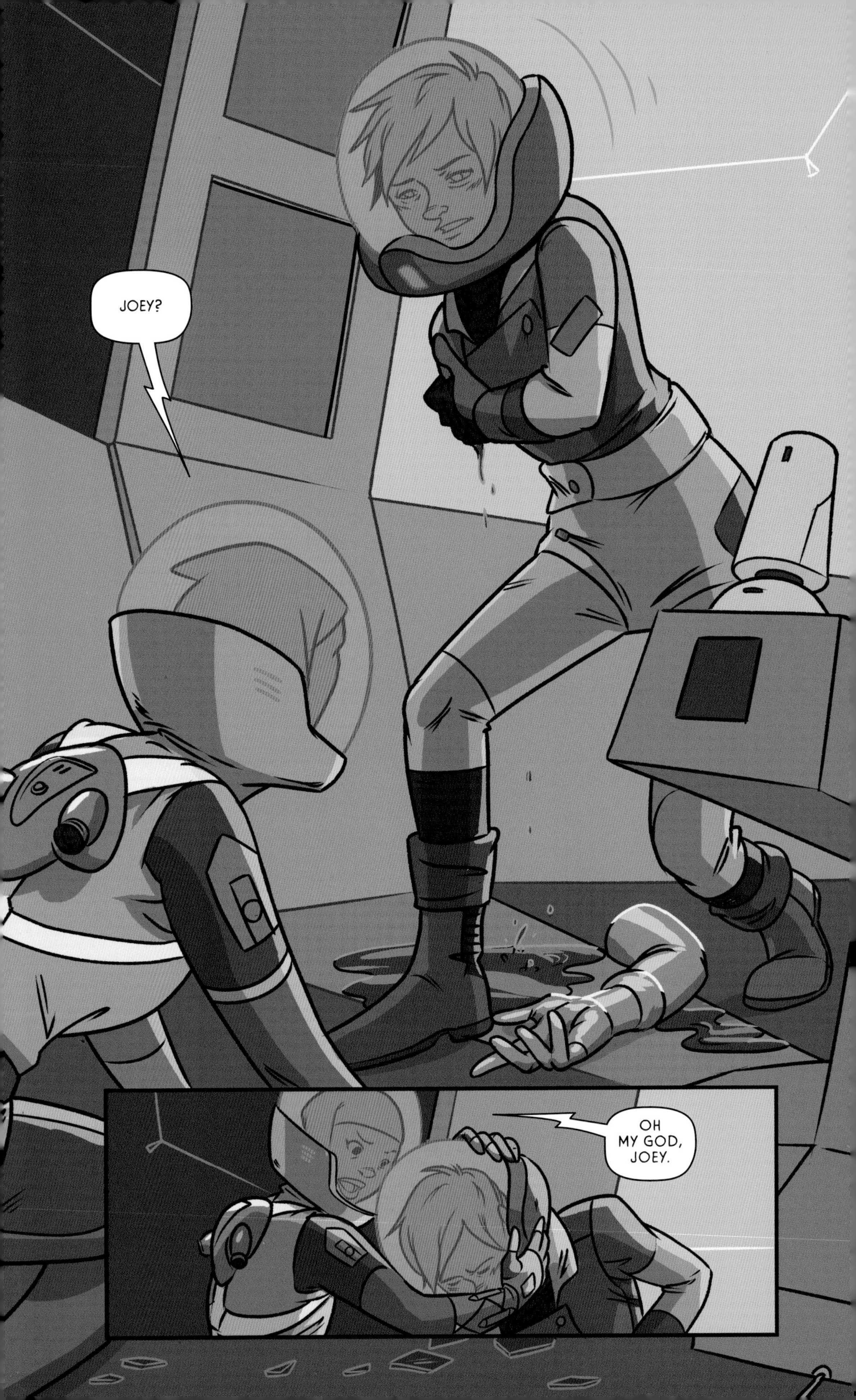
JOEY?
OH MY GOD, JOEY.

"REST IN
PIECES!"

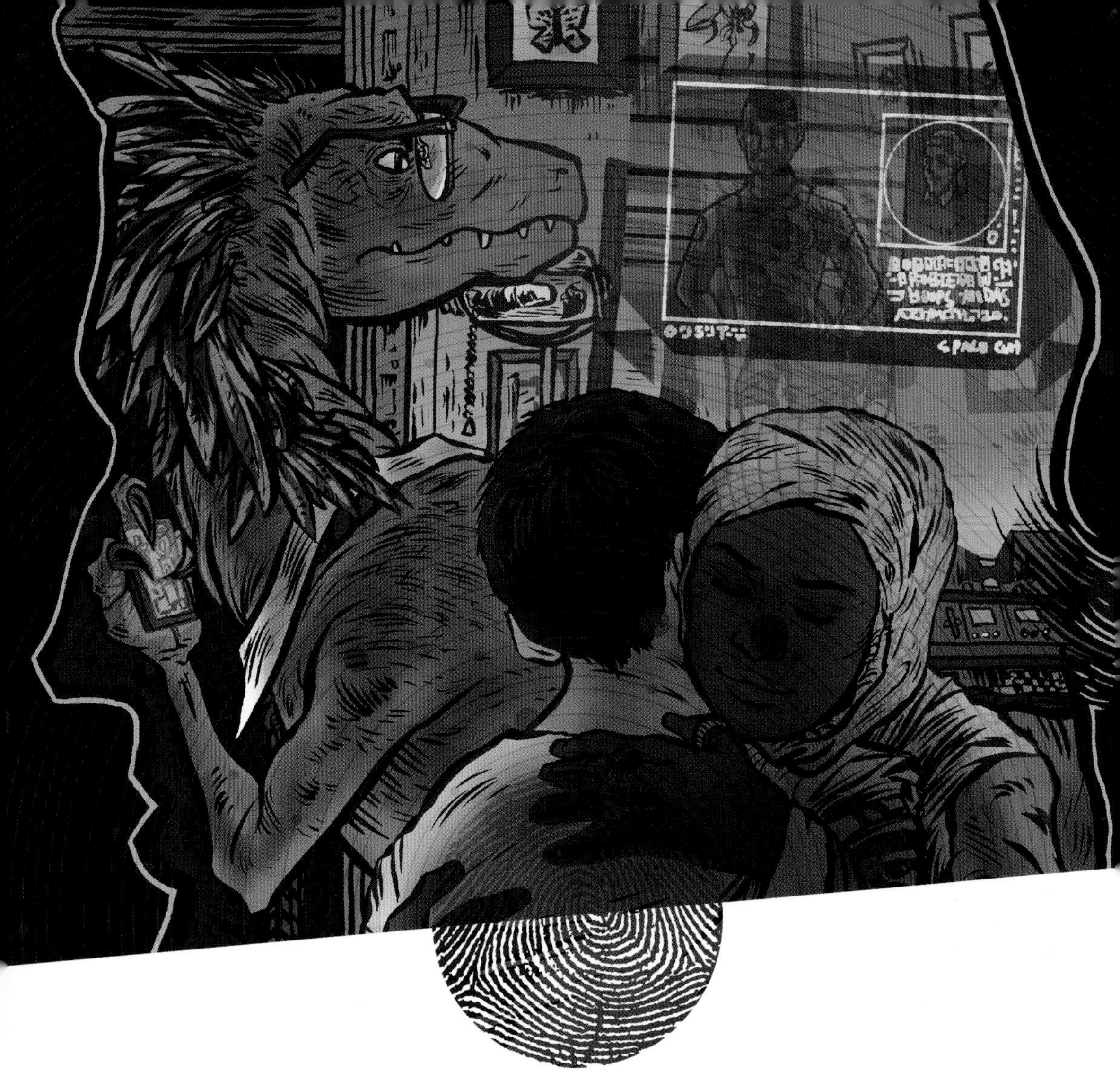

CHAPTER SIX

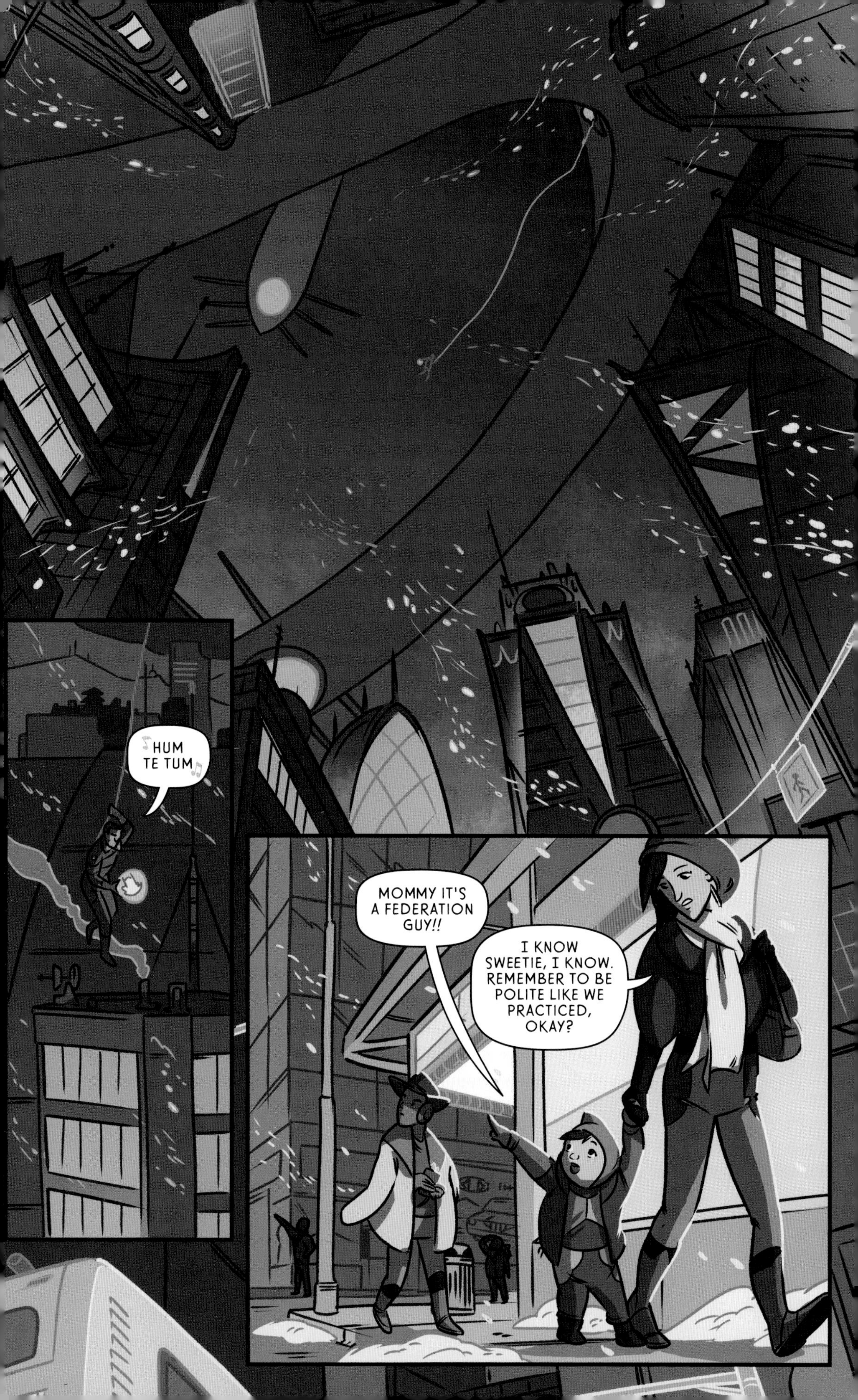

HUM TE TUM
MOMMY IT'S A FEDERATION GUY!!
I KNOW SWEETIE, I KNOW. REMEMBER TO BE POLITE LIKE WE PRACTICED, OKAY?

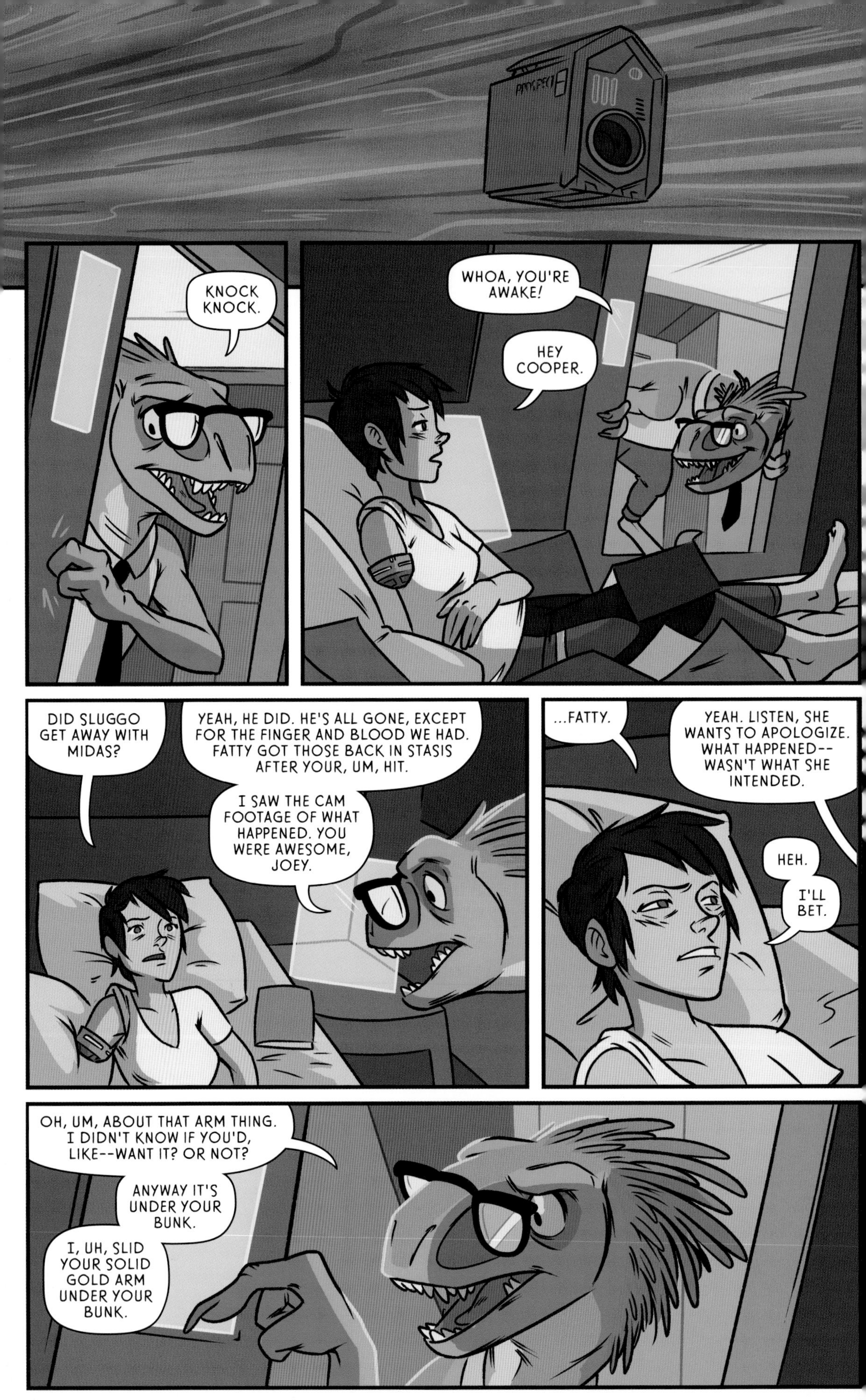
KNOCK KNOCK.
WHOA, YOU'RE AWAKE!
HEY COOPER.
DID SLUGGO GET AWAY WITH MIDAS?
YEAH, HE DID. HE'S ALL GONE, EXCEPT FOR THE FINGER AND BLOOD WE HAD. FATTY GOT THOSE BACK IN STASIS AFTER YOUR, UM, HIT.
I SAW THE CAM FOOTAGE OF WHAT HAPPENED. YOU WERE AWESOME, JOEY.
...FATTY.
YEAH. LISTEN, SHE WANTS TO APOLOGIZE. WHAT HAPPENED-- WASN'T WHAT SHE INTENDED.
HEH.
I'LL BET.
OH, UM, ABOUT THAT ARM THING. I DIDN'T KNOW IF YOU'D, LIKE--WANT IT? OR NOT?
ANYWAY IT'S UNDER YOUR BUNK.
I, UH, SLID YOUR SOLID GOLD ARM UNDER YOUR BUNK.

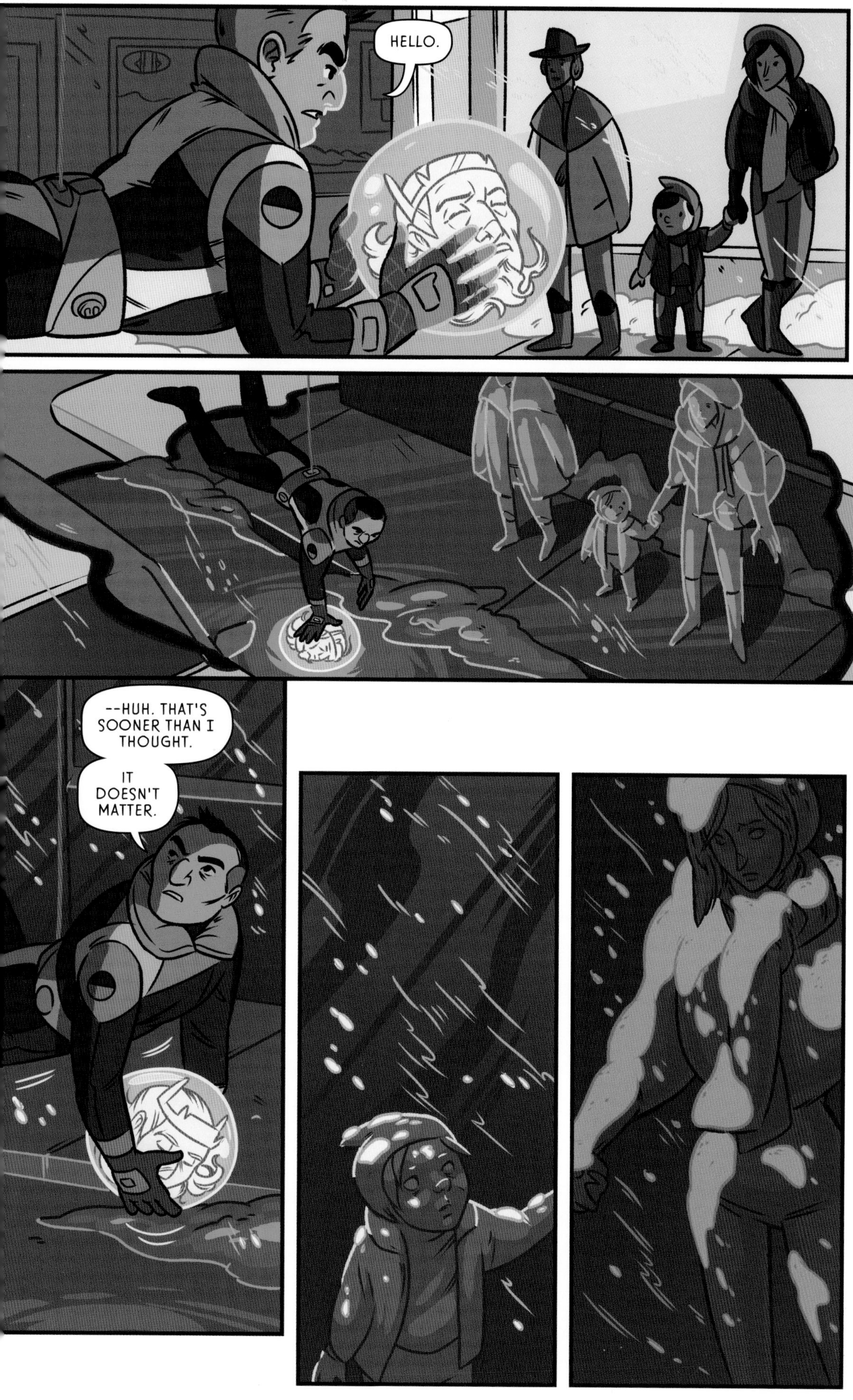
HELLO.
--HUH. THAT'S SOONER THAN I THOUGHT.
IT DOESN'T MATTER.

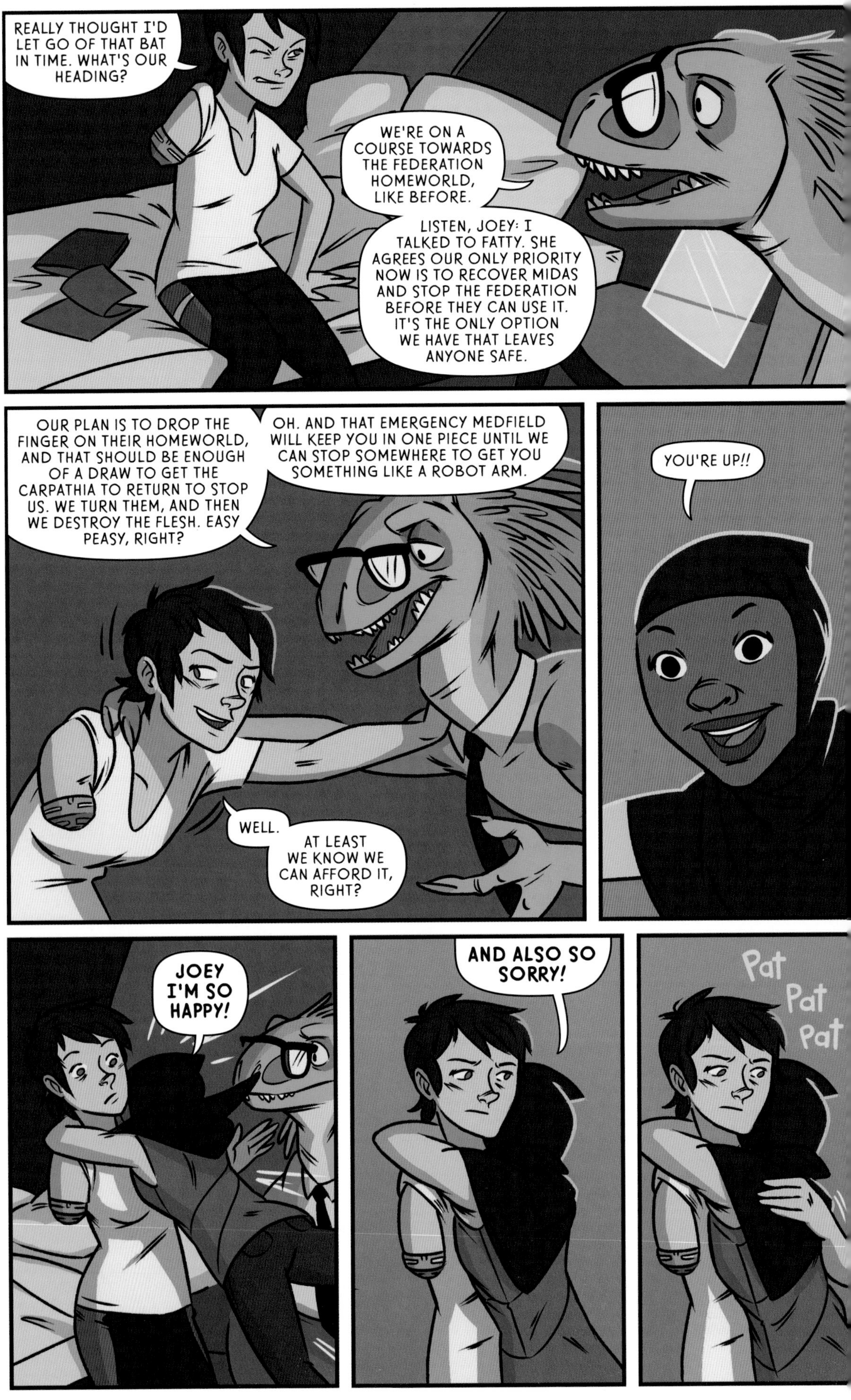
REALLY THOUGHT I'D LET GO OF THAT BAT IN TIME. WHAT'S OUR HEADING?
WE'RE ON A COURSE TOWARDS THE FEDERATION HOMEWORLD, LIKE BEFORE.
LISTEN, JOEY: I TALKED TO FATTY. SHE AGREES OUR ONLY PRIORITY NOW IS TO RECOVER MIDAS AND STOP THE FEDERATION BEFORE THEY CAN USE IT. IT'S THE ONLY OPTION WE HAVE THAT LEAVES ANYONE SAFE.
OUR PLAN IS TO DROP THE FINGER ON THEIR HOMEWORLD, AND THAT SHOULD BE ENOUGH OF A DRAW TO GET THE CARPATHIA TO RETURN TO STOP US. WE TURN THEM, AND THEN WE DESTROY THE FLESH. EASY PEASY, RIGHT?
OH. AND THAT EMERGENCY MEDFIELD WILL KEEP YOU IN ONE PIECE UNTIL WE CAN STOP SOMEWHERE TO GET YOU SOMETHING LIKE A ROBOT ARM.
WELL.
AT LEAST WE KNOW WE CAN AFFORD IT, RIGHT?
YOU'RE UP!!
JOEY I'M SO HAPPY!
AND ALSO SO SORRY!
Pat
Pat
Pat

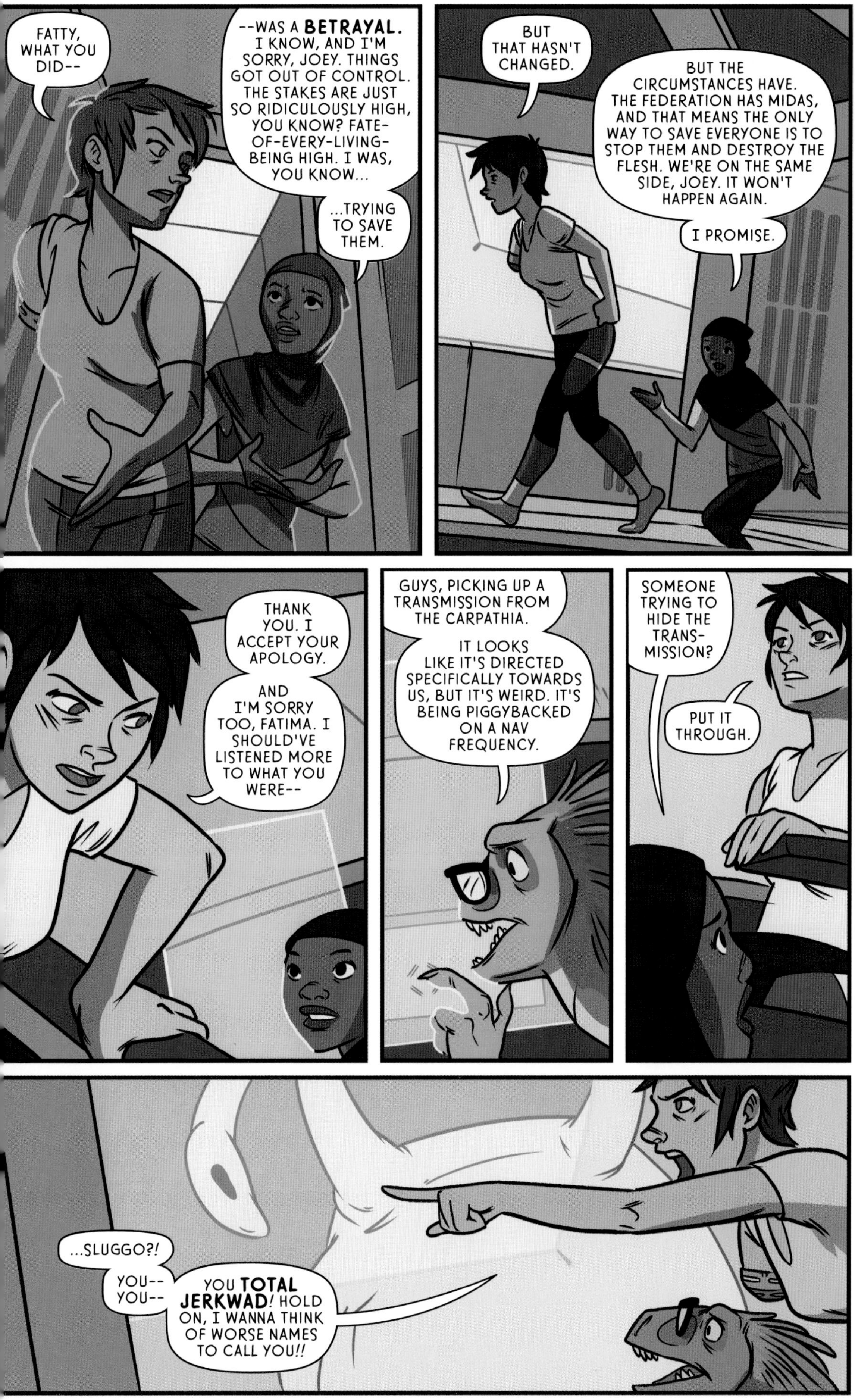
FATTY, WHAT YOU DID--
--WAS A **BETRAYAL.** I KNOW, AND I'M SORRY, JOEY. THINGS GOT OUT OF CONTROL. THE STAKES ARE JUST SO RIDICULOUSLY HIGH, YOU KNOW? FATE-OF-EVERY-LIVING-BEING HIGH. I WAS, YOU KNOW...
...TRYING TO SAVE THEM.
BUT THAT HASN'T CHANGED.
BUT THE CIRCUMSTANCES HAVE. THE FEDERATION HAS MIDAS, AND THAT MEANS THE ONLY WAY TO SAVE EVERYONE IS TO STOP THEM AND DESTROY THE FLESH. WE'RE ON THE SAME SIDE, JOEY. IT WON'T HAPPEN AGAIN.
I PROMISE.
THANK YOU. I ACCEPT YOUR APOLOGY.
AND I'M SORRY TOO, FATIMA. I SHOULD'VE LISTENED MORE TO WHAT YOU WERE--
GUYS, PICKING UP A TRANSMISSION FROM THE CARPATHIA.
IT LOOKS LIKE IT'S DIRECTED SPECIFICALLY TOWARDS US, BUT IT'S WEIRD. IT'S BEING PIGGYBACKED ON A NAV FREQUENCY.
SOMEONE TRYING TO HIDE THE TRANS-MISSION?
PUT IT THROUGH.
...SLUGGO?!
YOU-- YOU--
YOU **TOTAL JERKWAD**! HOLD ON, I WANNA THINK OF WORSE NAMES TO CALL YOU!!

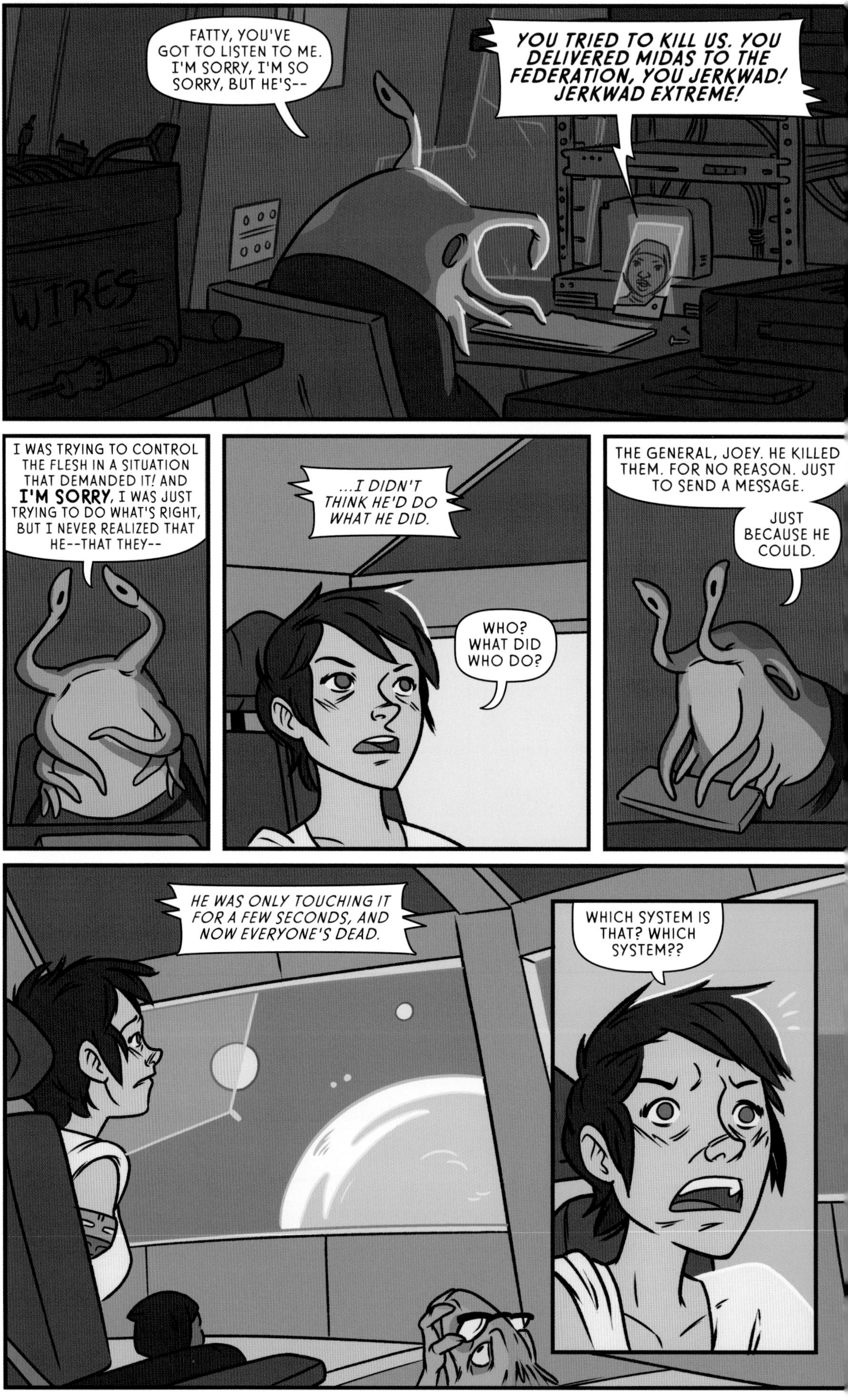
FATTY, YOU'VE GOT TO LISTEN TO ME. I'M SORRY, I'M SO SORRY, BUT HE'S--
YOU TRIED TO KILL US. YOU DELIVERED MIDAS TO THE FEDERATION, YOU JERKWAD! JERKWAD EXTREME!
WIRES
I WAS TRYING TO CONTROL THE FLESH IN A SITUATION THAT DEMANDED IT! AND I'M SORRY, I WAS JUST TRYING TO DO WHAT'S RIGHT, BUT I NEVER REALIZED THAT HE--THAT THEY--
...I DIDN'T THINK HE'D DO WHAT HE DID.
WHO? WHAT DID WHO DO?
THE GENERAL, JOEY. HE KILLED THEM. FOR NO REASON. JUST TO SEND A MESSAGE.
JUST BECAUSE HE COULD.
HE WAS ONLY TOUCHING IT FOR A FEW SECONDS, AND NOW EVERYONE'S DEAD.
WHICH SYSTEM IS THAT? WHICH SYSTEM??

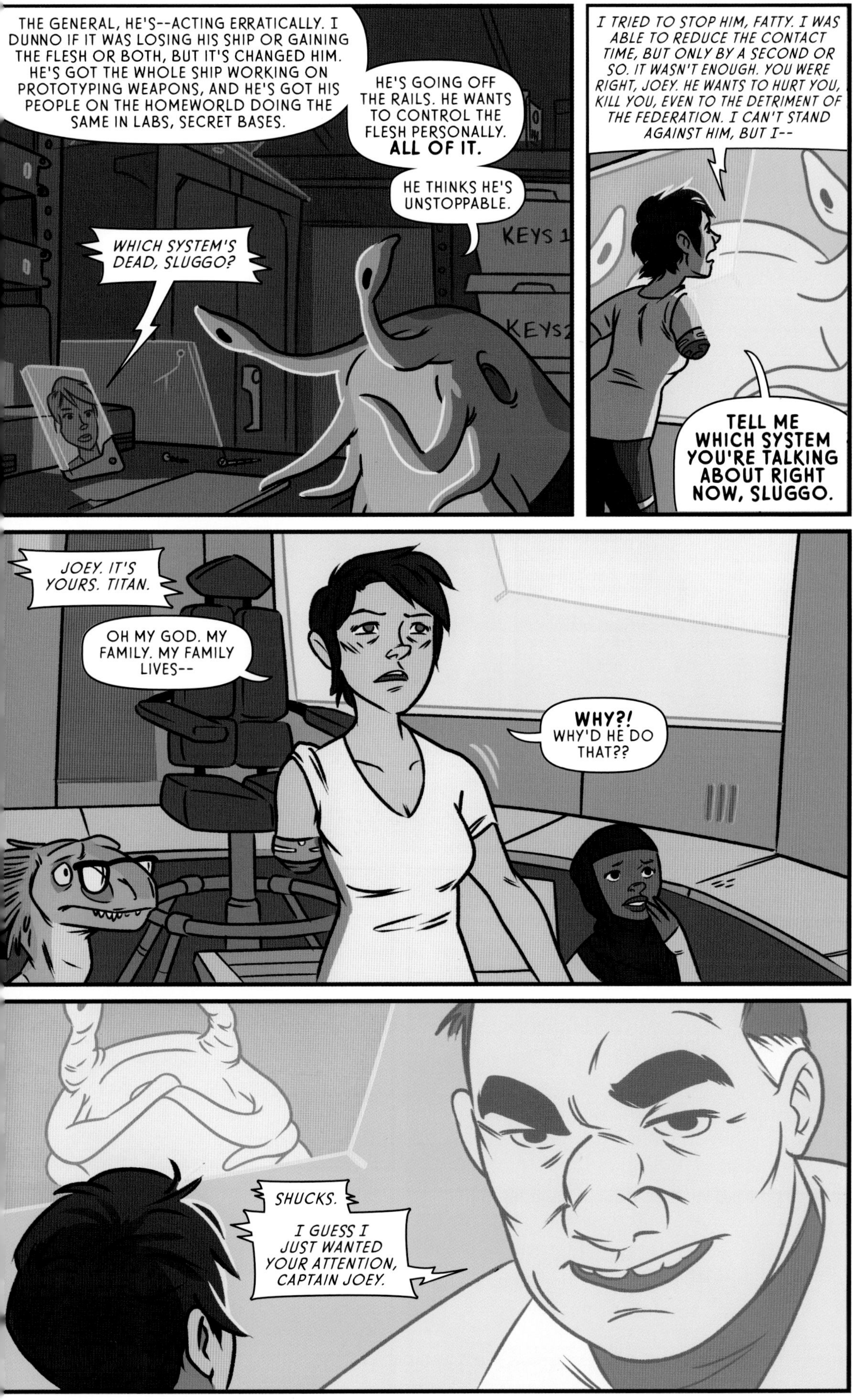
THE GENERAL, HE'S--ACTING ERRATICALLY. I DUNNO IF IT WAS LOSING HIS SHIP OR GAINING THE FLESH OR BOTH, BUT IT'S CHANGED HIM. HE'S GOT THE WHOLE SHIP WORKING ON PROTOTYPING WEAPONS, AND HE'S GOT HIS PEOPLE ON THE HOMEWORLD DOING THE SAME IN LABS, SECRET BASES.
HE'S GOING OFF THE RAILS. HE WANTS TO CONTROL THE FLESH PERSONALLY. ALL OF IT.
HE THINKS HE'S UNSTOPPABLE.
WHICH SYSTEM'S DEAD, SLUGGO?
KEYS 1
KEYS 2
I TRIED TO STOP HIM, FATTY. I WAS ABLE TO REDUCE THE CONTACT TIME, BUT ONLY BY A SECOND OR SO. IT WASN'T ENOUGH. YOU WERE RIGHT, JOEY. HE WANTS TO HURT YOU, KILL YOU, EVEN TO THE DETRIMENT OF THE FEDERATION. I CAN'T STAND AGAINST HIM, BUT I--
TELL ME WHICH SYSTEM YOU'RE TALKING ABOUT RIGHT NOW, SLUGGO.
JOEY. IT'S YOURS. TITAN.
OH MY GOD. MY FAMILY. MY FAMILY LIVES--
WHY?! WHY'D HE DO THAT??
SHUCKS.
I GUESS I JUST WANTED YOUR ATTENTION, CAPTAIN JOEY.

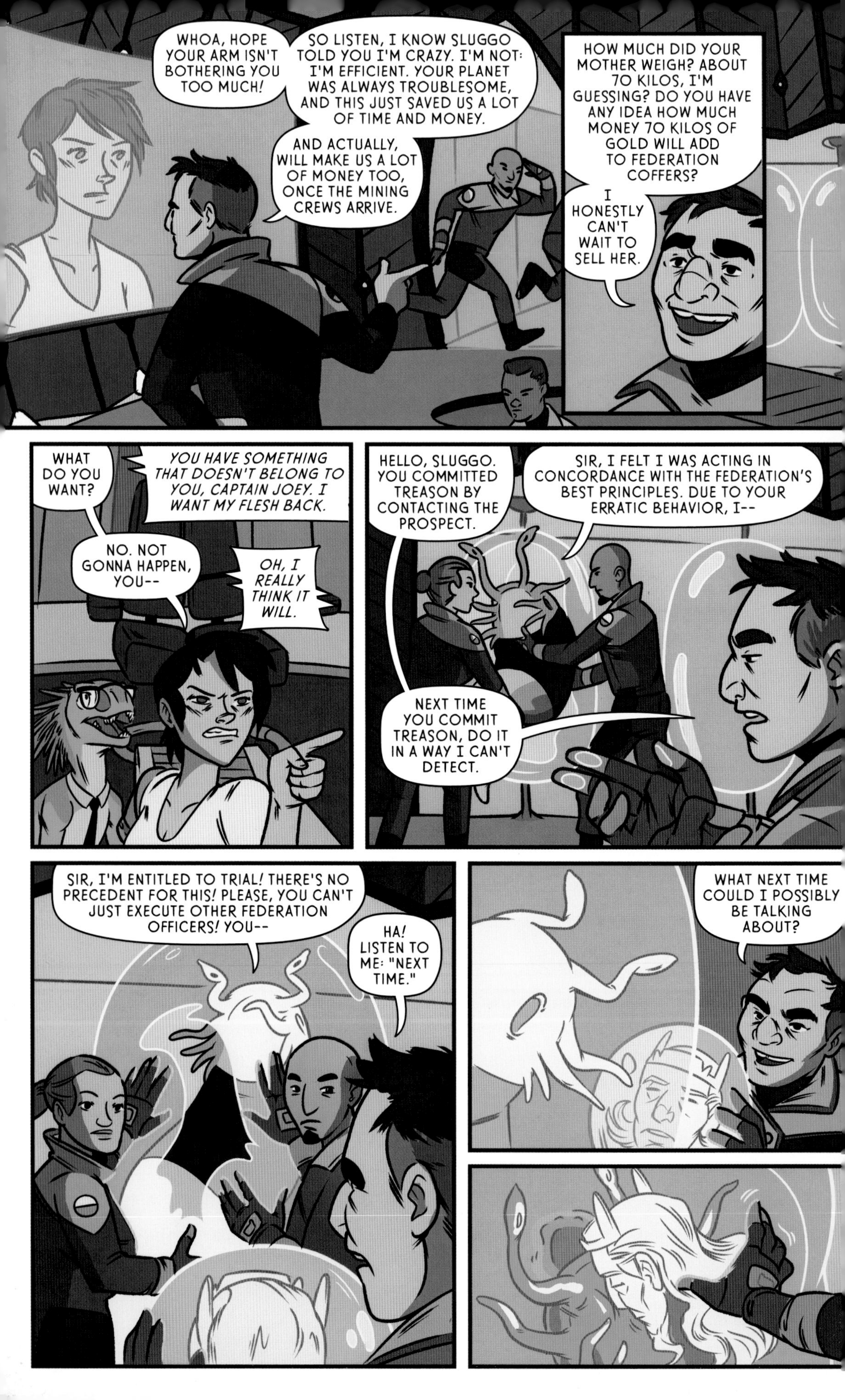
WHOA, HOPE YOUR ARM ISN'T BOTHERING YOU TOO MUCH!
SO LISTEN, I KNOW SLUGGO TOLD YOU I'M CRAZY. I'M NOT: I'M EFFICIENT. YOUR PLANET WAS ALWAYS TROUBLESOME, AND THIS JUST SAVED US A LOT OF TIME AND MONEY.
AND ACTUALLY, WILL MAKE US A LOT OF MONEY TOO, ONCE THE MINING CREWS ARRIVE.
HOW MUCH DID YOUR MOTHER WEIGH? ABOUT 70 KILOS, I'M GUESSING? DO YOU HAVE ANY IDEA HOW MUCH MONEY 70 KILOS OF GOLD WILL ADD TO FEDERATION COFFERS?
I HONESTLY CAN'T WAIT TO SELL HER.
WHAT DO YOU WANT?
YOU HAVE SOMETHING THAT DOESN'T BELONG TO YOU, CAPTAIN JOEY. I WANT MY FLESH BACK.
NO. NOT GONNA HAPPEN, YOU--
OH, I REALLY THINK IT WILL.
HELLO, SLUGGO. YOU COMMITTED TREASON BY CONTACTING THE PROSPECT.
SIR, I FELT I WAS ACTING IN CONCORDANCE WITH THE FEDERATION'S BEST PRINCIPLES. DUE TO YOUR ERRATIC BEHAVIOR, I--
NEXT TIME YOU COMMIT TREASON, DO IT IN A WAY I CAN'T DETECT.
SIR, I'M ENTITLED TO TRIAL! THERE'S NO PRECEDENT FOR THIS! PLEASE, YOU CAN'T JUST EXECUTE OTHER FEDERATION OFFICERS! YOU--
HA! LISTEN TO ME: "NEXT TIME."
WHAT NEXT TIME COULD I POSSIBLY BE TALKING ABOUT?

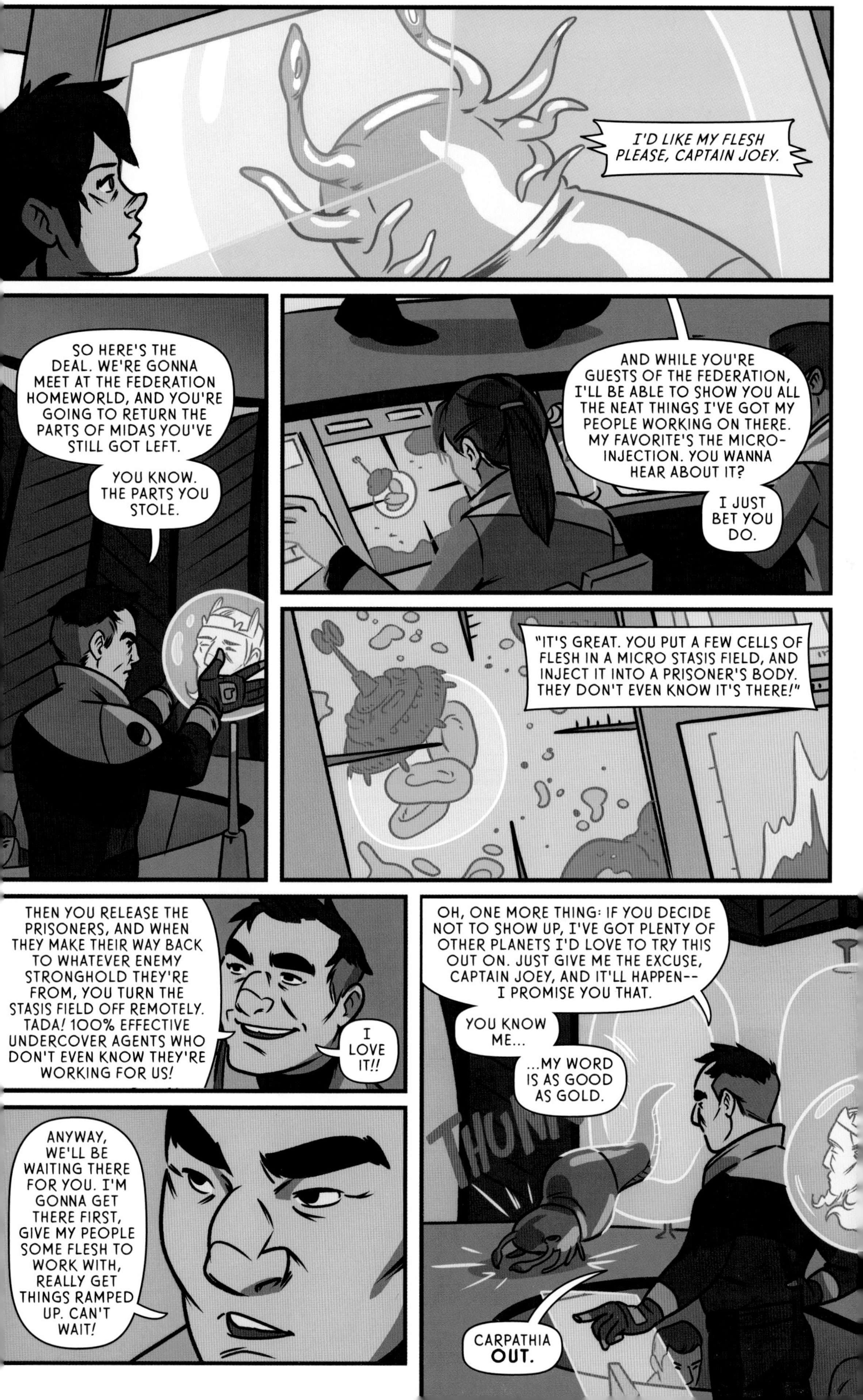
I'D LIKE MY FLESH PLEASE, CAPTAIN JOEY.
SO HERE'S THE DEAL. WE'RE GONNA MEET AT THE FEDERATION HOMEWORLD, AND YOU'RE GOING TO RETURN THE PARTS OF MIDAS YOU'VE STILL GOT LEFT.
YOU KNOW. THE PARTS YOU STOLE.
AND WHILE YOU'RE GUESTS OF THE FEDERATION, I'LL BE ABLE TO SHOW YOU ALL THE NEAT THINGS I'VE GOT MY PEOPLE WORKING ON THERE. MY FAVORITE'S THE MICRO-INJECTION. YOU WANNA HEAR ABOUT IT?
I JUST BET YOU DO.
"IT'S GREAT. YOU PUT A FEW CELLS OF FLESH IN A MICRO STASIS FIELD, AND INJECT IT INTO A PRISONER'S BODY. THEY DON'T EVEN KNOW IT'S THERE!"
THEN YOU RELEASE THE PRISONERS, AND WHEN THEY MAKE THEIR WAY BACK TO WHATEVER ENEMY STRONGHOLD THEY'RE FROM, YOU TURN THE STASIS FIELD OFF REMOTELY. TADA! 100% EFFECTIVE UNDERCOVER AGENTS WHO DON'T EVEN KNOW THEY'RE WORKING FOR US!
I LOVE IT!!
ANYWAY, WE'LL BE WAITING THERE FOR YOU. I'M GONNA GET THERE FIRST, GIVE MY PEOPLE SOME FLESH TO WORK WITH, REALLY GET THINGS RAMPED UP. CAN'T WAIT!
OH, ONE MORE THING: IF YOU DECIDE NOT TO SHOW UP, I'VE GOT PLENTY OF OTHER PLANETS I'D LOVE TO TRY THIS OUT ON. JUST GIVE ME THE EXCUSE, CAPTAIN JOEY, AND IT'LL HAPPEN-- I PROMISE YOU THAT.
YOU KNOW ME...
...MY WORD IS AS GOOD AS GOLD.
CARPATHIA **OUT.**

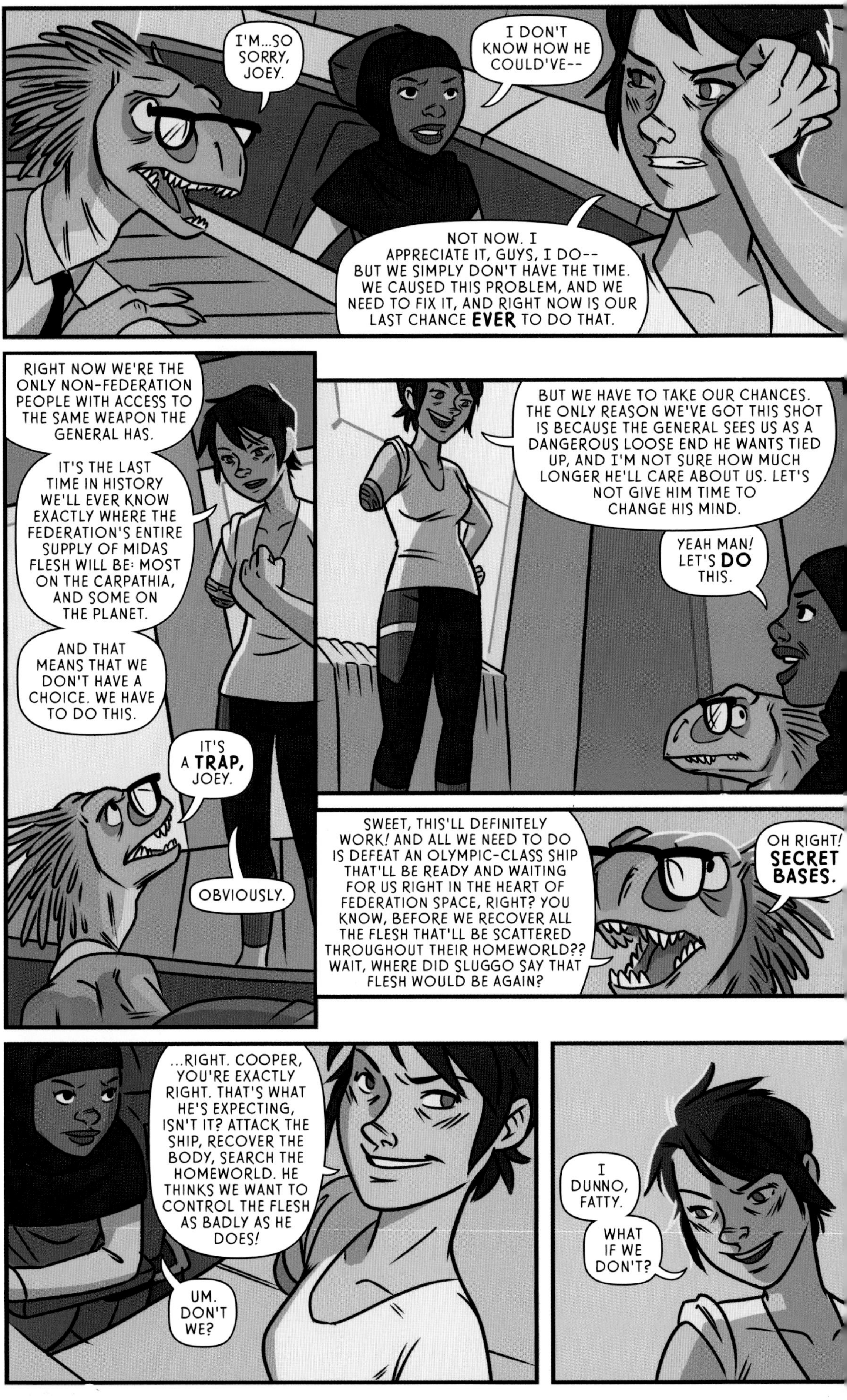
I'M...SO SORRY, JOEY.
I DON'T KNOW HOW HE COULD'VE--
NOT NOW. I APPRECIATE IT, GUYS, I DO-- BUT WE SIMPLY DON'T HAVE THE TIME. WE CAUSED THIS PROBLEM, AND WE NEED TO FIX IT, AND RIGHT NOW IS OUR LAST CHANCE EVER TO DO THAT.
RIGHT NOW WE'RE THE ONLY NON-FEDERATION PEOPLE WITH ACCESS TO THE SAME WEAPON THE GENERAL HAS.
IT'S THE LAST TIME IN HISTORY WE'LL EVER KNOW EXACTLY WHERE THE FEDERATION'S ENTIRE SUPPLY OF MIDAS FLESH WILL BE: MOST ON THE CARPATHIA, AND SOME ON THE PLANET.
AND THAT MEANS THAT WE DON'T HAVE A CHOICE. WE HAVE TO DO THIS.
IT'S A TRAP, JOEY.
OBVIOUSLY.
BUT WE HAVE TO TAKE OUR CHANCES. THE ONLY REASON WE'VE GOT THIS SHOT IS BECAUSE THE GENERAL SEES US AS A DANGEROUS LOOSE END HE WANTS TIED UP, AND I'M NOT SURE HOW MUCH LONGER HE'LL CARE ABOUT US. LET'S NOT GIVE HIM TIME TO CHANGE HIS MIND.
YEAH MAN! LET'S DO THIS.
SWEET, THIS'LL DEFINITELY WORK! AND ALL WE NEED TO DO IS DEFEAT AN OLYMPIC-CLASS SHIP THAT'LL BE READY AND WAITING FOR US RIGHT IN THE HEART OF FEDERATION SPACE, RIGHT? YOU KNOW, BEFORE WE RECOVER ALL THE FLESH THAT'LL BE SCATTERED THROUGHOUT THEIR HOMEWORLD?? WAIT, WHERE DID SLUGGO SAY THAT FLESH WOULD BE AGAIN?
OH RIGHT! SECRET BASES.
...RIGHT. COOPER, YOU'RE EXACTLY RIGHT. THAT'S WHAT HE'S EXPECTING, ISN'T IT? ATTACK THE SHIP, RECOVER THE BODY, SEARCH THE HOMEWORLD. HE THINKS WE WANT TO CONTROL THE FLESH AS BADLY AS HE DOES!
UM. DON'T WE?
I DUNNO, FATTY.
WHAT IF WE DON'T?

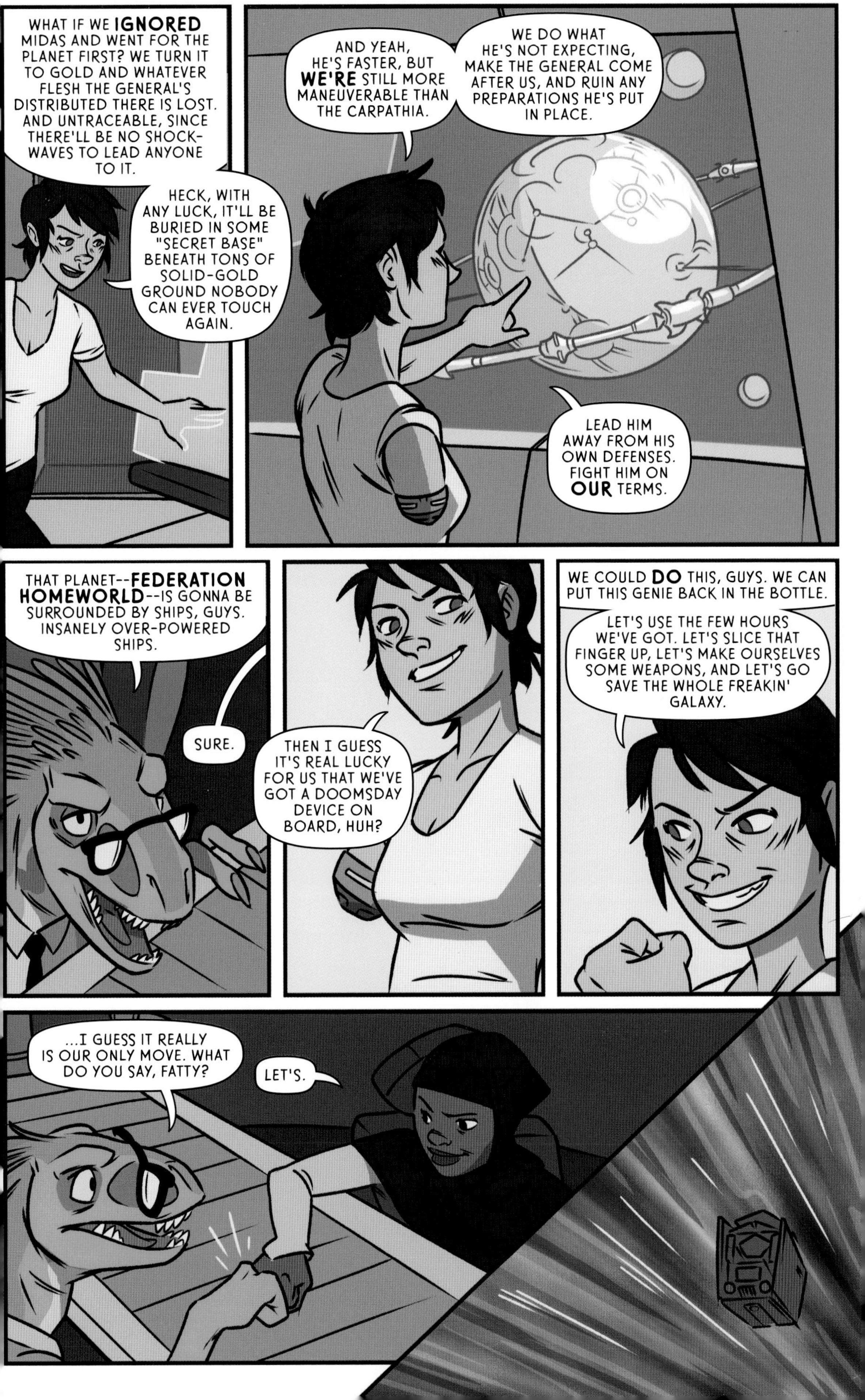
WHAT IF WE IGNORED MIDAS AND WENT FOR THE PLANET FIRST? WE TURN IT TO GOLD AND WHATEVER FLESH THE GENERAL'S DISTRIBUTED THERE IS LOST. AND UNTRACEABLE, SINCE THERE'LL BE NO SHOCK-WAVES TO LEAD ANYONE TO IT.
HECK, WITH ANY LUCK, IT'LL BE BURIED IN SOME "SECRET BASE" BENEATH TONS OF SOLID-GOLD GROUND NOBODY CAN EVER TOUCH AGAIN.
AND YEAH, HE'S FASTER, BUT WE'RE STILL MORE MANEUVERABLE THAN THE CARPATHIA.
WE DO WHAT HE'S NOT EXPECTING, MAKE THE GENERAL COME AFTER US, AND RUIN ANY PREPARATIONS HE'S PUT IN PLACE.
LEAD HIM AWAY FROM HIS OWN DEFENSES. FIGHT HIM ON OUR TERMS.
THAT PLANET--FEDERATION HOMEWORLD--IS GONNA BE SURROUNDED BY SHIPS, GUYS. INSANELY OVER-POWERED SHIPS.
SURE.
THEN I GUESS IT'S REAL LUCKY FOR US THAT WE'VE GOT A DOOMSDAY DEVICE ON BOARD, HUH?
WE COULD DO THIS, GUYS. WE CAN PUT THIS GENIE BACK IN THE BOTTLE.
LET'S USE THE FEW HOURS WE'VE GOT. LET'S SLICE THAT FINGER UP, LET'S MAKE OURSELVES SOME WEAPONS, AND LET'S GO SAVE THE WHOLE FREAKIN' GALAXY.
...I GUESS IT REALLY IS OUR ONLY MOVE. WHAT DO YOU SAY, FATTY?
LET'S.

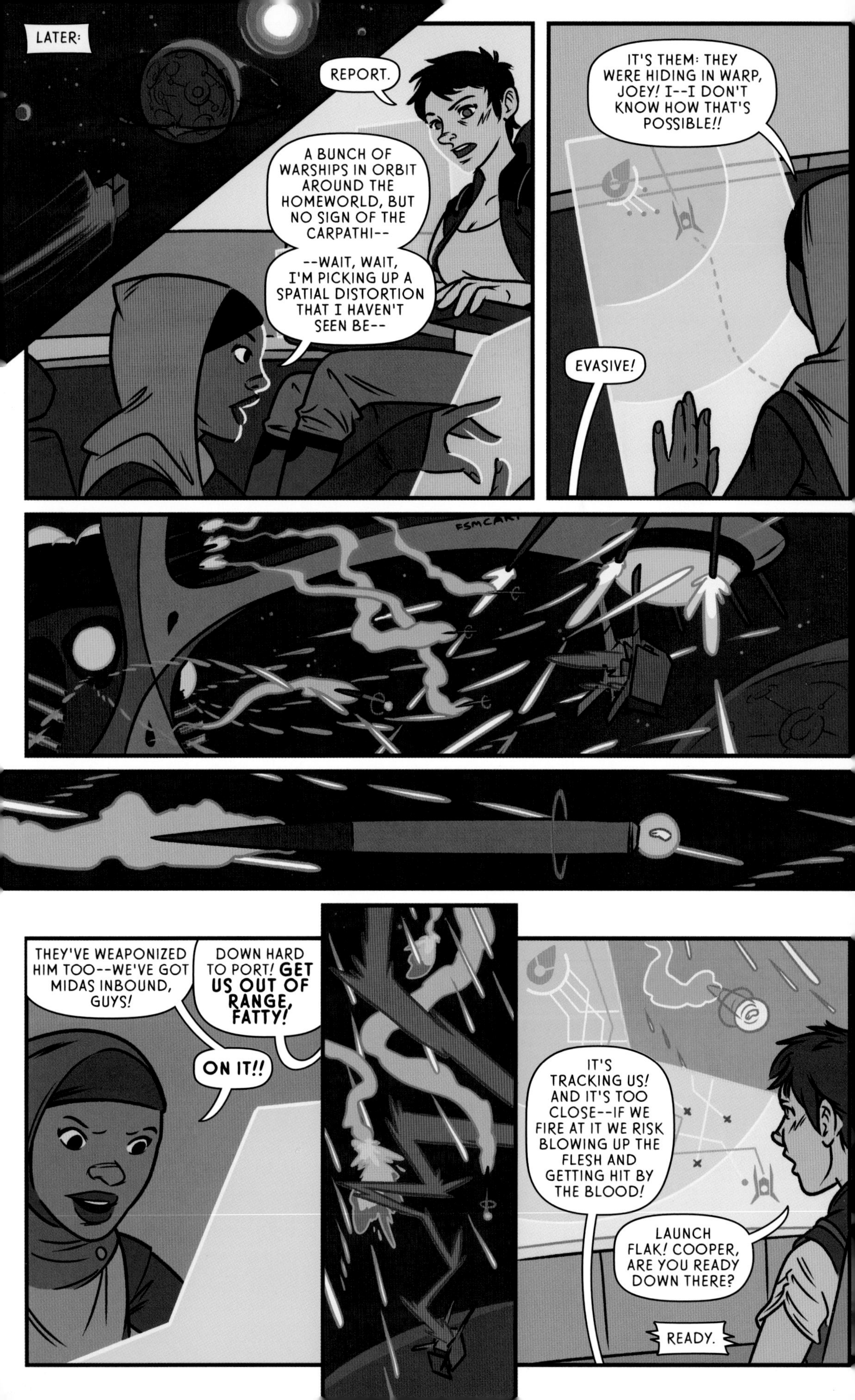
LATER:
REPORT.
A BUNCH OF WARSHIPS IN ORBIT AROUND THE HOMEWORLD, BUT NO SIGN OF THE CARPATHI--
--WAIT, WAIT, I'M PICKING UP A SPATIAL DISTORTION THAT I HAVEN'T SEEN BE--
IT'S THEM: THEY WERE HIDING IN WARP, JOEY! I--I DON'T KNOW HOW THAT'S POSSIBLE!!
EVASIVE!
FSMCART
THEY'VE WEAPONIZED HIM TOO--WE'VE GOT MIDAS INBOUND, GUYS!
DOWN HARD TO PORT! GET US OUT OF RANGE, FATTY!
ON IT!!
IT'S TRACKING US! AND IT'S TOO CLOSE--IF WE FIRE AT IT WE RISK BLOWING UP THE FLESH AND GETTING HIT BY THE BLOOD!
LAUNCH FLAK! COOPER, ARE YOU READY DOWN THERE?
READY.

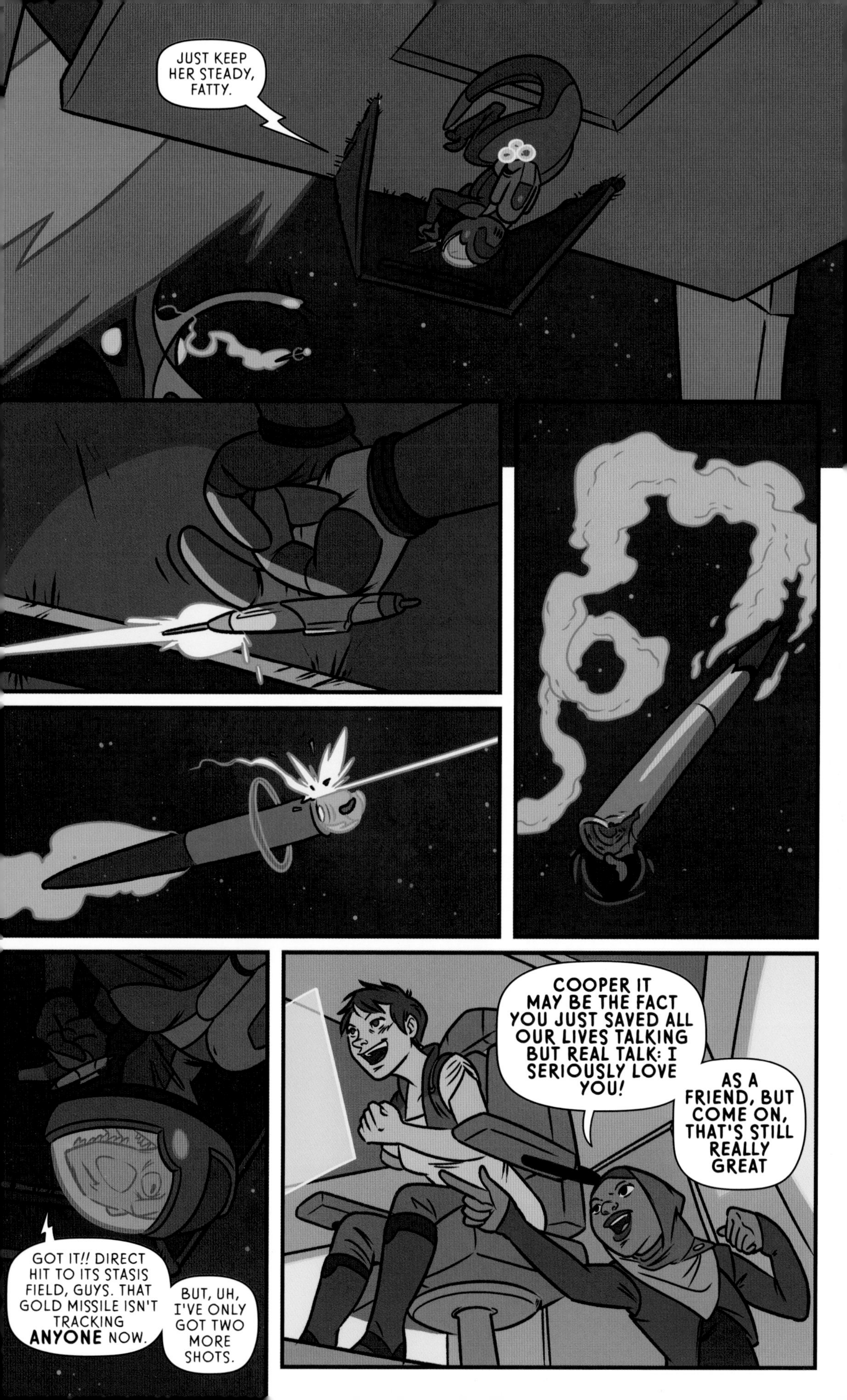
JUST KEEP HER STEADY, FATTY.
COOPER IT MAY BE THE FACT YOU JUST SAVED ALL OUR LIVES TALKING BUT REAL TALK: I SERIOUSLY LOVE YOU!
AS A FRIEND, BUT COME ON, THAT'S STILL REALLY GREAT
GOT IT!! DIRECT HIT TO ITS STASIS FIELD, GUYS. THAT GOLD MISSILE ISN'T TRACKING **ANYONE** NOW.
BUT, UH, I'VE ONLY GOT TWO MORE SHOTS.

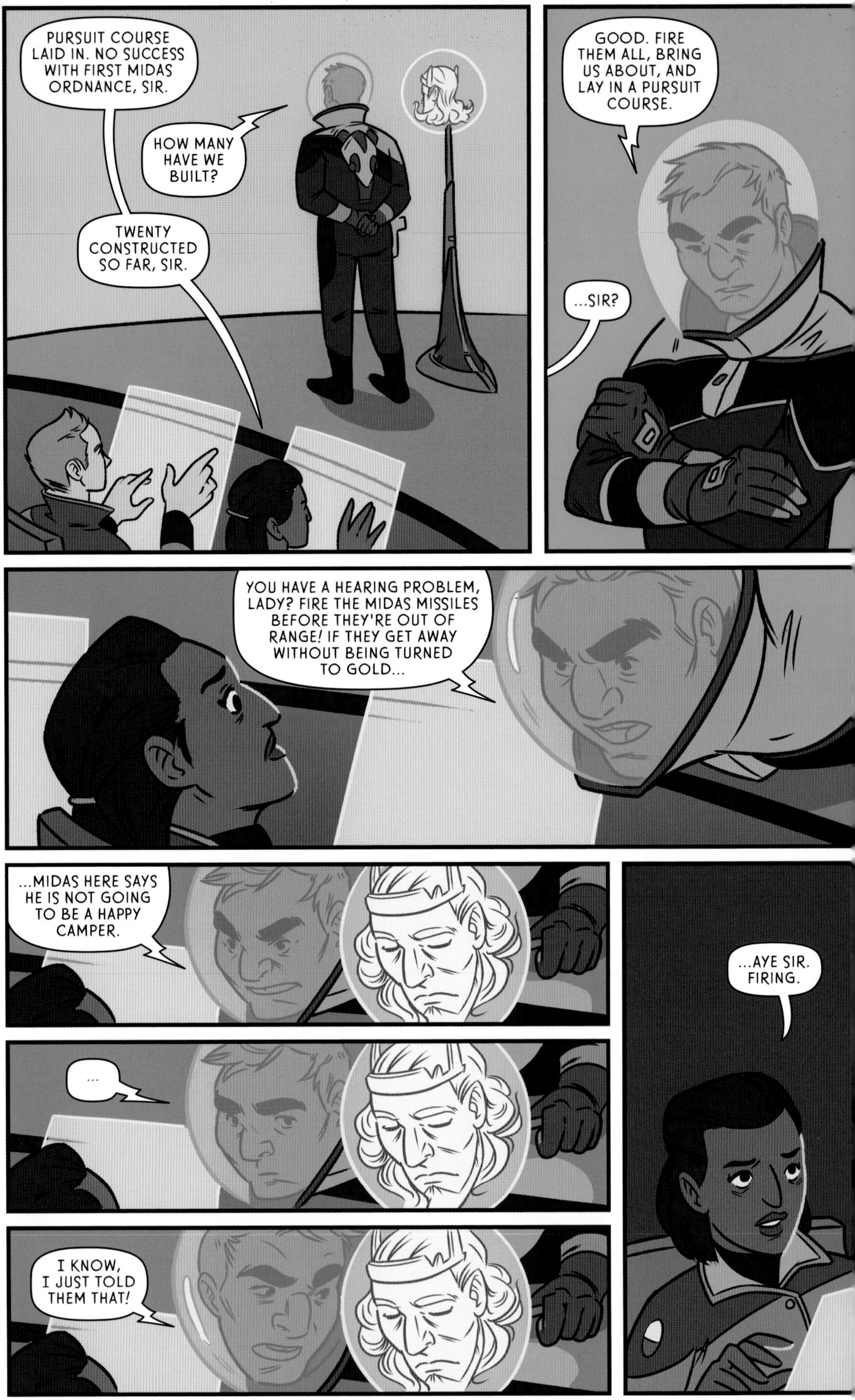
PURSUIT COURSE LAID IN. NO SUCCESS WITH FIRST MIDAS ORDNANCE, SIR.
HOW MANY HAVE WE BUILT?
TWENTY CONSTRUCTED SO FAR, SIR.
GOOD. FIRE THEM ALL, BRING US ABOUT, AND LAY IN A PURSUIT COURSE.
...SIR?
YOU HAVE A HEARING PROBLEM, LADY? FIRE THE MIDAS MISSILES BEFORE THEY'RE OUT OF RANGE! IF THEY GET AWAY WITHOUT BEING TURNED TO GOLD...
...MIDAS HERE SAYS HE IS NOT GOING TO BE A HAPPY CAMPER.
...
I KNOW, I JUST TOLD THEM THAT!
...AYE SIR. FIRING.

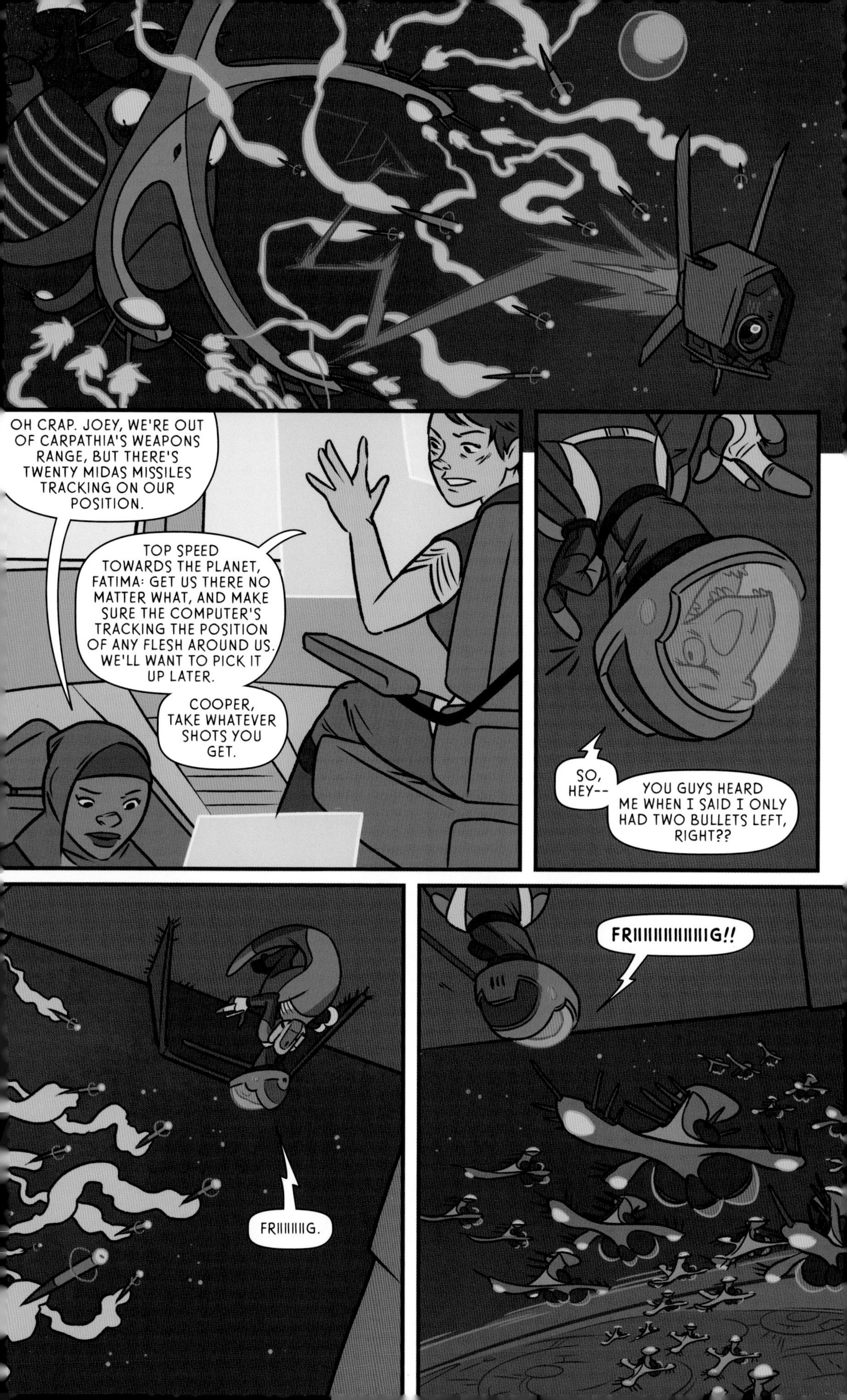
OH CRAP. JOEY, WE'RE OUT OF CARPATHIA'S WEAPONS RANGE, BUT THERE'S TWENTY MIDAS MISSILES TRACKING ON OUR POSITION.
TOP SPEED TOWARDS THE PLANET, FATIMA: GET US THERE NO MATTER WHAT, AND MAKE SURE THE COMPUTER'S TRACKING THE POSITION OF ANY FLESH AROUND US. WE'LL WANT TO PICK IT UP LATER.
COOPER, TAKE WHATEVER SHOTS YOU GET.
SO, HEY--
YOU GUYS HEARD ME WHEN I SAID I ONLY HAD TWO BULLETS LEFT, RIGHT??
FRIIIIIIIG.
FRIIIIIIIIIIIIIG!!

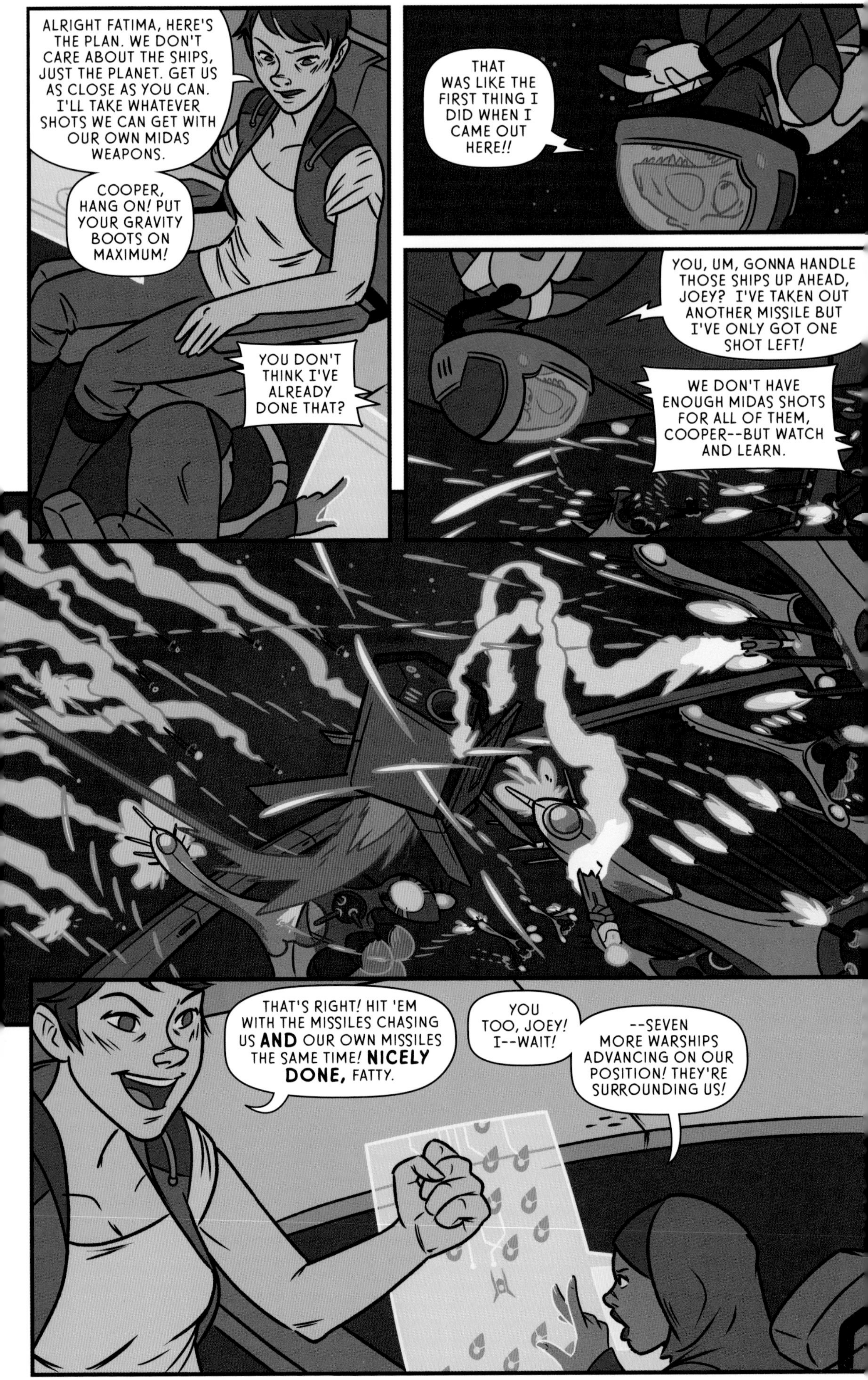
ALRIGHT FATIMA, HERE'S THE PLAN. WE DON'T CARE ABOUT THE SHIPS, JUST THE PLANET. GET US AS CLOSE AS YOU CAN. I'LL TAKE WHATEVER SHOTS WE CAN GET WITH OUR OWN MIDAS WEAPONS.
COOPER, HANG ON! PUT YOUR GRAVITY BOOTS ON MAXIMUM!
YOU DON'T THINK I'VE ALREADY DONE THAT?
THAT WAS LIKE THE FIRST THING I DID WHEN I CAME OUT HERE!!
YOU, UM, GONNA HANDLE THOSE SHIPS UP AHEAD, JOEY? I'VE TAKEN OUT ANOTHER MISSILE BUT I'VE ONLY GOT ONE SHOT LEFT!
WE DON'T HAVE ENOUGH MIDAS SHOTS FOR ALL OF THEM, COOPER--BUT WATCH AND LEARN.
THAT'S RIGHT! HIT 'EM WITH THE MISSILES CHASING US AND OUR OWN MISSILES THE SAME TIME! NICELY DONE, FATTY.
YOU TOO, JOEY! I--WAIT!
--SEVEN MORE WARSHIPS ADVANCING ON OUR POSITION! THEY'RE SURROUNDING US!

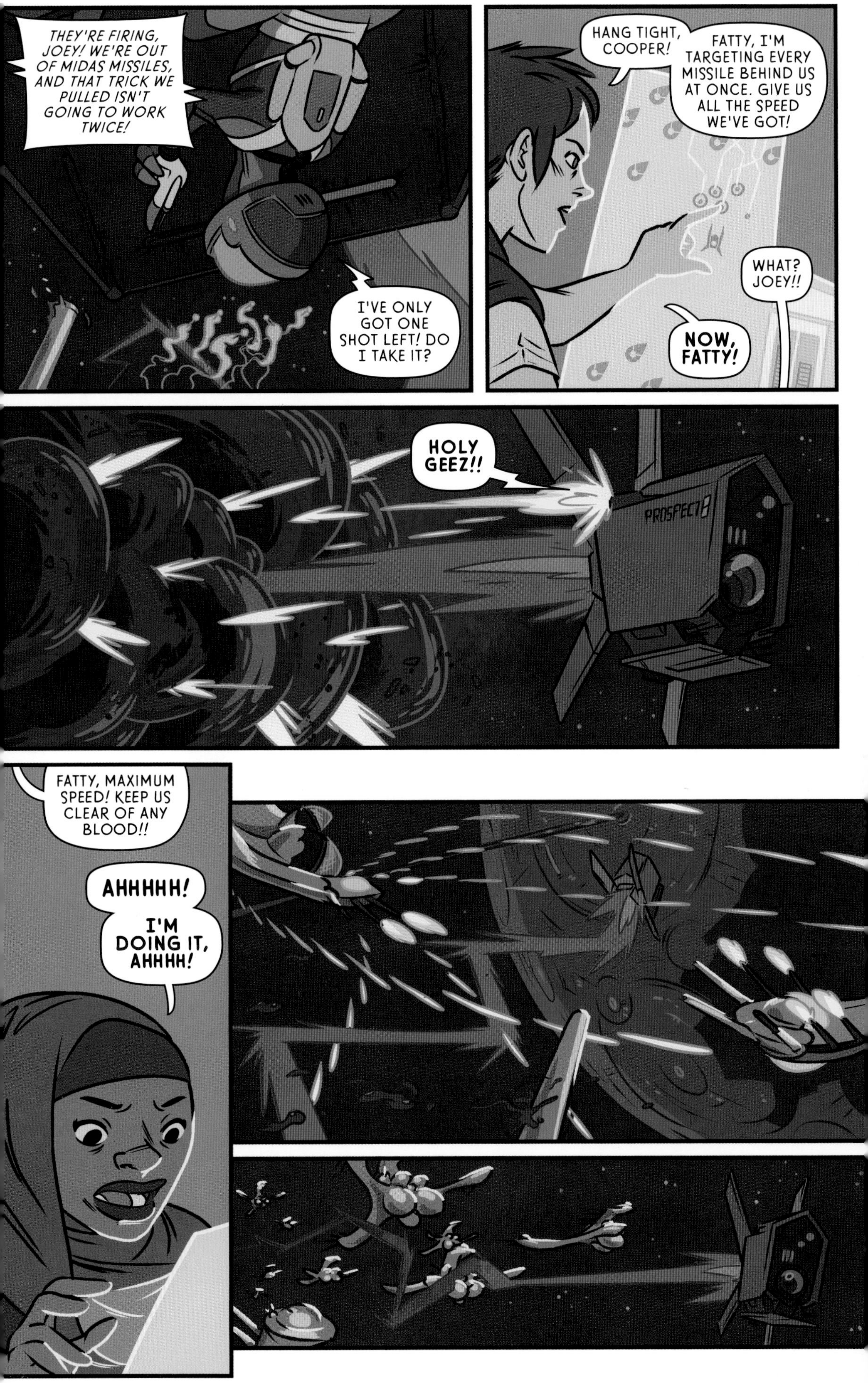
THEY'RE FIRING, JOEY! WE'RE OUT OF MIDAS MISSILES, AND THAT TRICK WE PULLED ISN'T GOING TO WORK TWICE!
I'VE ONLY GOT ONE SHOT LEFT! DO I TAKE IT?
HANG TIGHT, COOPER!
FATTY, I'M TARGETING EVERY MISSILE BEHIND US AT ONCE. GIVE US ALL THE SPEED WE'VE GOT!
WHAT? JOEY!!
NOW, FATTY!
HOLY GEEZ!!
PROSPECT 8
FATTY, MAXIMUM SPEED! KEEP US CLEAR OF ANY BLOOD!!
AHHHHH!
I'M DOING IT, AHHHH!

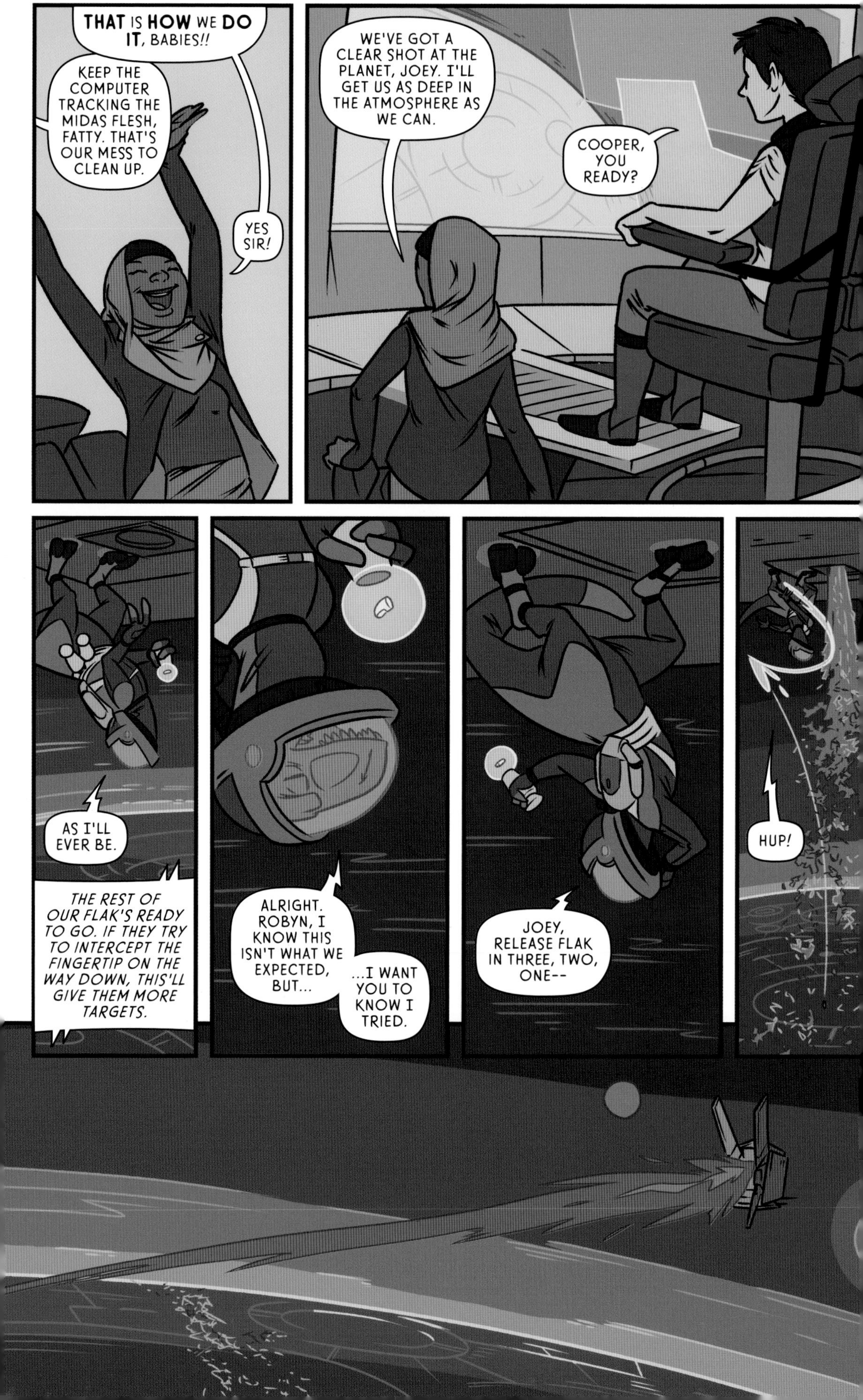
THAT IS HOW WE DO IT, BABIES!!
KEEP THE COMPUTER TRACKING THE MIDAS FLESH, FATTY. THAT'S OUR MESS TO CLEAN UP.
YES SIR!
WE'VE GOT A CLEAR SHOT AT THE PLANET, JOEY. I'LL GET US AS DEEP IN THE ATMOSPHERE AS WE CAN.
COOPER, YOU READY?
AS I'LL EVER BE.
THE REST OF OUR FLAK'S READY TO GO. IF THEY TRY TO INTERCEPT THE FINGERTIP ON THE WAY DOWN, THIS'LL GIVE THEM MORE TARGETS.
ALRIGHT. ROBYN, I KNOW THIS ISN'T WHAT WE EXPECTED, BUT...
...I WANT YOU TO KNOW I TRIED.
JOEY, RELEASE FLAK IN THREE, TWO, ONE--
HUP!

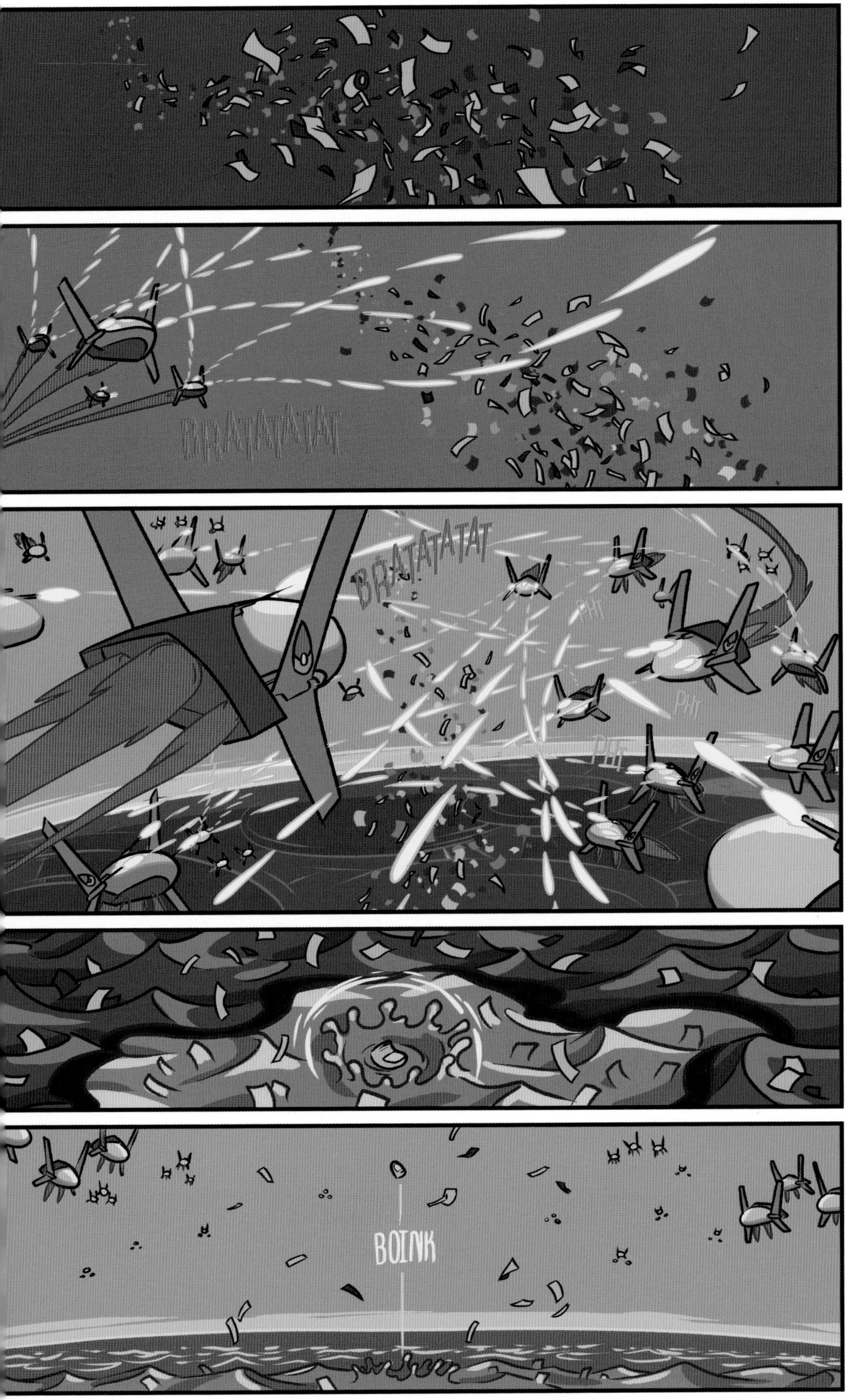
BRATATATAT
BRATATATAT
PHT
PHT
PHT
BOINK

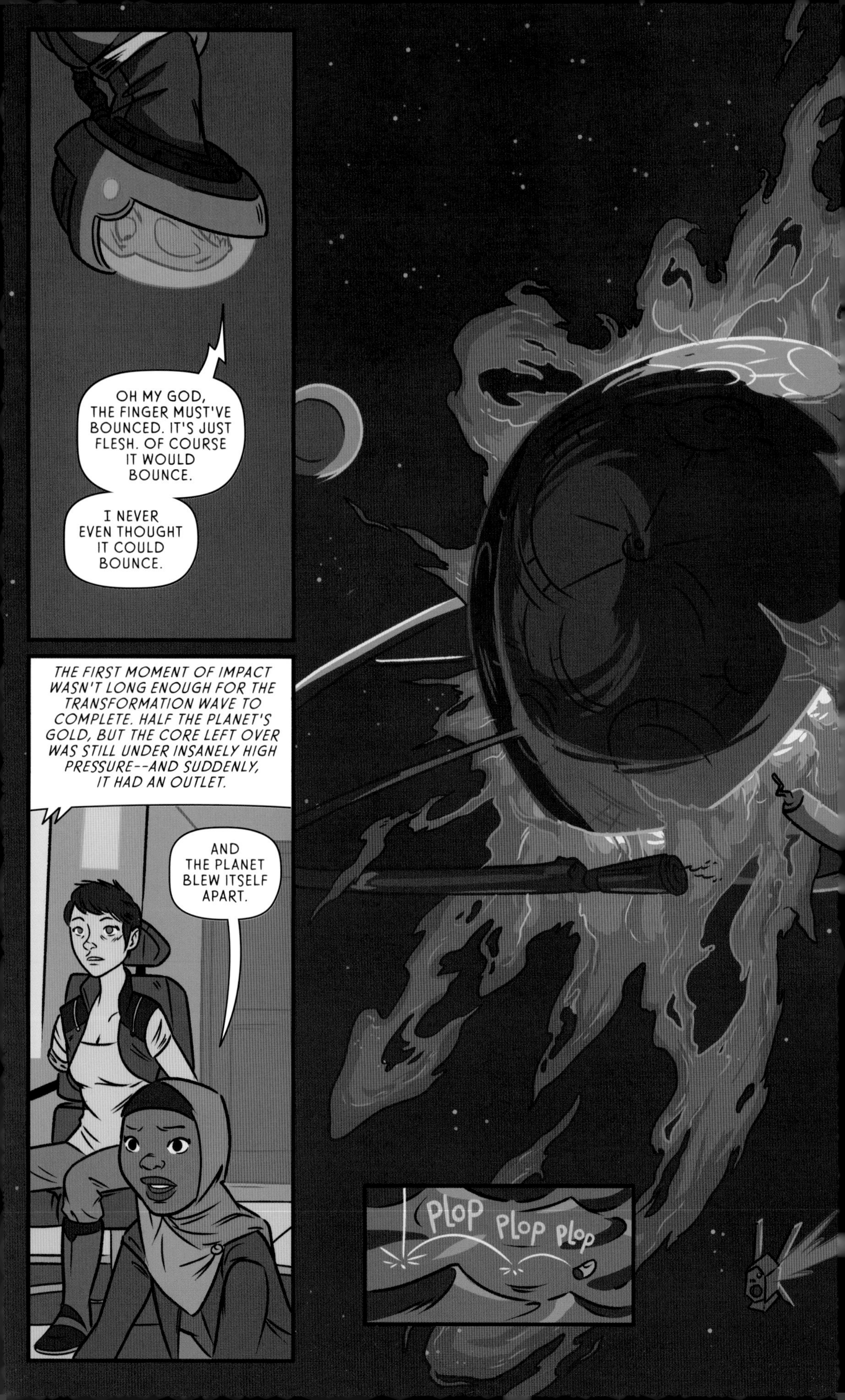

OH MY GOD, THE FINGER MUST'VE BOUNCED. IT'S JUST FLESH. OF COURSE IT WOULD BOUNCE.
I NEVER EVEN THOUGHT IT COULD BOUNCE.
THE FIRST MOMENT OF IMPACT WASN'T LONG ENOUGH FOR THE TRANSFORMATION WAVE TO COMPLETE. HALF THE PLANET'S GOLD, BUT THE CORE LEFT OVER WAS STILL UNDER INSANELY HIGH PRESSURE--AND SUDDENLY, IT HAD AN OUTLET.
AND THE PLANET BLEW ITSELF APART.
PLOP PLOP PLOP

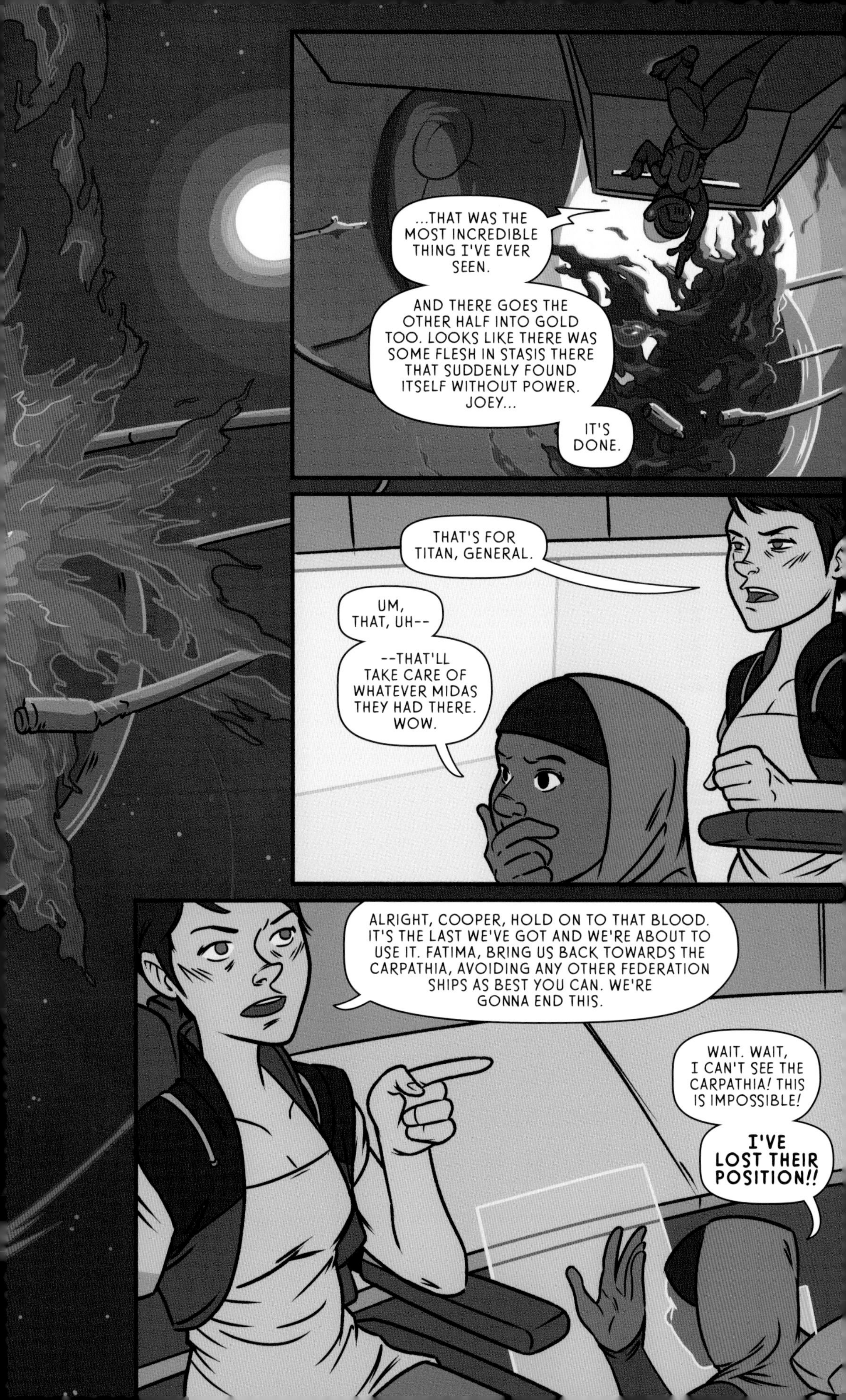
...THAT WAS THE MOST INCREDIBLE THING I'VE EVER SEEN.
AND THERE GOES THE OTHER HALF INTO GOLD TOO. LOOKS LIKE THERE WAS SOME FLESH IN STASIS THERE THAT SUDDENLY FOUND ITSELF WITHOUT POWER. JOEY...
IT'S DONE.
THAT'S FOR TITAN, GENERAL.
UM, THAT, UH--
--THAT'LL TAKE CARE OF WHATEVER MIDAS THEY HAD THERE. WOW.
ALRIGHT, COOPER, HOLD ON TO THAT BLOOD. IT'S THE LAST WE'VE GOT AND WE'RE ABOUT TO USE IT. FATIMA, BRING US BACK TOWARDS THE CARPATHIA, AVOIDING ANY OTHER FEDERATION SHIPS AS BEST YOU CAN. WE'RE GONNA END THIS.
WAIT. WAIT, I CAN'T SEE THE CARPATHIA! THIS IS IMPOSSIBLE!
I'VE LOST THEIR POSITION!!

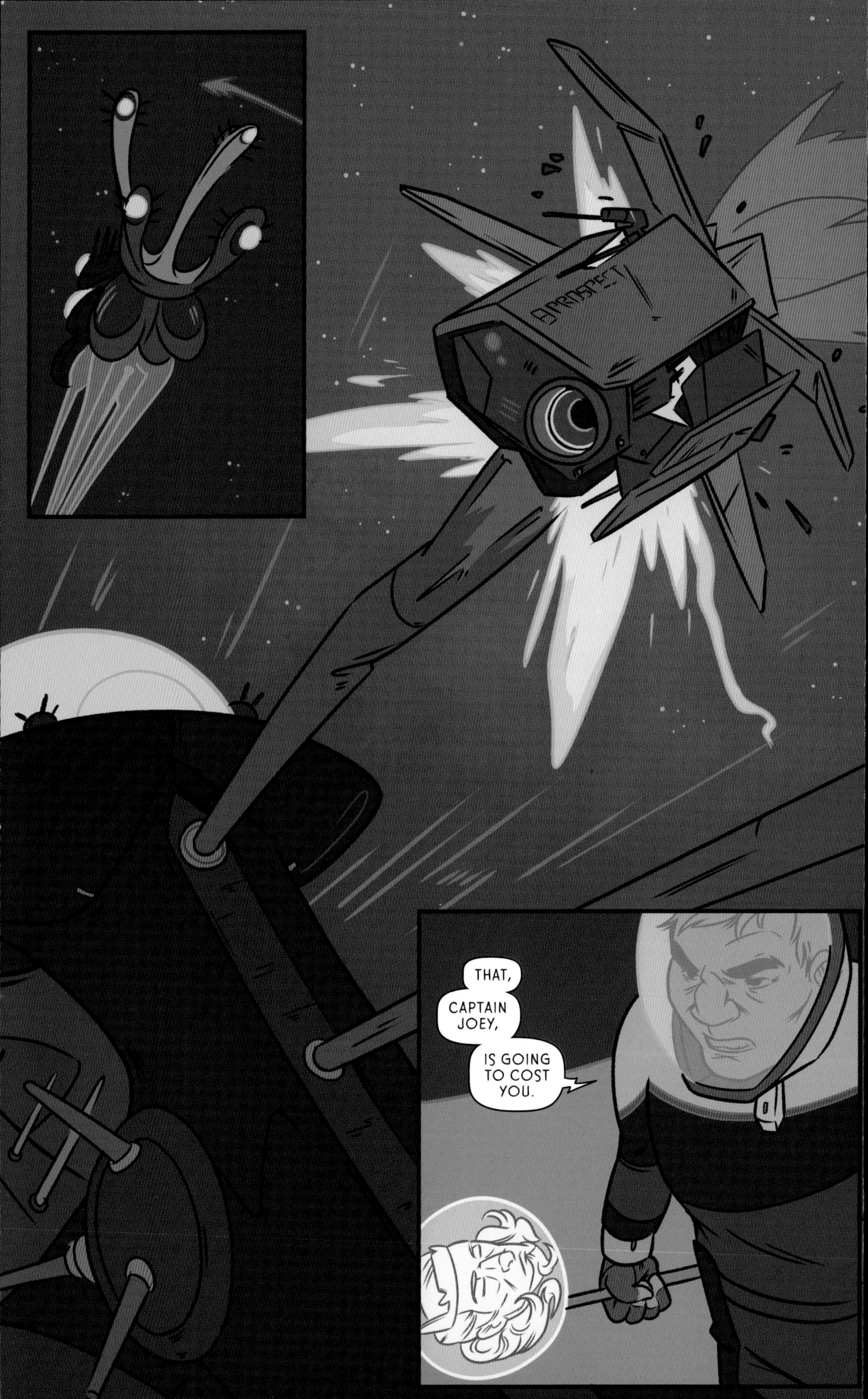
PROSPECT
THAT,
CAPTAIN JOEY,
IS GOING TO COST YOU.

"HOLY GEEZ!!"

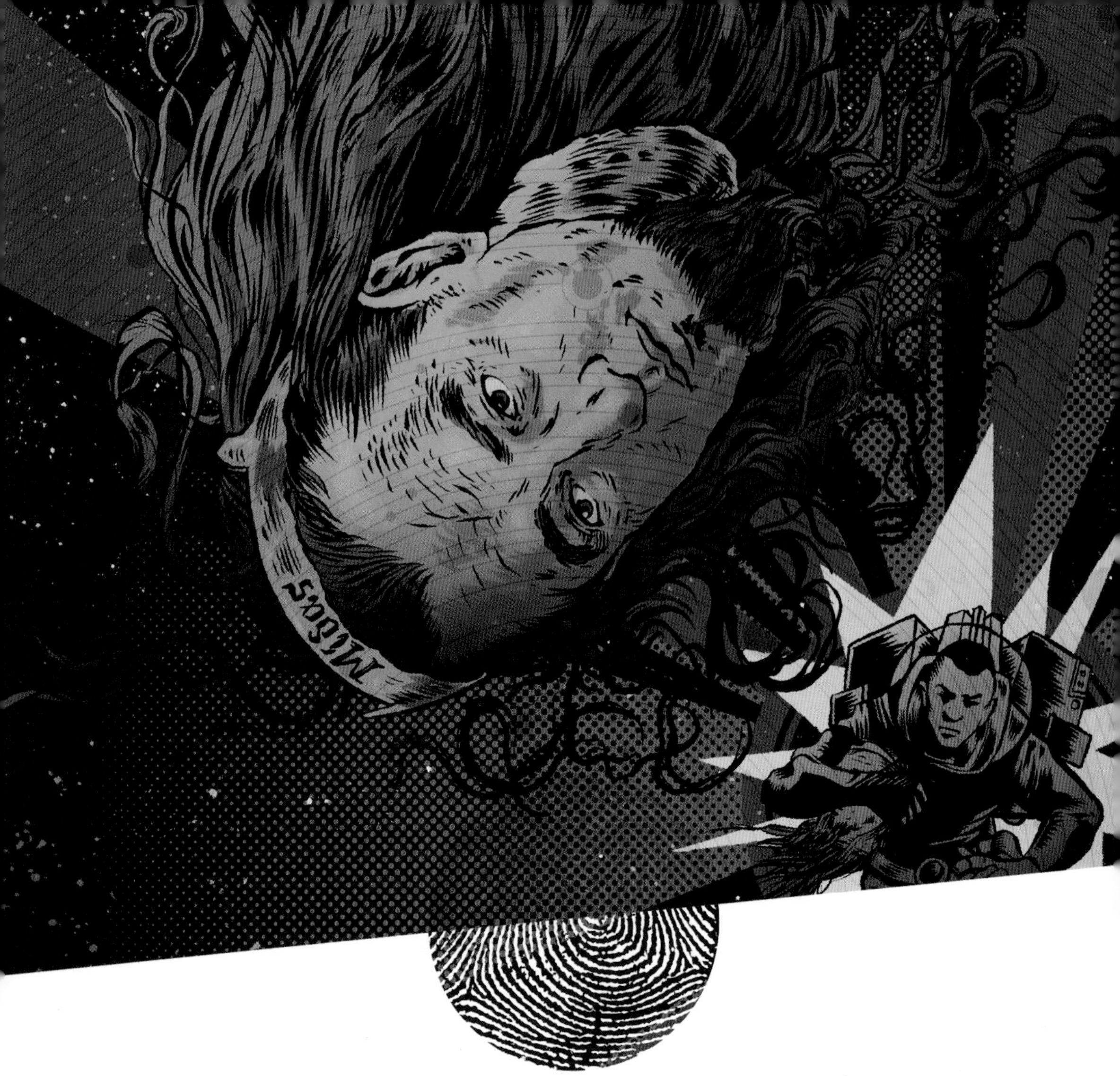

CHAPTER SEVEN

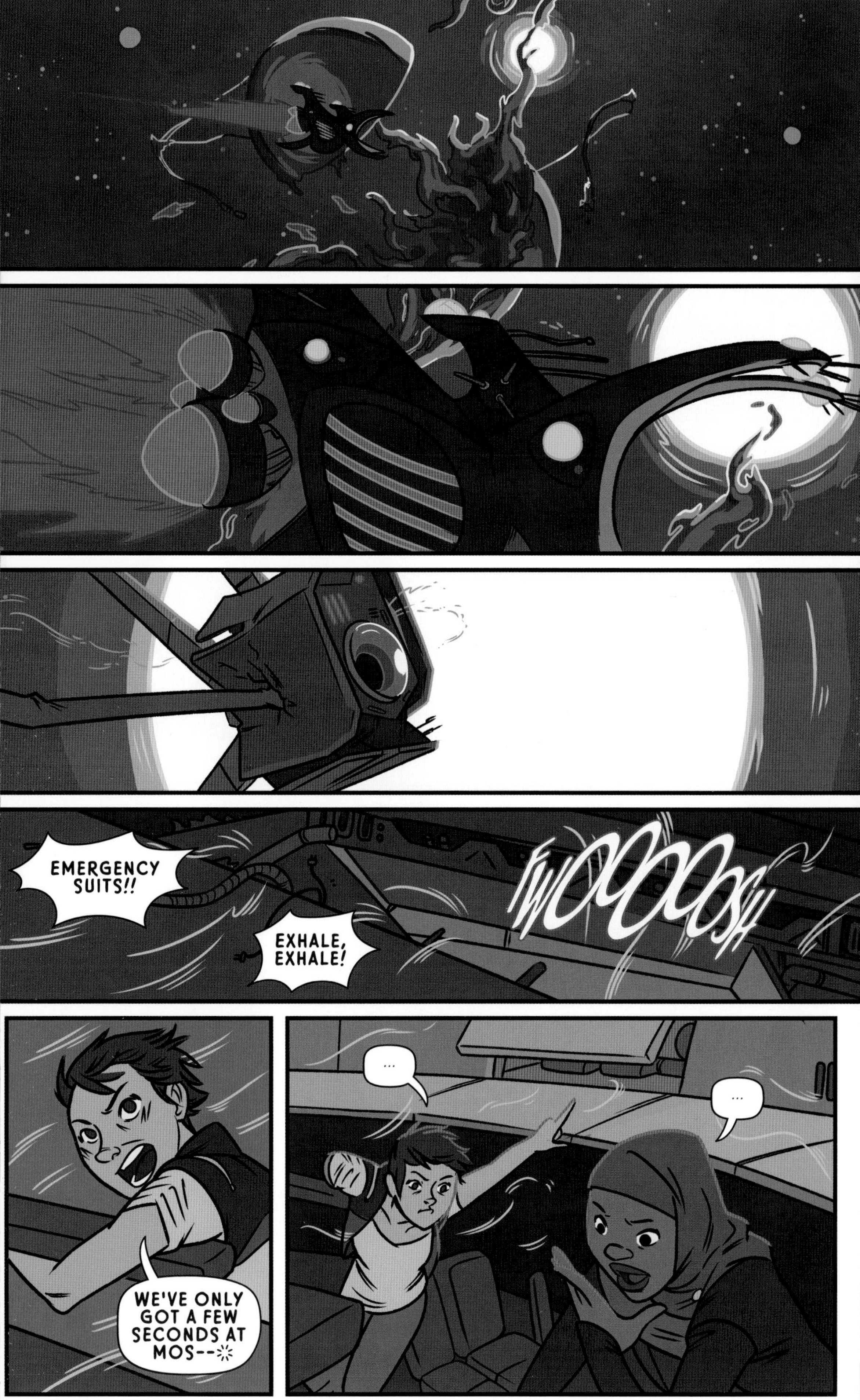

EMERGENCY SUITS!!
EXHALE, EXHALE!
FWOOOOSH
WE'VE ONLY GOT A FEW SECONDS AT MOS--
...
...

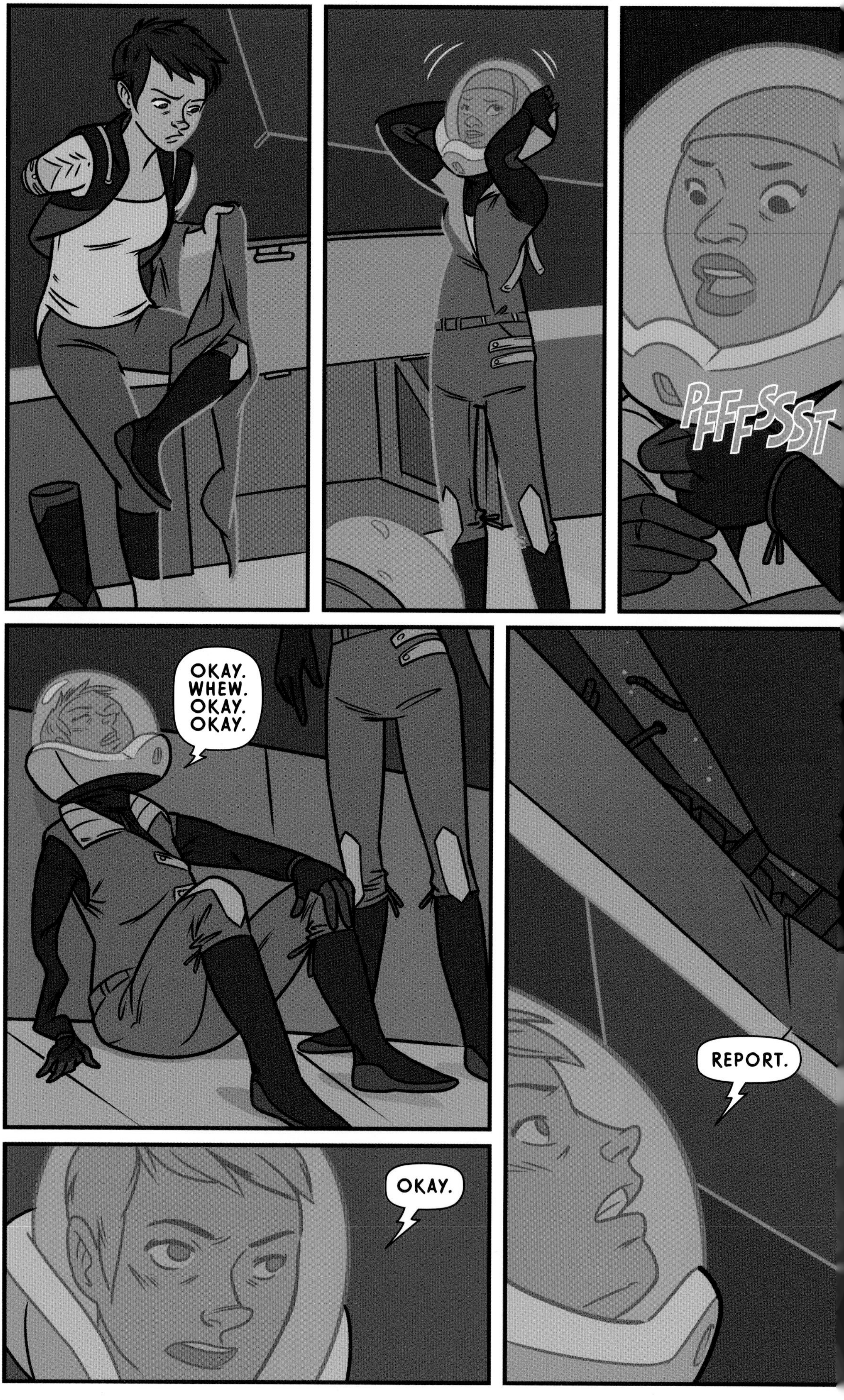
PFFFSSST
OKAY. WHEW. OKAY. OKAY.
REPORT.
OKAY.

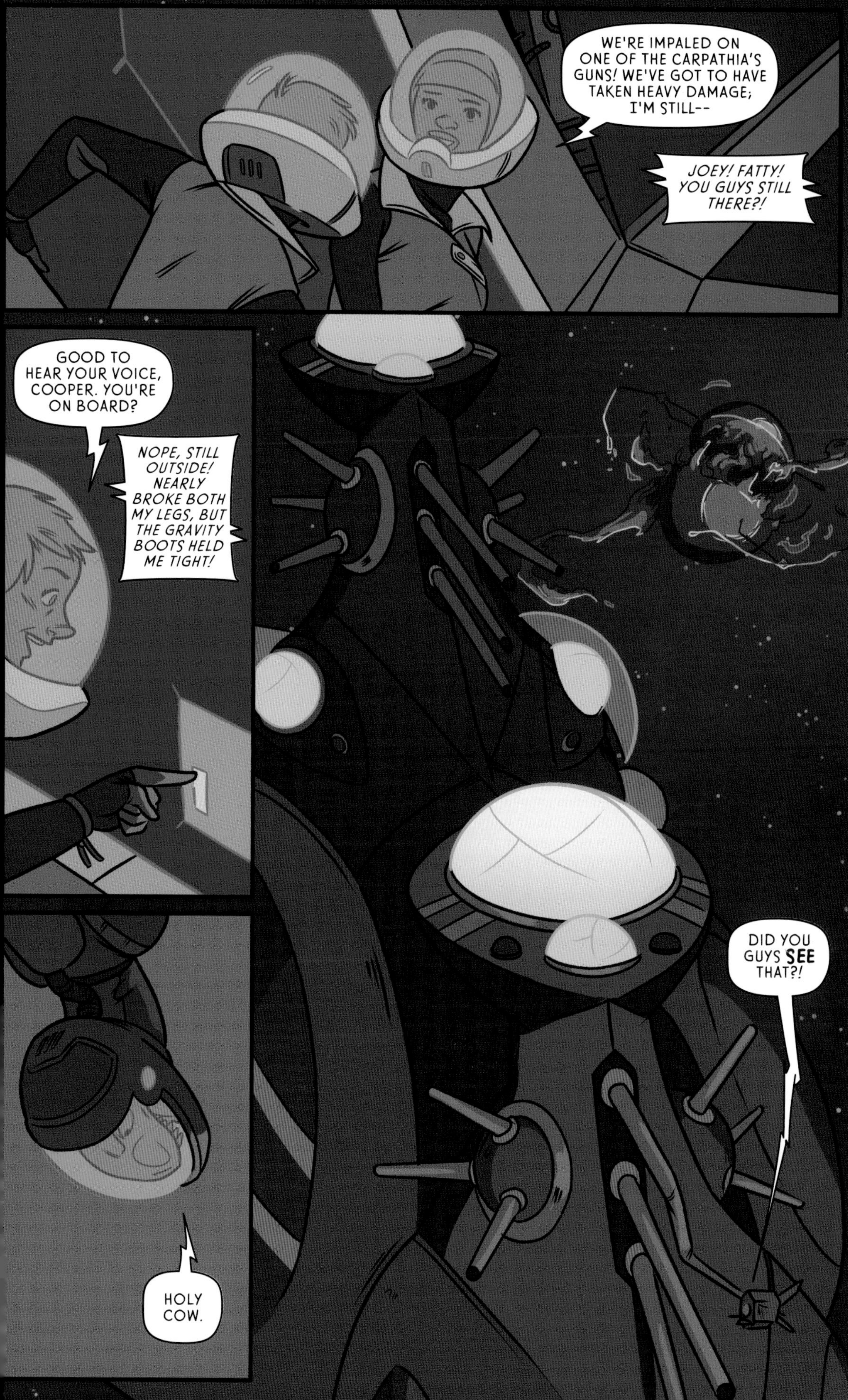

WE'RE IMPALED ON ONE OF THE CARPATHIA'S GUNS! WE'VE GOT TO HAVE TAKEN HEAVY DAMAGE; I'M STILL--
JOEY! FATTY! YOU GUYS STILL THERE?!
GOOD TO HEAR YOUR VOICE, COOPER. YOU'RE ON BOARD?
NOPE, STILL OUTSIDE! NEARLY BROKE BOTH MY LEGS, BUT THE GRAVITY BOOTS HELD ME TIGHT!
DID YOU GUYS **SEE** THAT?!
HOLY COW.

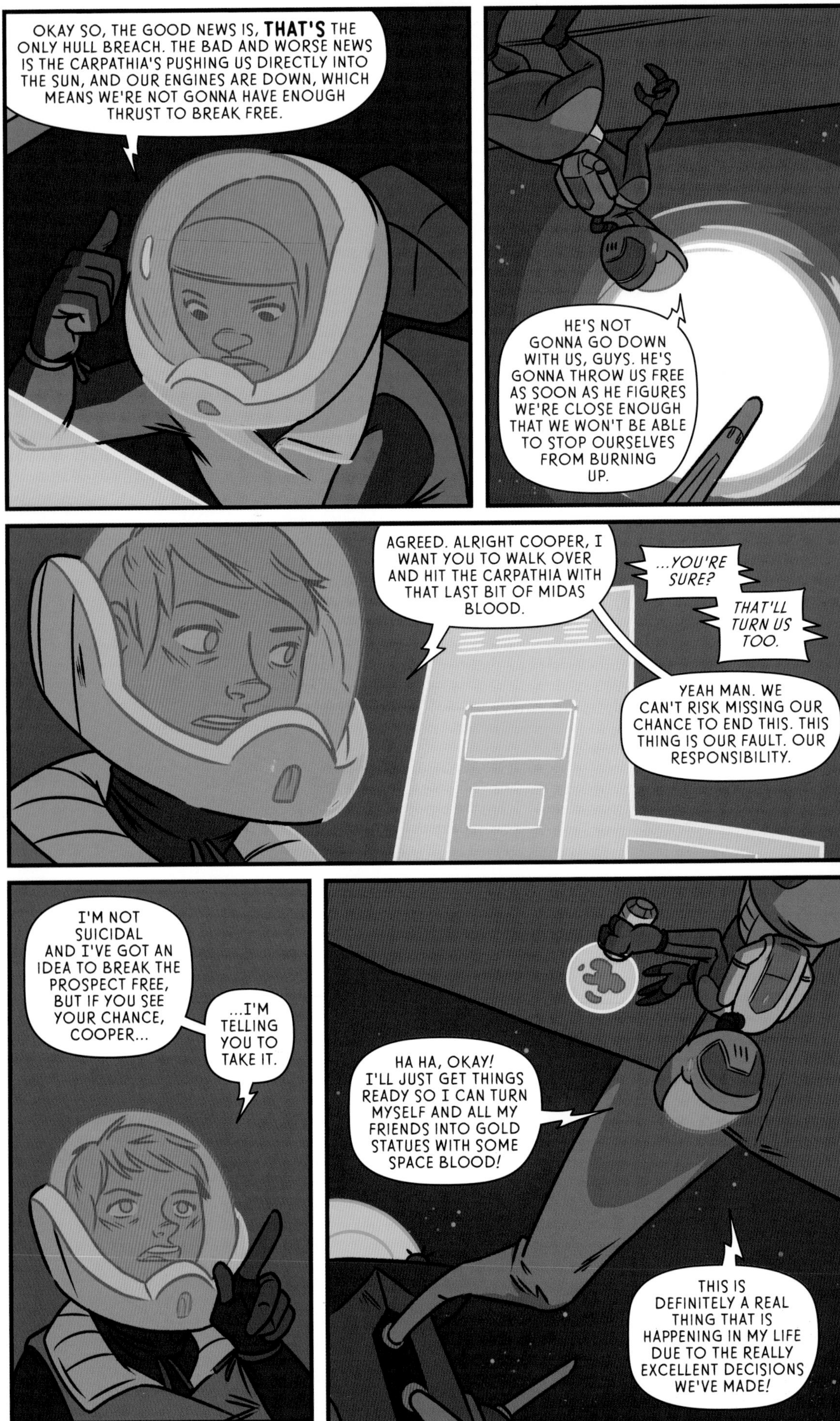

OKAY SO, THE GOOD NEWS IS, **THAT'S** THE ONLY HULL BREACH. THE BAD AND WORSE NEWS IS THE CARPATHIA'S PUSHING US DIRECTLY INTO THE SUN, AND OUR ENGINES ARE DOWN, WHICH MEANS WE'RE NOT GONNA HAVE ENOUGH THRUST TO BREAK FREE.
HE'S NOT GONNA GO DOWN WITH US, GUYS. HE'S GONNA THROW US FREE AS SOON AS HE FIGURES WE'RE CLOSE ENOUGH THAT WE WON'T BE ABLE TO STOP OURSELVES FROM BURNING UP.
AGREED. ALRIGHT COOPER, I WANT YOU TO WALK OVER AND HIT THE CARPATHIA WITH THAT LAST BIT OF MIDAS BLOOD.
...YOU'RE SURE?
THAT'LL TURN US TOO.
YEAH MAN. WE CAN'T RISK MISSING OUR CHANCE TO END THIS. THIS THING IS OUR FAULT. OUR RESPONSIBILITY.
I'M NOT SUICIDAL AND I'VE GOT AN IDEA TO BREAK THE PROSPECT FREE, BUT IF YOU SEE YOUR CHANCE, COOPER...
...I'M TELLING YOU TO TAKE IT.
HA HA, OKAY! I'LL JUST GET THINGS READY SO I CAN TURN MYSELF AND ALL MY FRIENDS INTO GOLD STATUES WITH SOME SPACE BLOOD!
THIS IS DEFINITELY A REAL THING THAT IS HAPPENING IN MY LIFE DUE TO THE REALLY EXCELLENT DECISIONS WE'VE MADE!

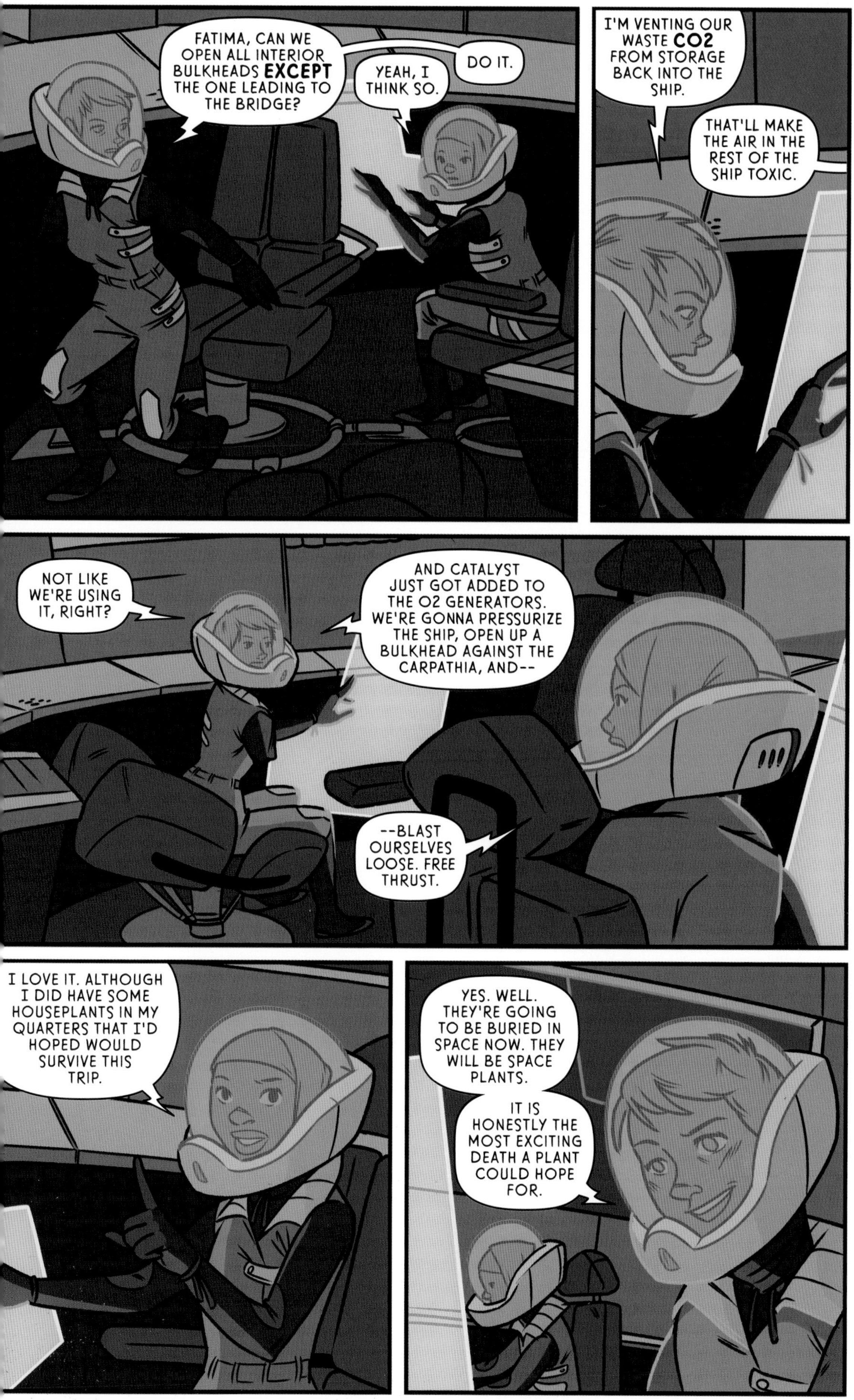
FATIMA, CAN WE OPEN ALL INTERIOR BULKHEADS **EXCEPT** THE ONE LEADING TO THE BRIDGE?
YEAH, I THINK SO.
DO IT.
I'M VENTING OUR WASTE **CO2** FROM STORAGE BACK INTO THE SHIP.
THAT'LL MAKE THE AIR IN THE REST OF THE SHIP TOXIC.
NOT LIKE WE'RE USING IT, RIGHT?
AND CATALYST JUST GOT ADDED TO THE O2 GENERATORS. WE'RE GONNA PRESSURIZE THE SHIP, OPEN UP A BULKHEAD AGAINST THE CARPATHIA, AND--
--BLAST OURSELVES LOOSE. FREE THRUST.
I LOVE IT. ALTHOUGH I DID HAVE SOME HOUSEPLANTS IN MY QUARTERS THAT I'D HOPED WOULD SURVIVE THIS TRIP.
YES. WELL. THEY'RE GOING TO BE BURIED IN SPACE NOW. THEY WILL BE SPACE PLANTS.
IT IS HONESTLY THE MOST EXCITING DEATH A PLANT COULD HOPE FOR.

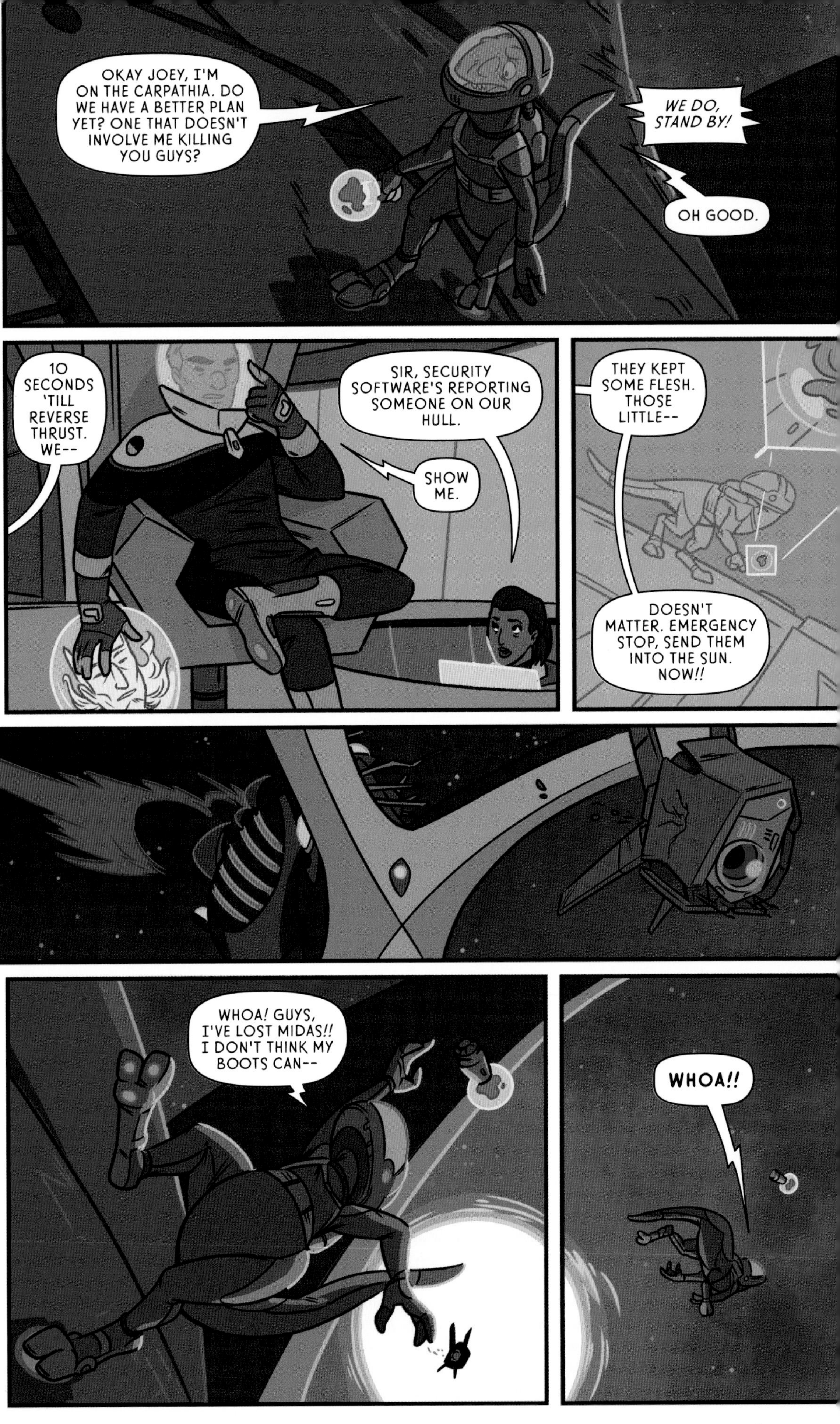
OKAY JOEY, I'M ON THE CARPATHIA. DO WE HAVE A BETTER PLAN YET? ONE THAT DOESN'T INVOLVE ME KILLING YOU GUYS?
WE DO, STAND BY!
OH GOOD.
10 SECONDS 'TILL REVERSE THRUST. WE--
SIR, SECURITY SOFTWARE'S REPORTING SOMEONE ON OUR HULL.
SHOW ME.
THEY KEPT SOME FLESH. THOSE LITTLE--
DOESN'T MATTER. EMERGENCY STOP, SEND THEM INTO THE SUN. NOW!!
WHOA! GUYS, I'VE LOST MIDAS!! I DON'T THINK MY BOOTS CAN--
WHOA!!

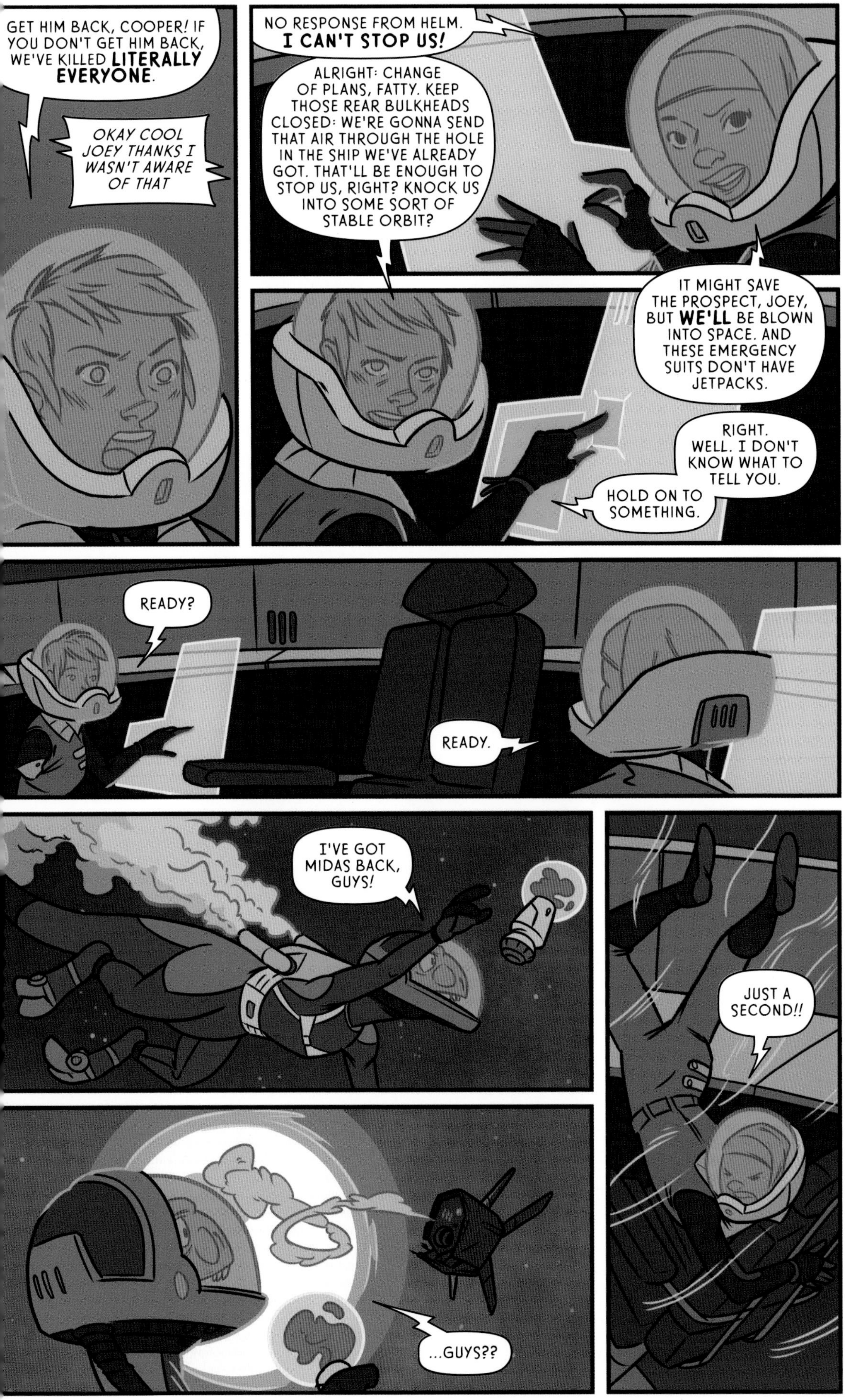
GET HIM BACK, COOPER! IF YOU DON'T GET HIM BACK, WE'VE KILLED LITERALLY EVERYONE.
OKAY COOL JOEY THANKS I WASN'T AWARE OF THAT
NO RESPONSE FROM HELM. I CAN'T STOP US!
ALRIGHT: CHANGE OF PLANS, FATTY. KEEP THOSE REAR BULKHEADS CLOSED: WE'RE GONNA SEND THAT AIR THROUGH THE HOLE IN THE SHIP WE'VE ALREADY GOT. THAT'LL BE ENOUGH TO STOP US, RIGHT? KNOCK US INTO SOME SORT OF STABLE ORBIT?
IT MIGHT SAVE THE PROSPECT, JOEY, BUT WE'LL BE BLOWN INTO SPACE. AND THESE EMERGENCY SUITS DON'T HAVE JETPACKS.
RIGHT. WELL. I DON'T KNOW WHAT TO TELL YOU.
HOLD ON TO SOMETHING.
READY?
READY.
I'VE GOT MIDAS BACK, GUYS!
JUST A SECOND!!
...GUYS??

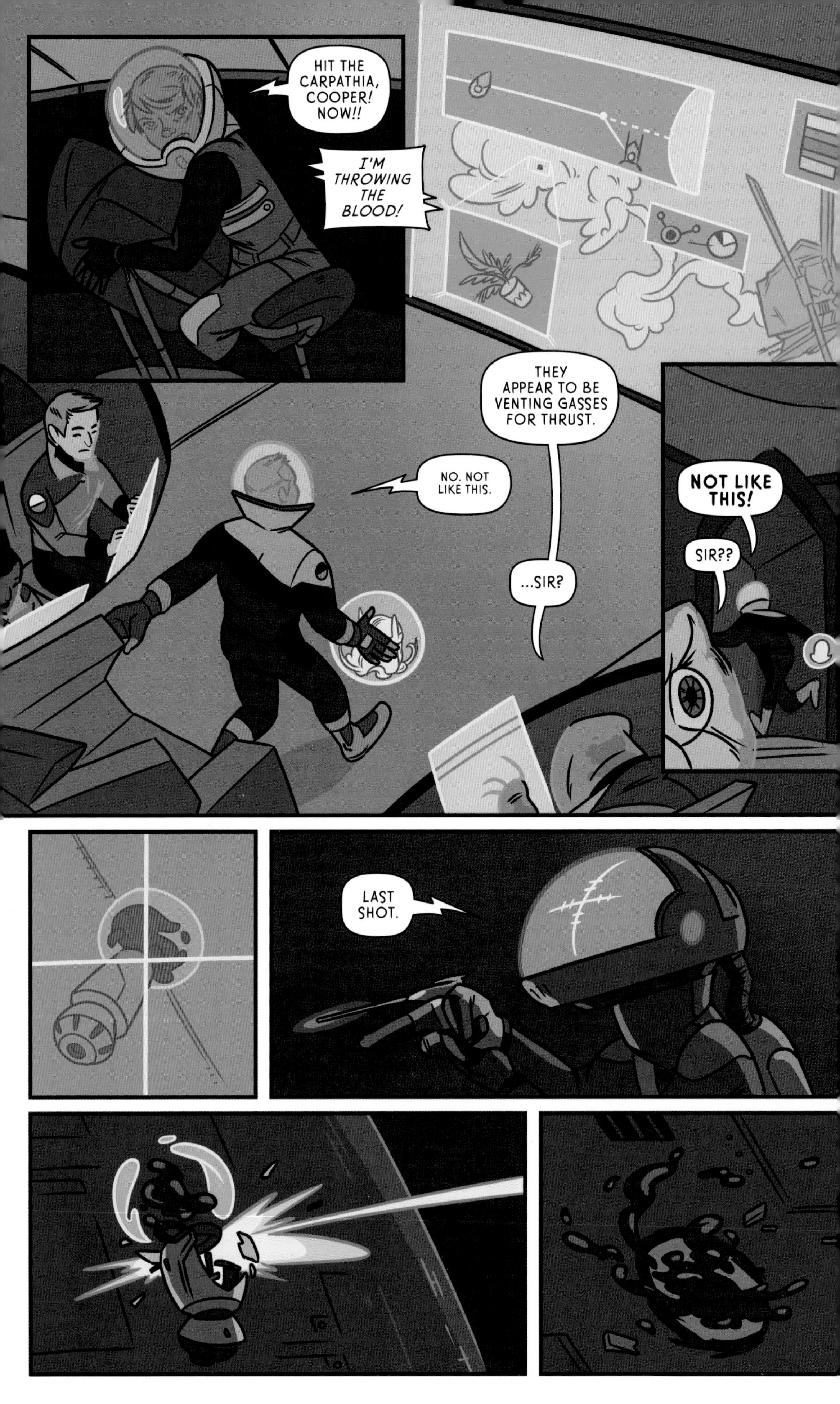
HIT THE CARPATHIA, COOPER! NOW!!
I'M THROWING THE BLOOD!
THEY APPEAR TO BE VENTING GASSES FOR THRUST.
NO. NOT LIKE THIS.
...SIR?
NOT LIKE THIS!
SIR??
LAST SHOT.

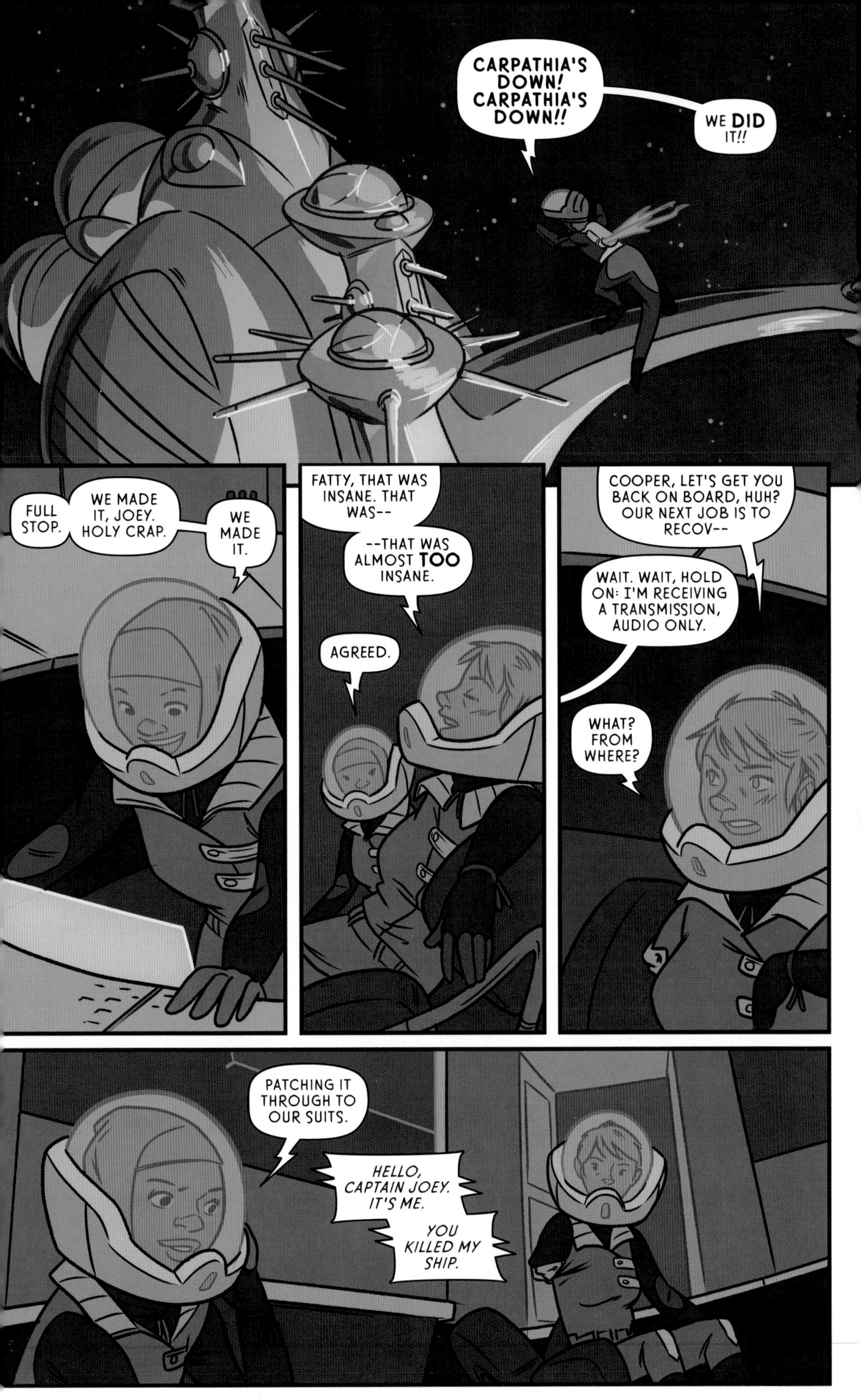
CARPATHIA'S DOWN! CARPATHIA'S DOWN!!
WE DID IT!!
FULL STOP.
WE MADE IT, JOEY. HOLY CRAP.
WE MADE IT.
FATTY, THAT WAS INSANE. THAT WAS--
--THAT WAS ALMOST TOO INSANE.
AGREED.
COOPER, LET'S GET YOU BACK ON BOARD, HUH? OUR NEXT JOB IS TO RECOV--
WAIT. WAIT, HOLD ON: I'M RECEIVING A TRANSMISSION, AUDIO ONLY.
WHAT? FROM WHERE?
PATCHING IT THROUGH TO OUR SUITS.
HELLO, CAPTAIN JOEY. IT'S ME.
YOU KILLED MY SHIP.

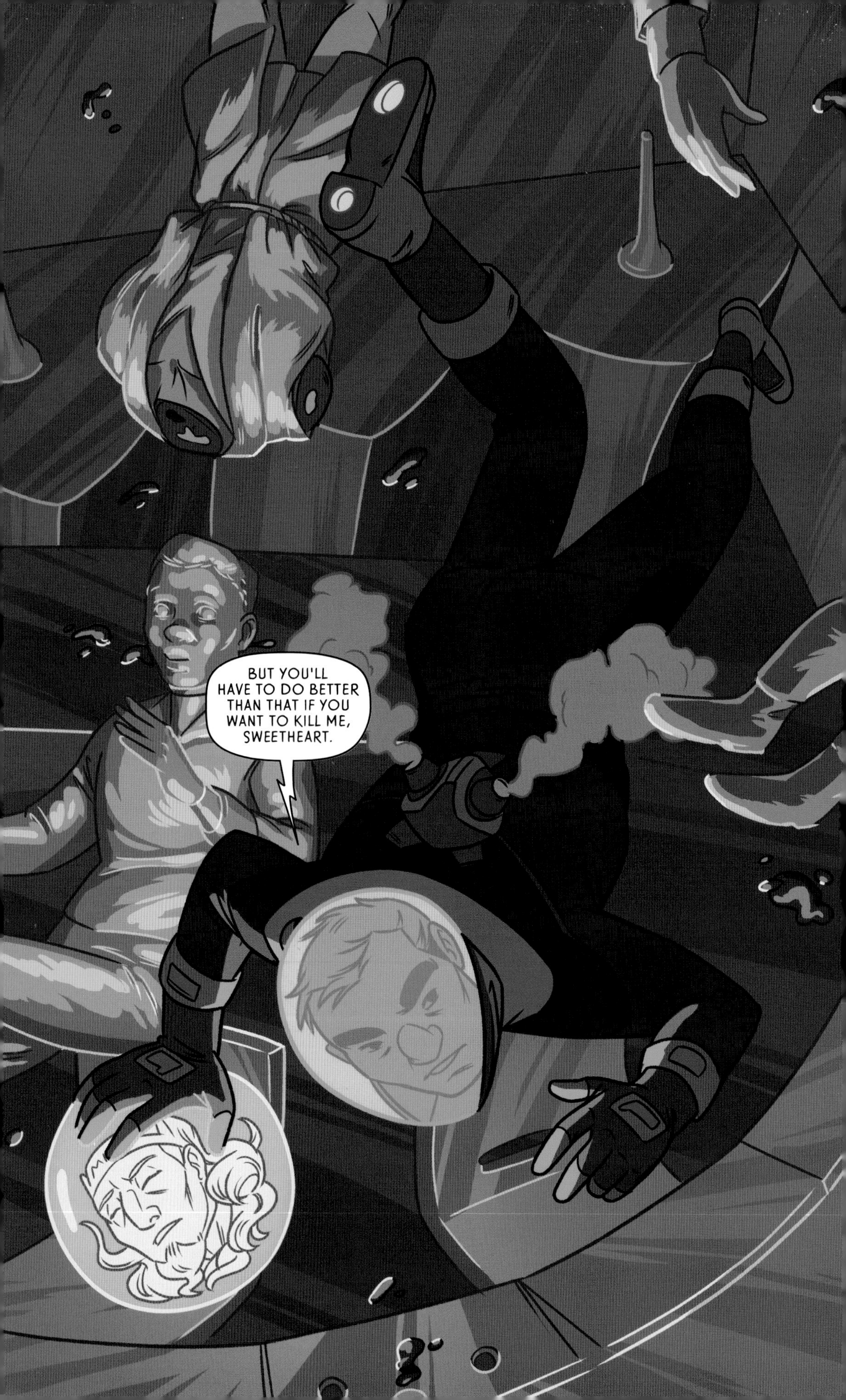
BUT YOU'LL HAVE TO DO BETTER THAN THAT IF YOU WANT TO KILL ME, SWEETHEART.

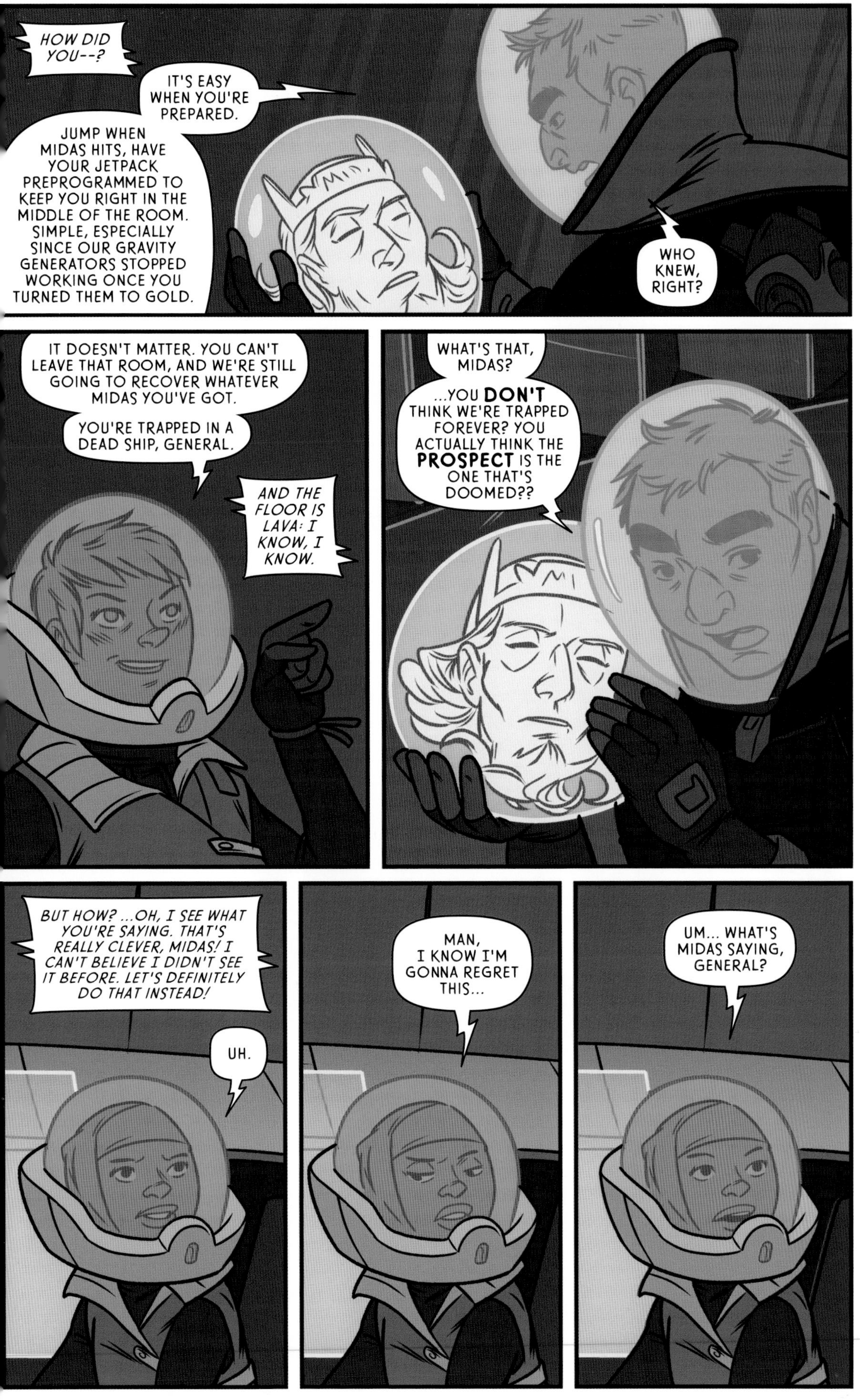
HOW DID YOU--?
IT'S EASY WHEN YOU'RE PREPARED.
JUMP WHEN MIDAS HITS, HAVE YOUR JETPACK PREPROGRAMMED TO KEEP YOU RIGHT IN THE MIDDLE OF THE ROOM. SIMPLE, ESPECIALLY SINCE OUR GRAVITY GENERATORS STOPPED WORKING ONCE YOU TURNED THEM TO GOLD.
WHO KNEW, RIGHT?
IT DOESN'T MATTER. YOU CAN'T LEAVE THAT ROOM, AND WE'RE STILL GOING TO RECOVER WHATEVER MIDAS YOU'VE GOT.
YOU'RE TRAPPED IN A DEAD SHIP, GENERAL.
AND THE FLOOR IS LAVA: I KNOW, I KNOW.
WHAT'S THAT, MIDAS?
...YOU **DON'T** THINK WE'RE TRAPPED FOREVER? YOU ACTUALLY THINK THE **PROSPECT** IS THE ONE THAT'S DOOMED??
BUT HOW? ...OH, I SEE WHAT YOU'RE SAYING. THAT'S REALLY CLEVER, MIDAS! I CAN'T BELIEVE I DIDN'T SEE IT BEFORE. LET'S DEFINITELY DO THAT INSTEAD!
UH.
MAN, I KNOW I'M GONNA REGRET THIS...
UM... WHAT'S MIDAS SAYING, GENERAL?

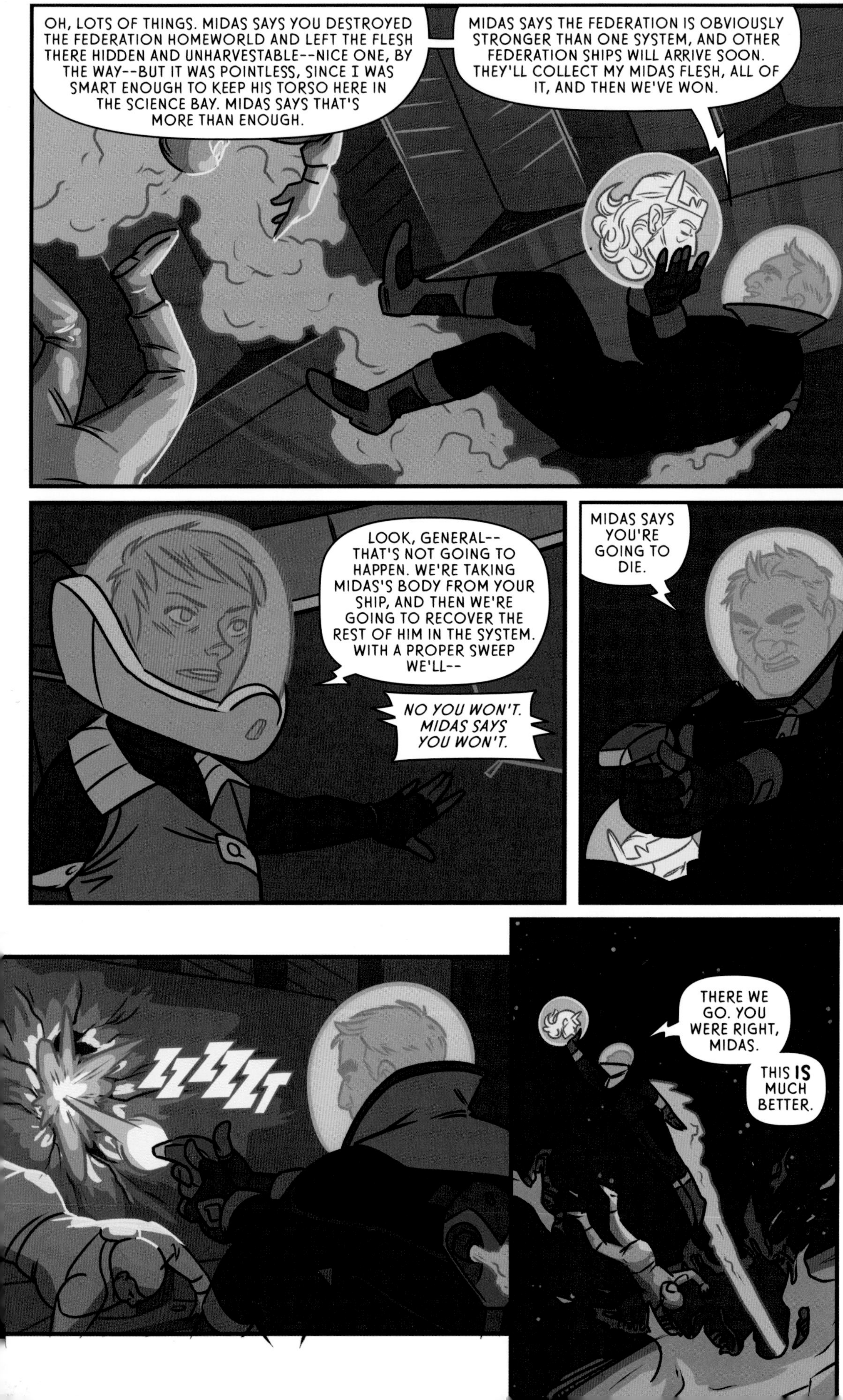
OH, LOTS OF THINGS. MIDAS SAYS YOU DESTROYED THE FEDERATION HOMEWORLD AND LEFT THE FLESH THERE HIDDEN AND UNHARVESTABLE--NICE ONE, BY THE WAY--BUT IT WAS POINTLESS, SINCE I WAS SMART ENOUGH TO KEEP HIS TORSO HERE IN THE SCIENCE BAY. MIDAS SAYS THAT'S MORE THAN ENOUGH.
MIDAS SAYS THE FEDERATION IS OBVIOUSLY STRONGER THAN ONE SYSTEM, AND OTHER FEDERATION SHIPS WILL ARRIVE SOON. THEY'LL COLLECT MY MIDAS FLESH, ALL OF IT, AND THEN WE'VE WON.
LOOK, GENERAL-- THAT'S NOT GOING TO HAPPEN. WE'RE TAKING MIDAS'S BODY FROM YOUR SHIP, AND THEN WE'RE GOING TO RECOVER THE REST OF HIM IN THE SYSTEM. WITH A PROPER SWEEP WE'LL--
NO YOU WON'T. MIDAS SAYS YOU WON'T.
MIDAS SAYS YOU'RE GOING TO DIE.
ZZZZZT
THERE WE GO. YOU WERE RIGHT, MIDAS.
THIS **IS** MUCH BETTER.

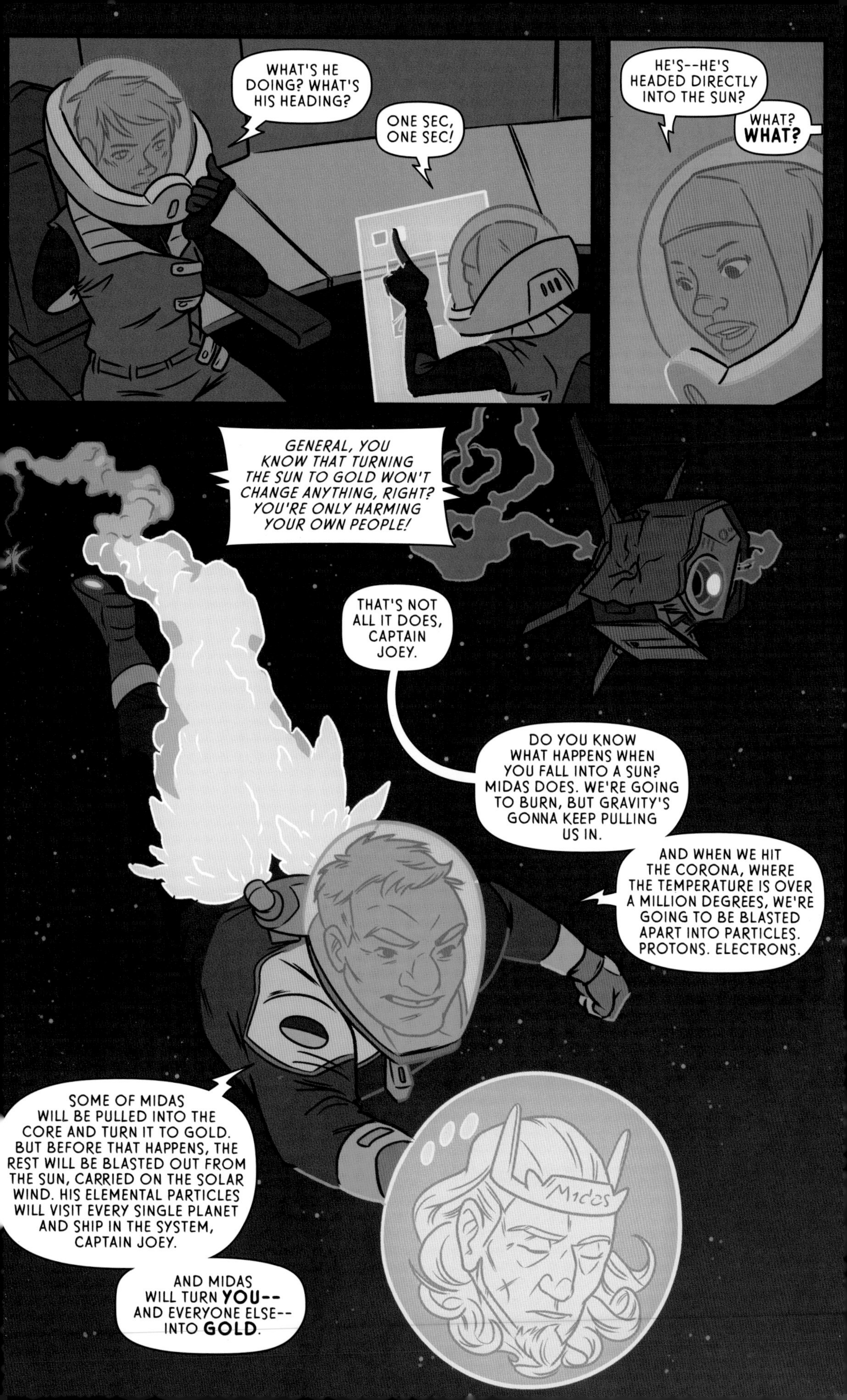
WHAT'S HE DOING? WHAT'S HIS HEADING?
ONE SEC, ONE SEC!
HE'S--HE'S HEADED DIRECTLY INTO THE SUN?
WHAT? **WHAT?**
GENERAL, YOU KNOW THAT TURNING THE SUN TO GOLD WON'T CHANGE ANYTHING, RIGHT? YOU'RE ONLY HARMING YOUR OWN PEOPLE!
THAT'S NOT ALL IT DOES, CAPTAIN JOEY.
DO YOU KNOW WHAT HAPPENS WHEN YOU FALL INTO A SUN? MIDAS DOES. WE'RE GOING TO BURN, BUT GRAVITY'S GONNA KEEP PULLING US IN.
AND WHEN WE HIT THE CORONA, WHERE THE TEMPERATURE IS OVER A MILLION DEGREES, WE'RE GOING TO BE BLASTED APART INTO PARTICLES. PROTONS. ELECTRONS.
SOME OF MIDAS WILL BE PULLED INTO THE CORE AND TURN IT TO GOLD. BUT BEFORE THAT HAPPENS, THE REST WILL BE BLASTED OUT FROM THE SUN, CARRIED ON THE SOLAR WIND. HIS ELEMENTAL PARTICLES WILL VISIT EVERY SINGLE PLANET AND SHIP IN THE SYSTEM, CAPTAIN JOEY.
AND MIDAS WILL TURN **YOU--** AND EVERYONE ELSE-- INTO **GOLD**.
Midas

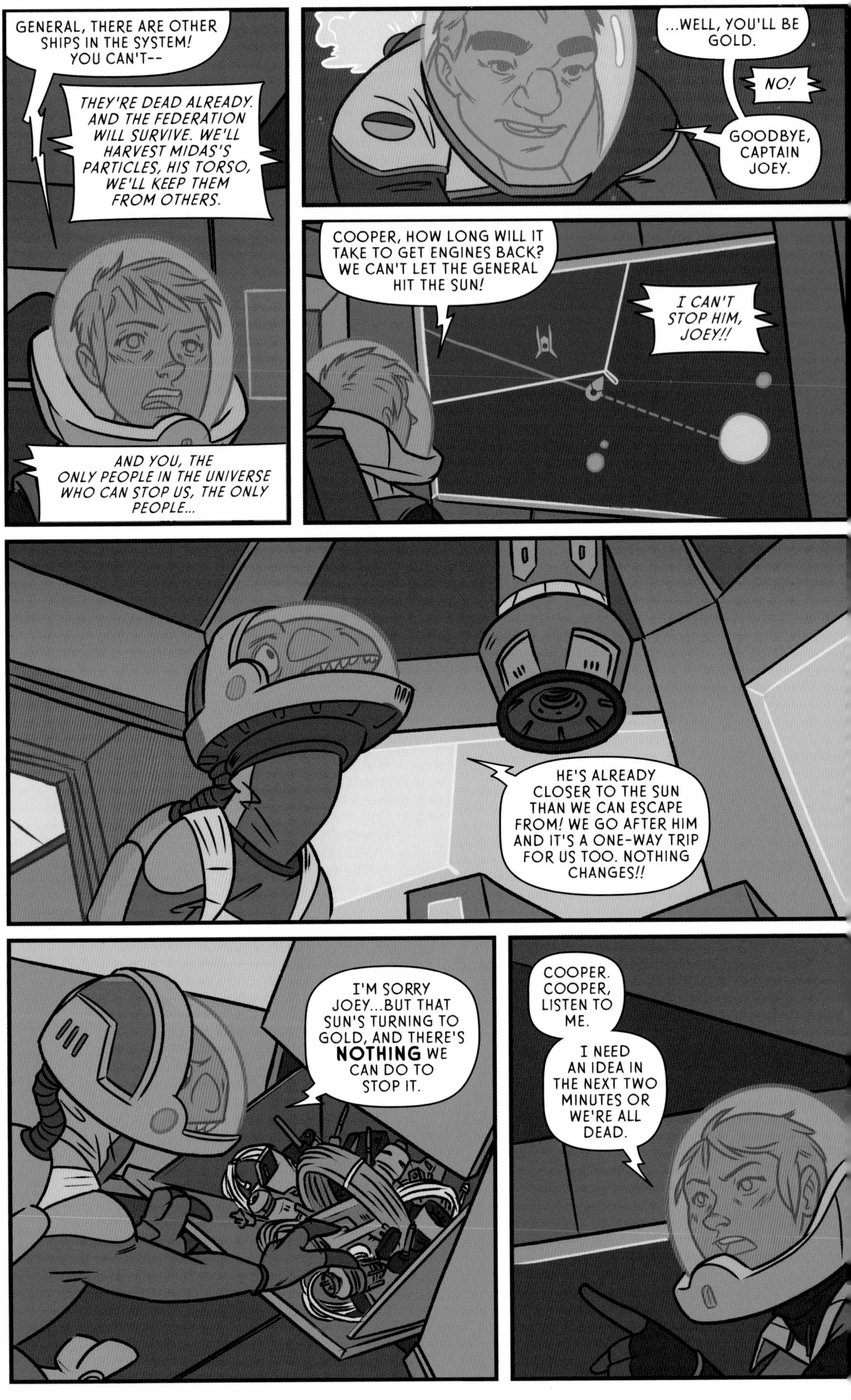
GENERAL, THERE ARE OTHER SHIPS IN THE SYSTEM! YOU CAN'T--
THEY'RE DEAD ALREADY. AND THE FEDERATION WILL SURVIVE. WE'LL HARVEST MIDAS'S PARTICLES, HIS TORSO, WE'LL KEEP THEM FROM OTHERS.
AND YOU, THE ONLY PEOPLE IN THE UNIVERSE WHO CAN STOP US, THE ONLY PEOPLE...
...WELL, YOU'LL BE GOLD.
NO!
GOODBYE, CAPTAIN JOEY.
COOPER, HOW LONG WILL IT TAKE TO GET ENGINES BACK? WE CAN'T LET THE GENERAL HIT THE SUN!
I CAN'T STOP HIM, JOEY!!
HE'S ALREADY CLOSER TO THE SUN THAN WE CAN ESCAPE FROM! WE GO AFTER HIM AND IT'S A ONE-WAY TRIP FOR US TOO. NOTHING CHANGES!!
I'M SORRY JOEY...BUT THAT SUN'S TURNING TO GOLD, AND THERE'S **NOTHING** WE CAN DO TO STOP IT.
COOPER. COOPER, LISTEN TO ME.
I NEED AN IDEA IN THE NEXT TWO MINUTES OR WE'RE ALL DEAD.

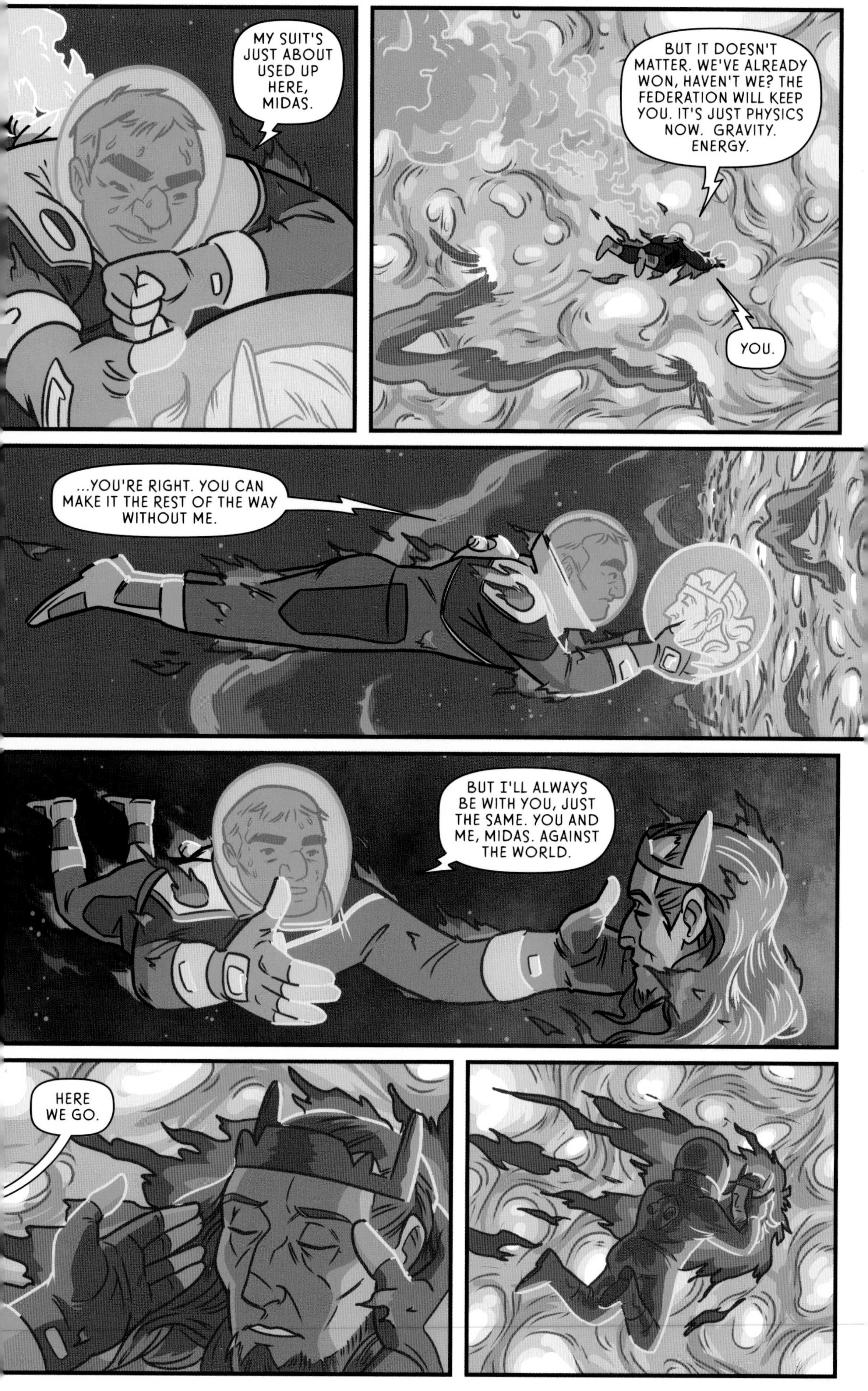
MY SUIT'S JUST ABOUT USED UP HERE, MIDAS.
BUT IT DOESN'T MATTER. WE'VE ALREADY WON, HAVEN'T WE? THE FEDERATION WILL KEEP YOU. IT'S JUST PHYSICS NOW. GRAVITY. ENERGY.
YOU.
...YOU'RE RIGHT. YOU CAN MAKE IT THE REST OF THE WAY WITHOUT ME.
BUT I'LL ALWAYS BE WITH YOU, JUST THE SAME. YOU AND ME, MIDAS. AGAINST THE WORLD.
HERE WE GO.

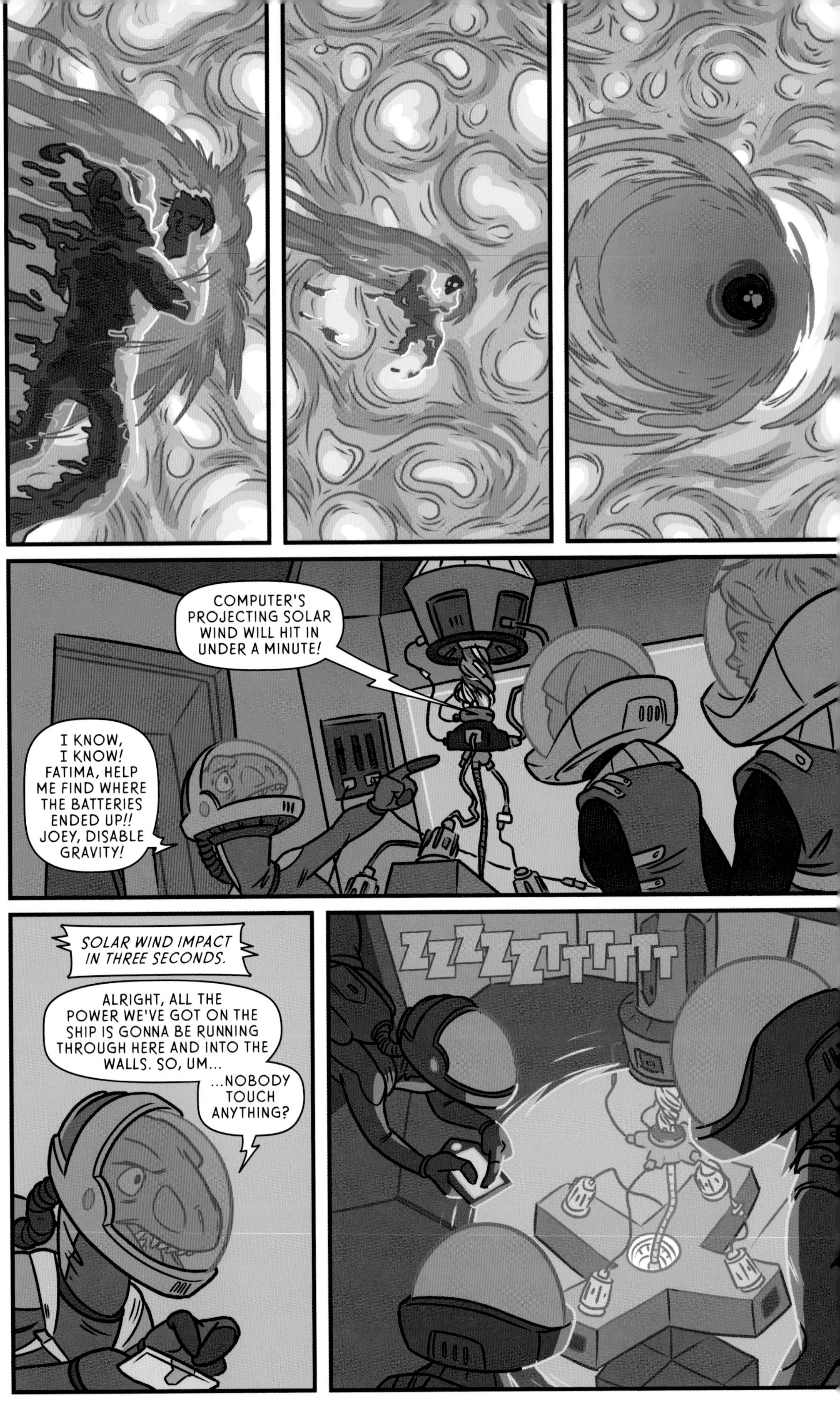
COMPUTER'S PROJECTING SOLAR WIND WILL HIT IN UNDER A MINUTE!
I KNOW, I KNOW! FATIMA, HELP ME FIND WHERE THE BATTERIES ENDED UP!! JOEY, DISABLE GRAVITY!
SOLAR WIND IMPACT IN THREE SECONDS.
ALRIGHT, ALL THE POWER WE'VE GOT ON THE SHIP IS GONNA BE RUNNING THROUGH HERE AND INTO THE WALLS. SO, UM...
...NOBODY TOUCH ANYTHING?
ZZZZZTTTTTT

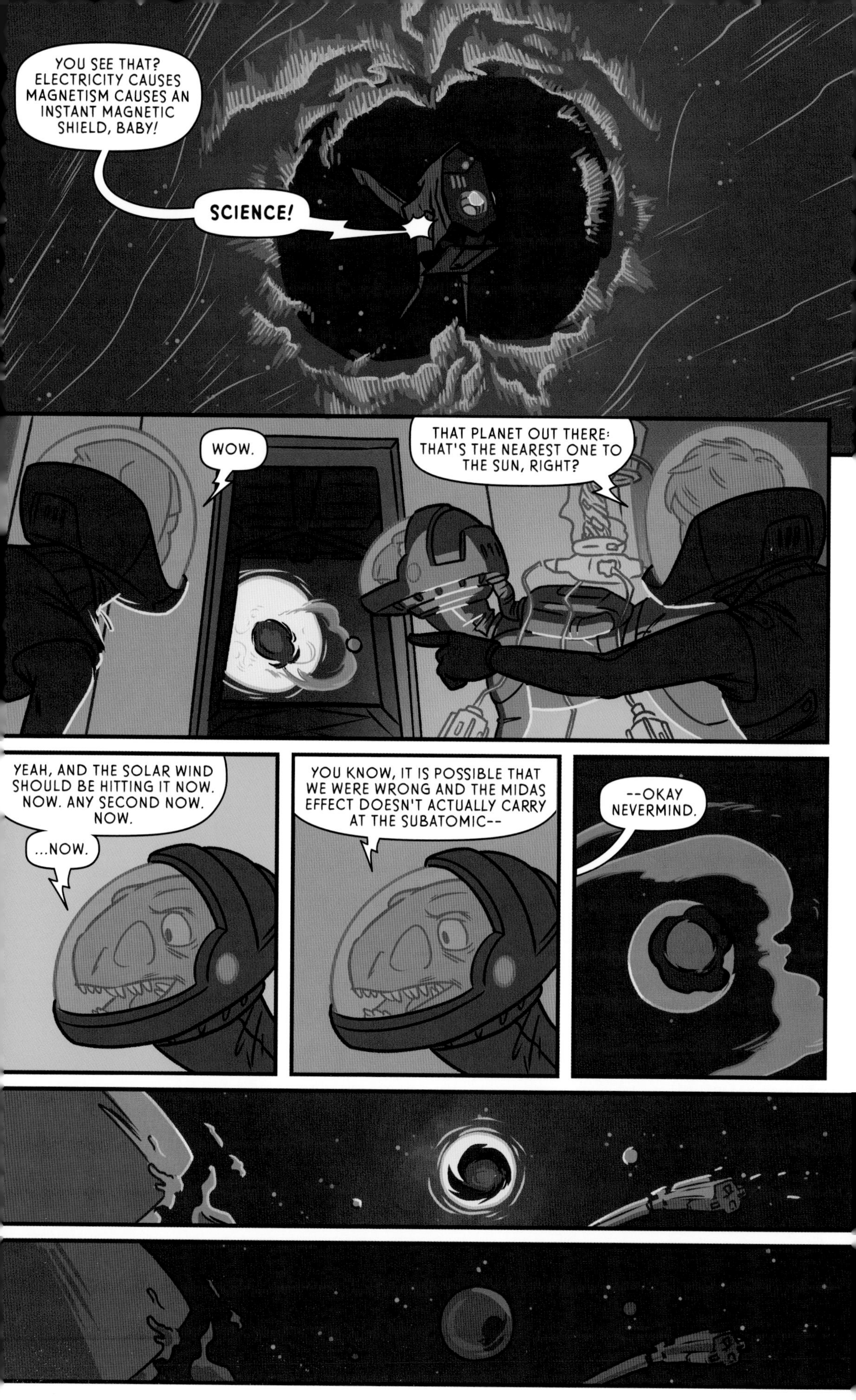
YOU SEE THAT? ELECTRICITY CAUSES MAGNETISM CAUSES AN INSTANT MAGNETIC SHIELD, BABY!
SCIENCE!
WOW.
THAT PLANET OUT THERE: THAT'S THE NEAREST ONE TO THE SUN, RIGHT?
YEAH, AND THE SOLAR WIND SHOULD BE HITTING IT NOW. NOW. ANY SECOND NOW. NOW.
...NOW.
YOU KNOW, IT IS POSSIBLE THAT WE WERE WRONG AND THE MIDAS EFFECT DOESN'T ACTUALLY CARRY AT THE SUBATOMIC--
--OKAY NEVERMIND.

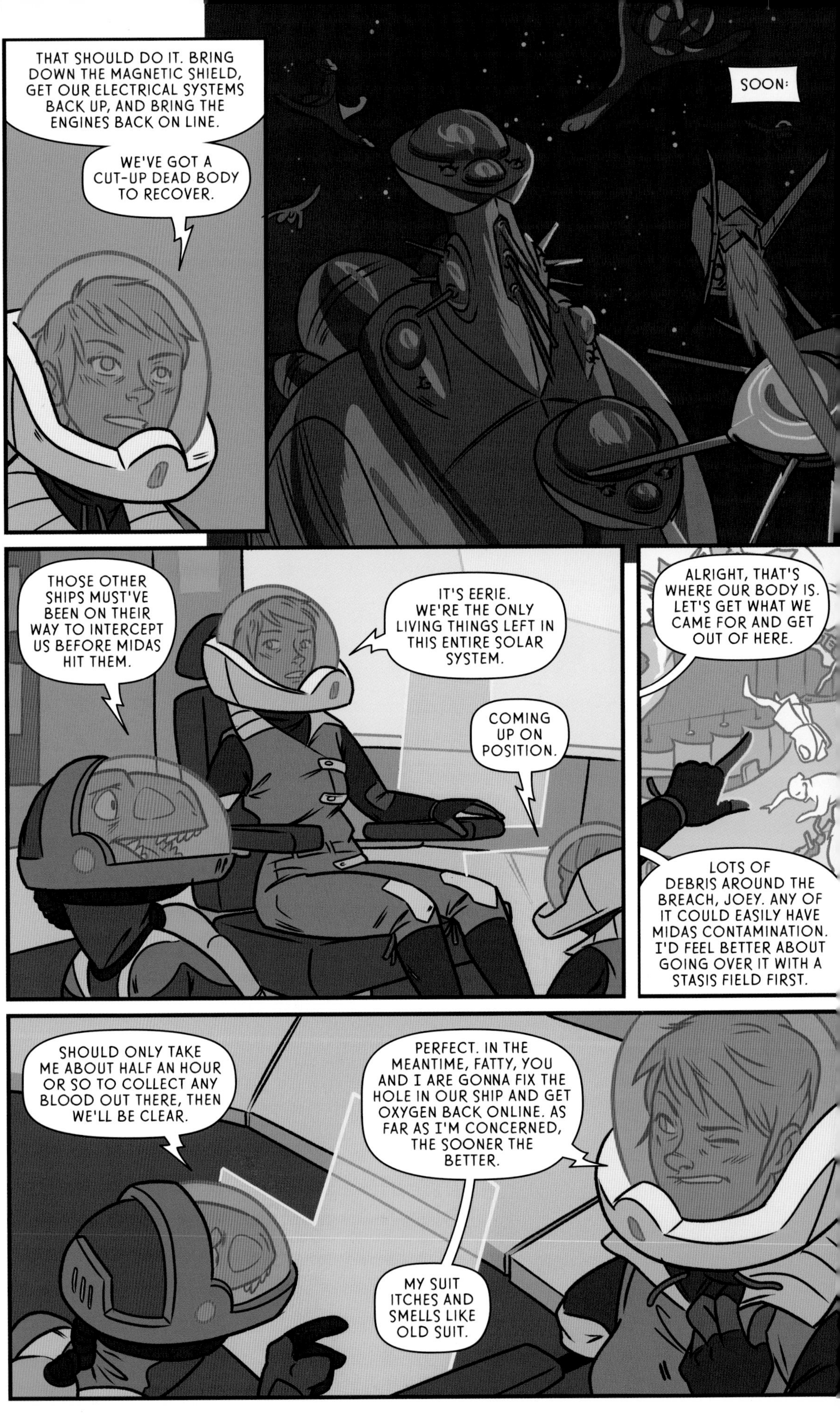
THAT SHOULD DO IT. BRING DOWN THE MAGNETIC SHIELD, GET OUR ELECTRICAL SYSTEMS BACK UP, AND BRING THE ENGINES BACK ON LINE.
WE'VE GOT A CUT-UP DEAD BODY TO RECOVER.
SOON:
THOSE OTHER SHIPS MUST'VE BEEN ON THEIR WAY TO INTERCEPT US BEFORE MIDAS HIT THEM.
IT'S EERIE. WE'RE THE ONLY LIVING THINGS LEFT IN THIS ENTIRE SOLAR SYSTEM.
COMING UP ON POSITION.
ALRIGHT, THAT'S WHERE OUR BODY IS. LET'S GET WHAT WE CAME FOR AND GET OUT OF HERE.
LOTS OF DEBRIS AROUND THE BREACH, JOEY. ANY OF IT COULD EASILY HAVE MIDAS CONTAMINATION. I'D FEEL BETTER ABOUT GOING OVER IT WITH A STASIS FIELD FIRST.
SHOULD ONLY TAKE ME ABOUT HALF AN HOUR OR SO TO COLLECT ANY BLOOD OUT THERE, THEN WE'LL BE CLEAR.
PERFECT. IN THE MEANTIME, FATTY, YOU AND I ARE GONNA FIX THE HOLE IN OUR SHIP AND GET OXYGEN BACK ONLINE. AS FAR AS I'M CONCERNED, THE SOONER THE BETTER.
MY SUIT ITCHES AND SMELLS LIKE OLD SUIT.

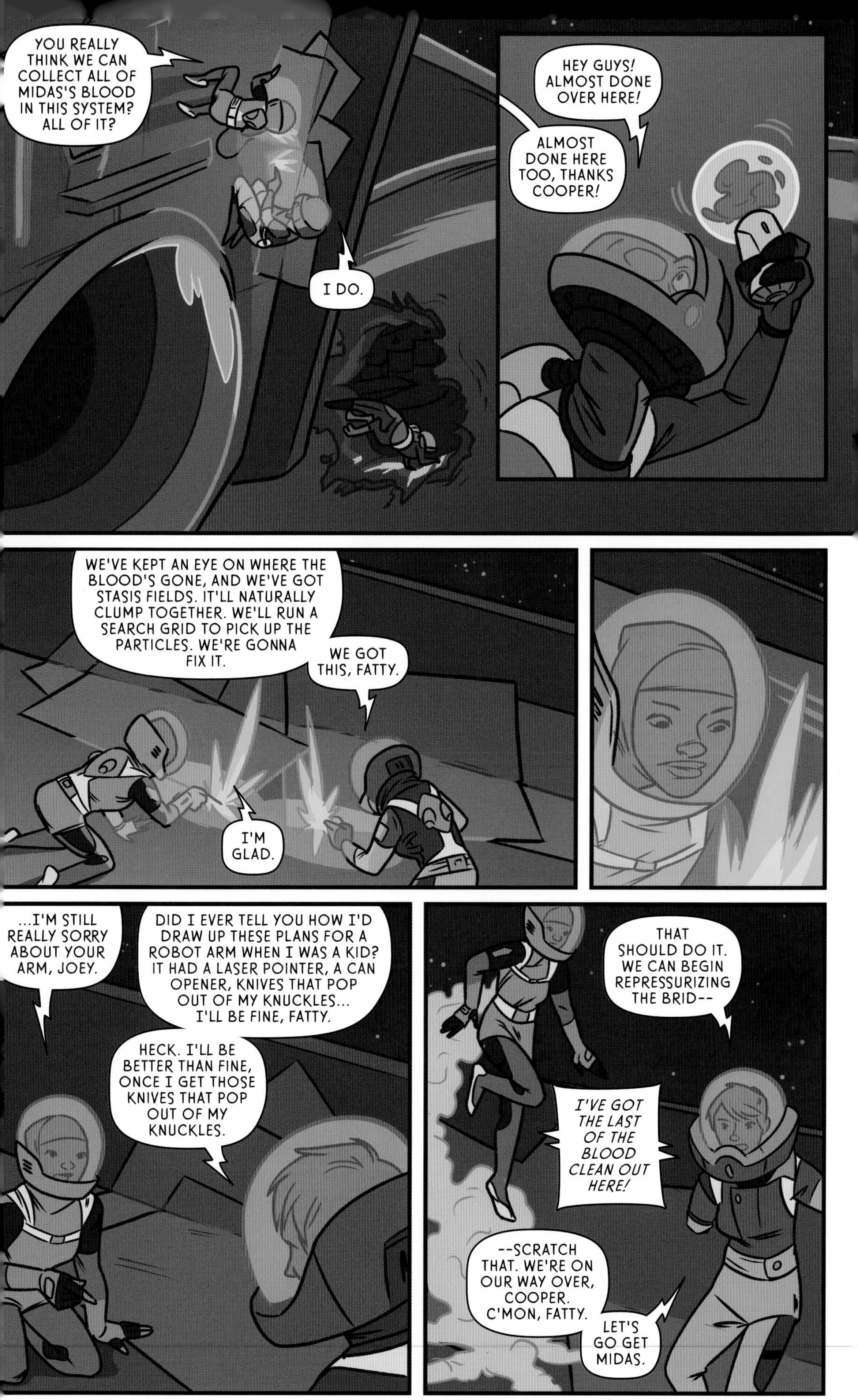
YOU REALLY THINK WE CAN COLLECT ALL OF MIDAS'S BLOOD IN THIS SYSTEM? ALL OF IT?
I DO.
HEY GUYS! ALMOST DONE OVER HERE!
ALMOST DONE HERE TOO, THANKS COOPER!
WE'VE KEPT AN EYE ON WHERE THE BLOOD'S GONE, AND WE'VE GOT STASIS FIELDS. IT'LL NATURALLY CLUMP TOGETHER. WE'LL RUN A SEARCH GRID TO PICK UP THE PARTICLES. WE'RE GONNA FIX IT.
WE GOT THIS, FATTY.
I'M GLAD.
...I'M STILL REALLY SORRY ABOUT YOUR ARM, JOEY.
DID I EVER TELL YOU HOW I'D DRAW UP THESE PLANS FOR A ROBOT ARM WHEN I WAS A KID? IT HAD A LASER POINTER, A CAN OPENER, KNIVES THAT POP OUT OF MY KNUCKLES... I'LL BE FINE, FATTY.
HECK. I'LL BE BETTER THAN FINE, ONCE I GET THOSE KNIVES THAT POP OUT OF MY KNUCKLES.
THAT SHOULD DO IT. WE CAN BEGIN REPRESSURIZING THE BRID--
I'VE GOT THE LAST OF THE BLOOD CLEAN OUT HERE!
--SCRATCH THAT. WE'RE ON OUR WAY OVER, COOPER. C'MON, FATTY.
LET'S GO GET MIDAS.

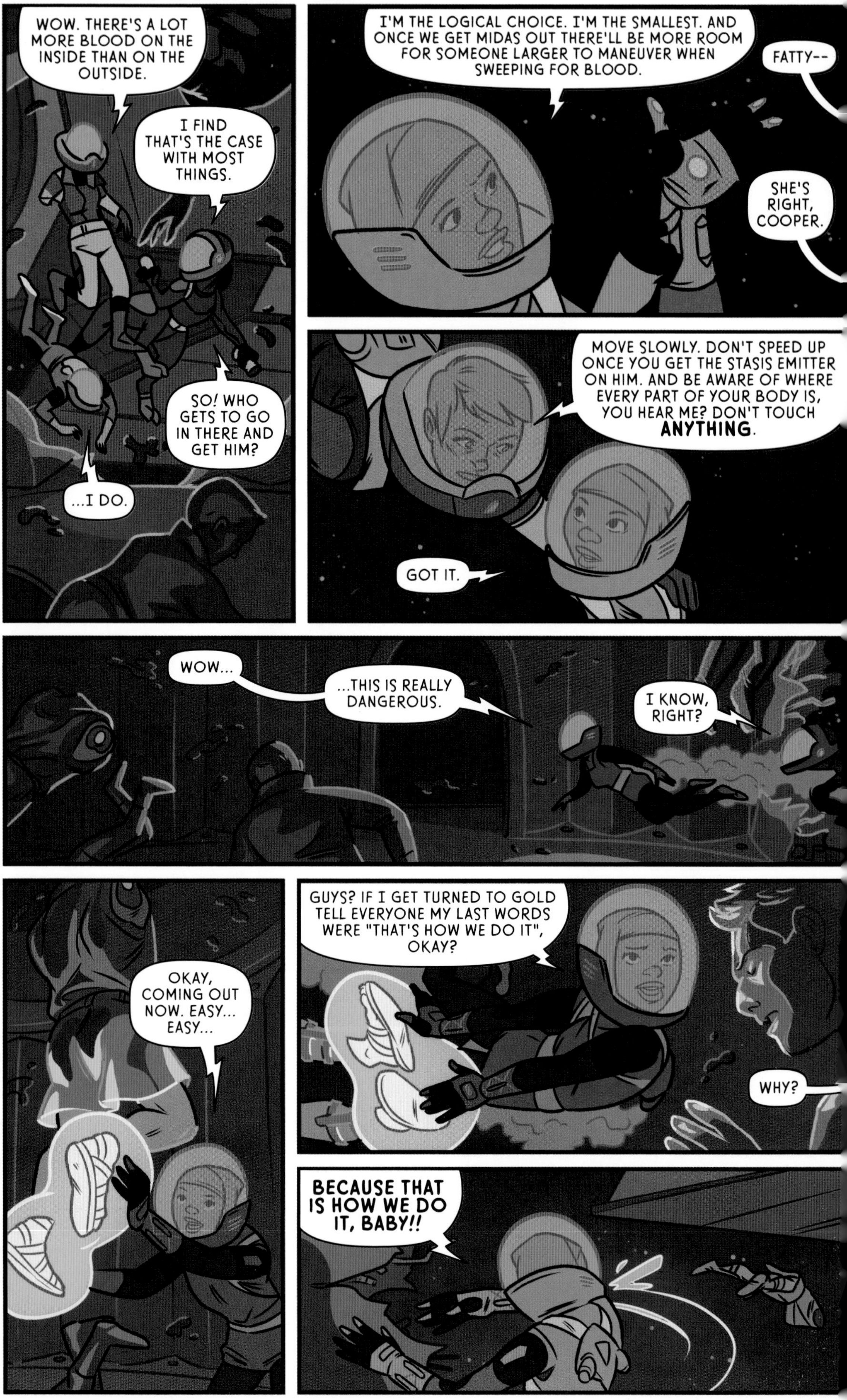
WOW. THERE'S A LOT MORE BLOOD ON THE INSIDE THAN ON THE OUTSIDE.
I FIND THAT'S THE CASE WITH MOST THINGS.
SO! WHO GETS TO GO IN THERE AND GET HIM?
...I DO.
I'M THE LOGICAL CHOICE. I'M THE SMALLEST. AND ONCE WE GET MIDAS OUT THERE'LL BE MORE ROOM FOR SOMEONE LARGER TO MANEUVER WHEN SWEEPING FOR BLOOD.
FATTY--
SHE'S RIGHT, COOPER.
MOVE SLOWLY. DON'T SPEED UP ONCE YOU GET THE STASIS EMITTER ON HIM. AND BE AWARE OF WHERE EVERY PART OF YOUR BODY IS, YOU HEAR ME? DON'T TOUCH **ANYTHING**.
GOT IT.
WOW...
...THIS IS REALLY DANGEROUS.
I KNOW, RIGHT?
OKAY, COMING OUT NOW. EASY... EASY...
GUYS? IF I GET TURNED TO GOLD TELL EVERYONE MY LAST WORDS WERE "THAT'S HOW WE DO IT", OKAY?
WHY?
BECAUSE THAT IS HOW WE DO IT, BABY!!

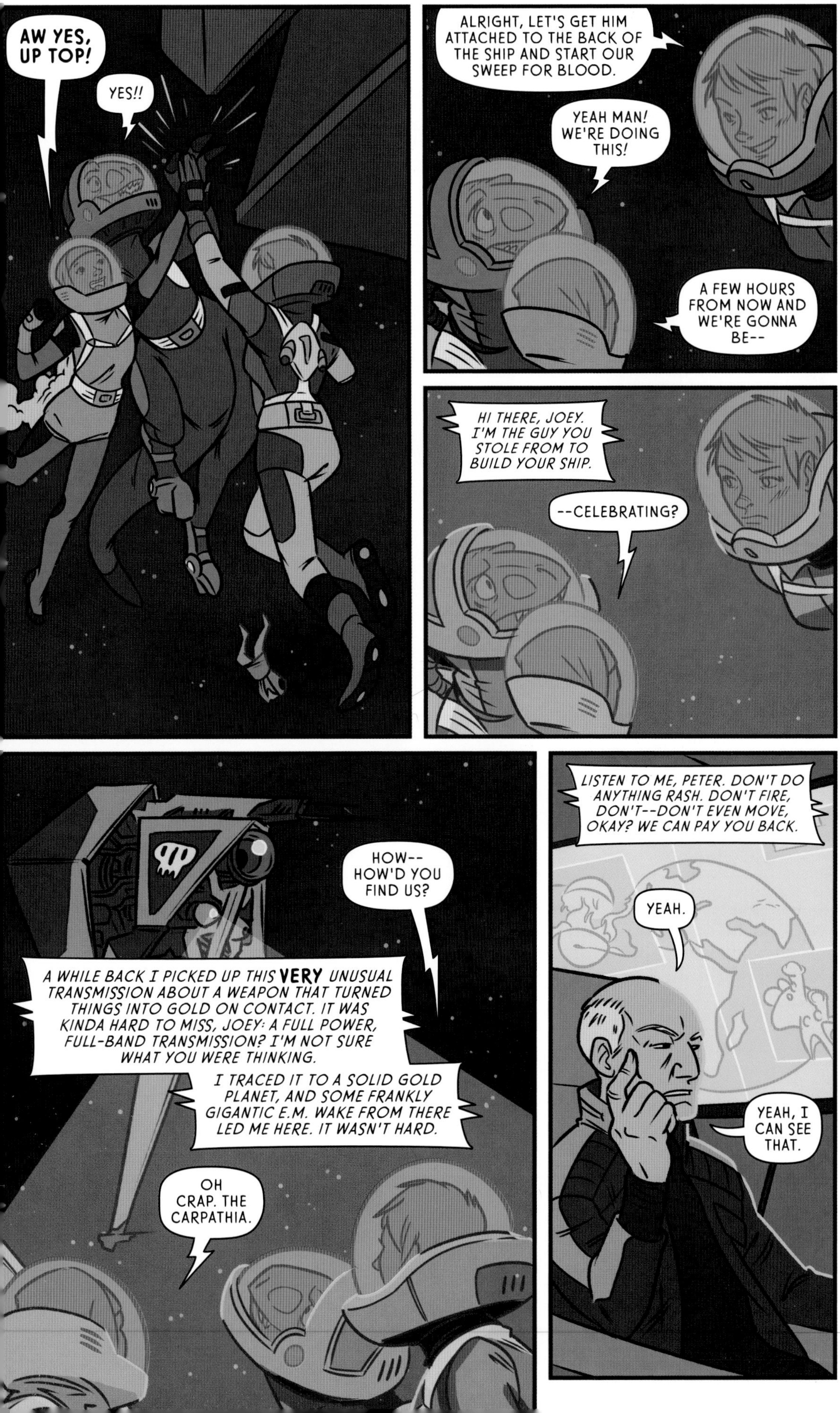

AW YES, UP TOP!
YES!!
ALRIGHT, LET'S GET HIM ATTACHED TO THE BACK OF THE SHIP AND START OUR SWEEP FOR BLOOD.
YEAH MAN! WE'RE DOING THIS!
A FEW HOURS FROM NOW AND WE'RE GONNA BE--
HI THERE, JOEY. I'M THE GUY YOU STOLE FROM TO BUILD YOUR SHIP.
--CELEBRATING?
HOW-- HOW'D YOU FIND US?
A WHILE BACK I PICKED UP THIS VERY UNUSUAL TRANSMISSION ABOUT A WEAPON THAT TURNED THINGS INTO GOLD ON CONTACT. IT WAS KINDA HARD TO MISS, JOEY: A FULL POWER, FULL-BAND TRANSMISSION? I'M NOT SURE WHAT YOU WERE THINKING.
I TRACED IT TO A SOLID GOLD PLANET, AND SOME FRANKLY GIGANTIC E.M. WAKE FROM THERE LED ME HERE. IT WASN'T HARD.
OH CRAP. THE CARPATHIA.
LISTEN TO ME, PETER. DON'T DO ANYTHING RASH. DON'T FIRE, DON'T--DON'T EVEN MOVE, OKAY? WE CAN PAY YOU BACK.
YEAH.
YEAH, I CAN SEE THAT.

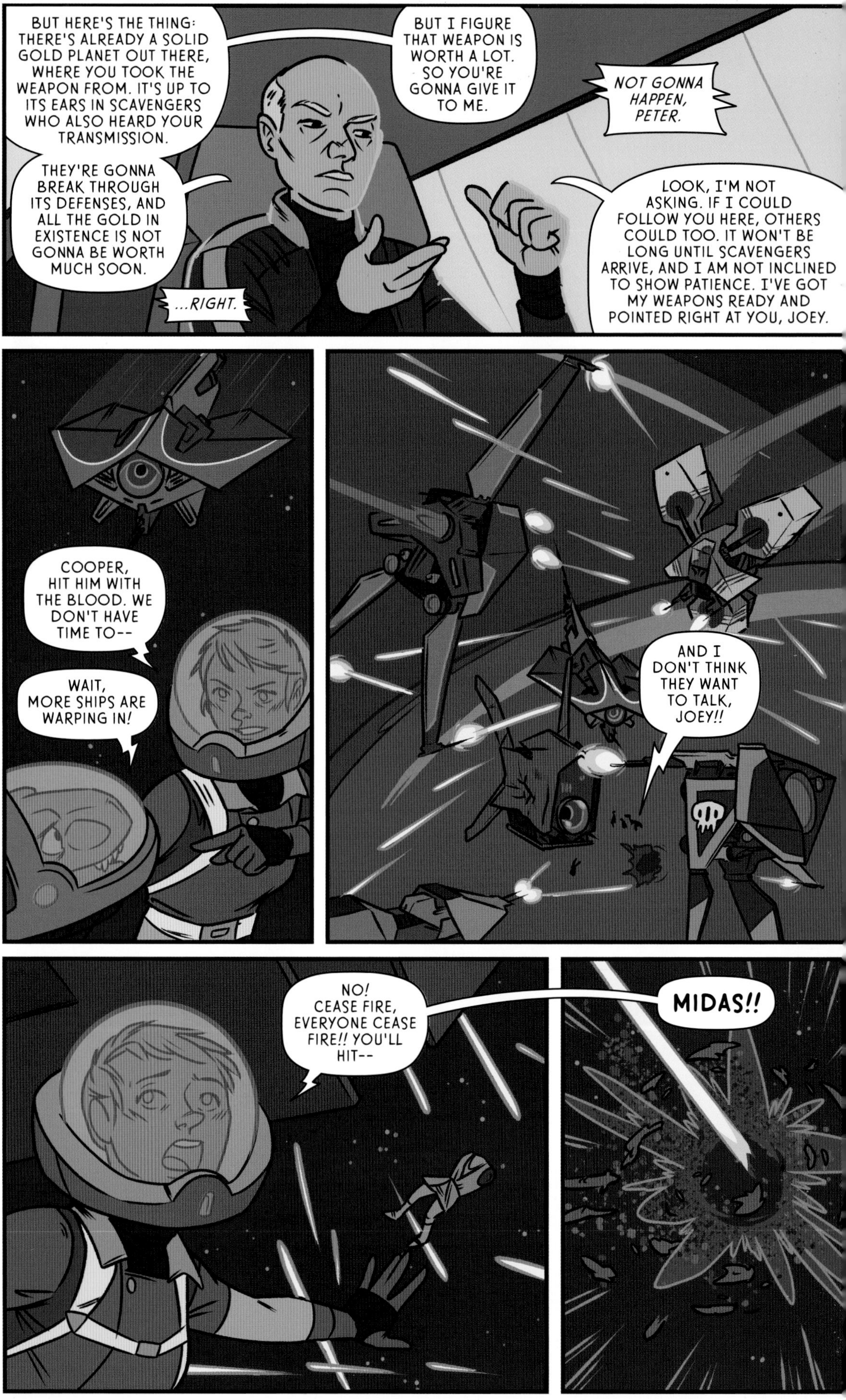
BUT HERE'S THE THING: THERE'S ALREADY A SOLID GOLD PLANET OUT THERE, WHERE YOU TOOK THE WEAPON FROM. IT'S UP TO ITS EARS IN SCAVENGERS WHO ALSO HEARD YOUR TRANSMISSION.
THEY'RE GONNA BREAK THROUGH ITS DEFENSES, AND ALL THE GOLD IN EXISTENCE IS NOT GONNA BE WORTH MUCH SOON.
...RIGHT.
BUT I FIGURE THAT WEAPON IS WORTH A LOT. SO YOU'RE GONNA GIVE IT TO ME.
NOT GONNA HAPPEN, PETER.
LOOK, I'M NOT ASKING. IF I COULD FOLLOW YOU HERE, OTHERS COULD TOO. IT WON'T BE LONG UNTIL SCAVENGERS ARRIVE, AND I AM NOT INCLINED TO SHOW PATIENCE. I'VE GOT MY WEAPONS READY AND POINTED RIGHT AT YOU, JOEY.
COOPER, HIT HIM WITH THE BLOOD. WE DON'T HAVE TIME TO--
WAIT, MORE SHIPS ARE WARPING IN!
AND I DON'T THINK THEY WANT TO TALK, JOEY!!
NO! CEASE FIRE, EVERYONE CEASE FIRE!! YOU'LL HIT--
MIDAS!!

"I'LL JUST GET THINGS READY SO I CAN TURN MYSELF AND ALL MY FRIENDS INTO **GOLD STATUES** WITH SOME **SPACE BLOOD.**"

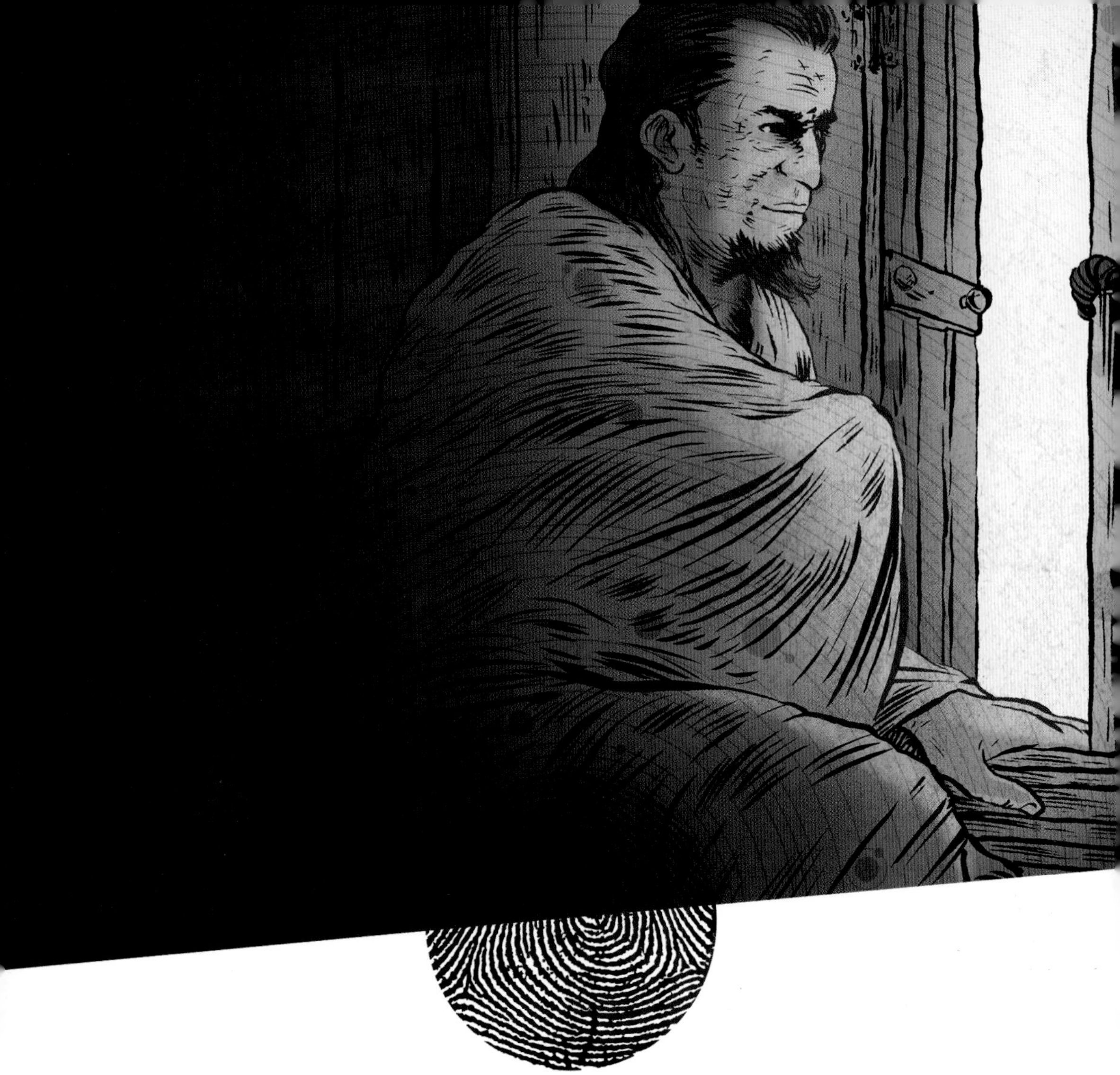

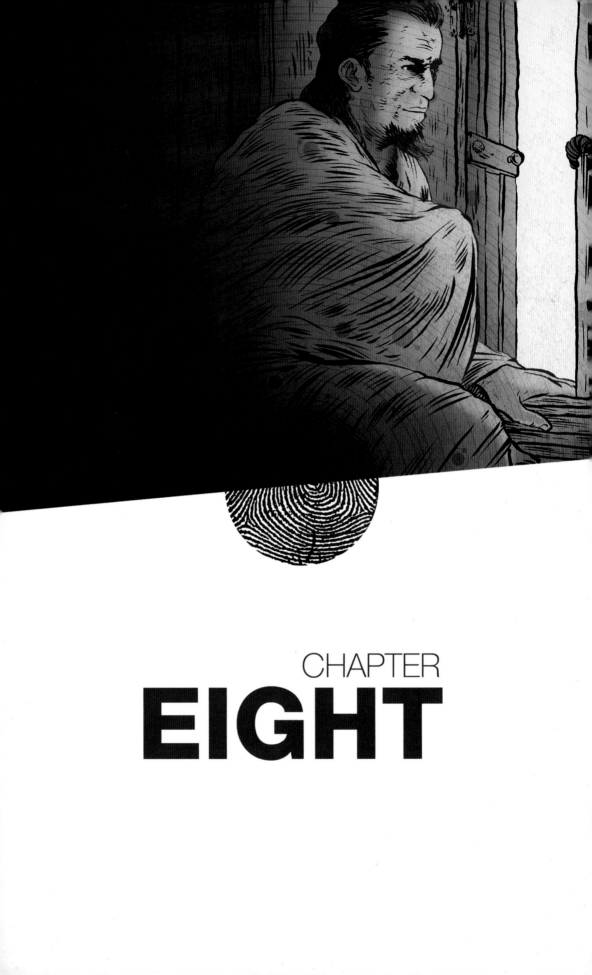

CHAPTER
EIGHT

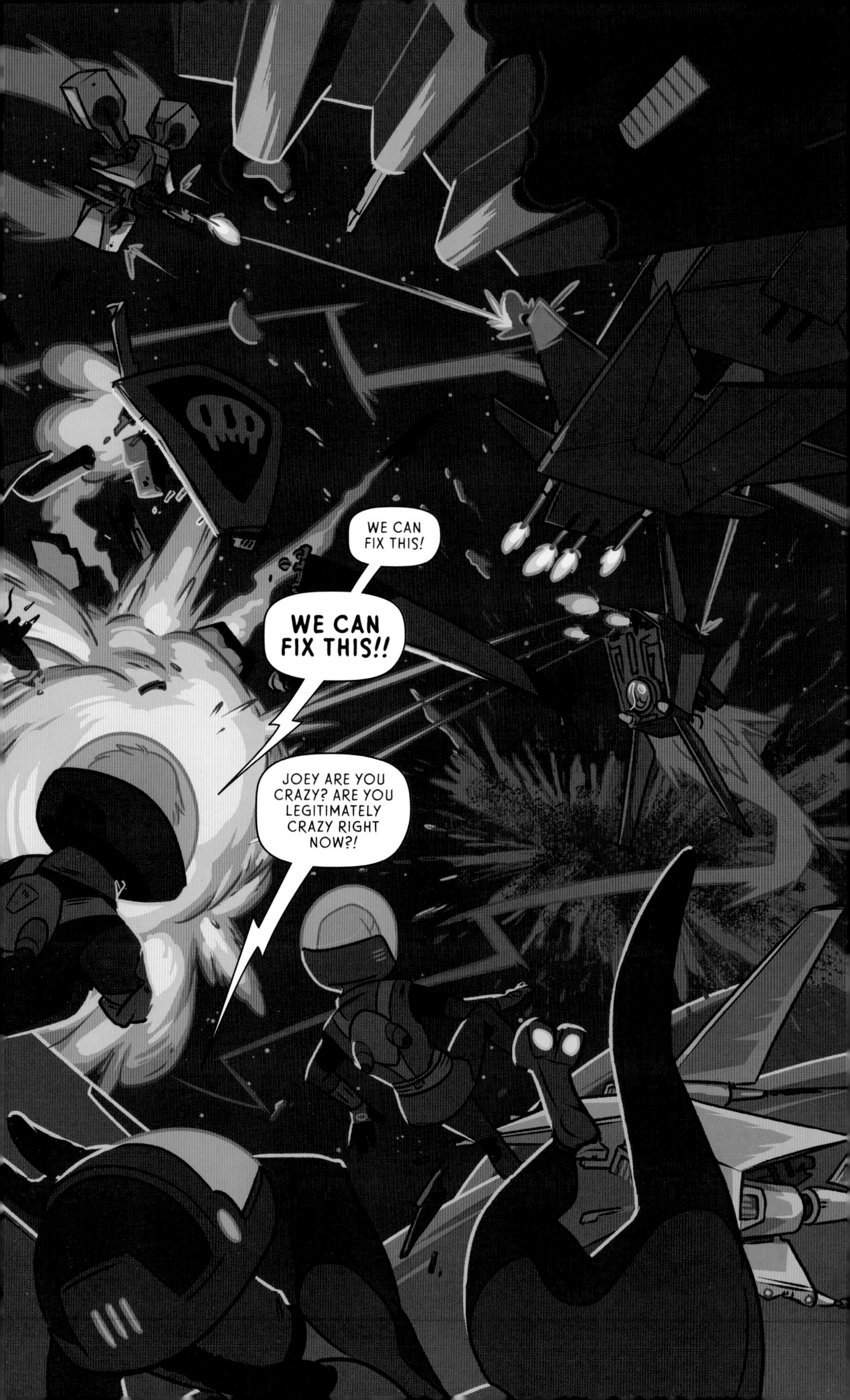
WE CAN FIX THIS!
WE CAN FIX THIS!!
JOEY ARE YOU CRAZY? ARE YOU LEGITIMATELY CRAZY RIGHT NOW?!

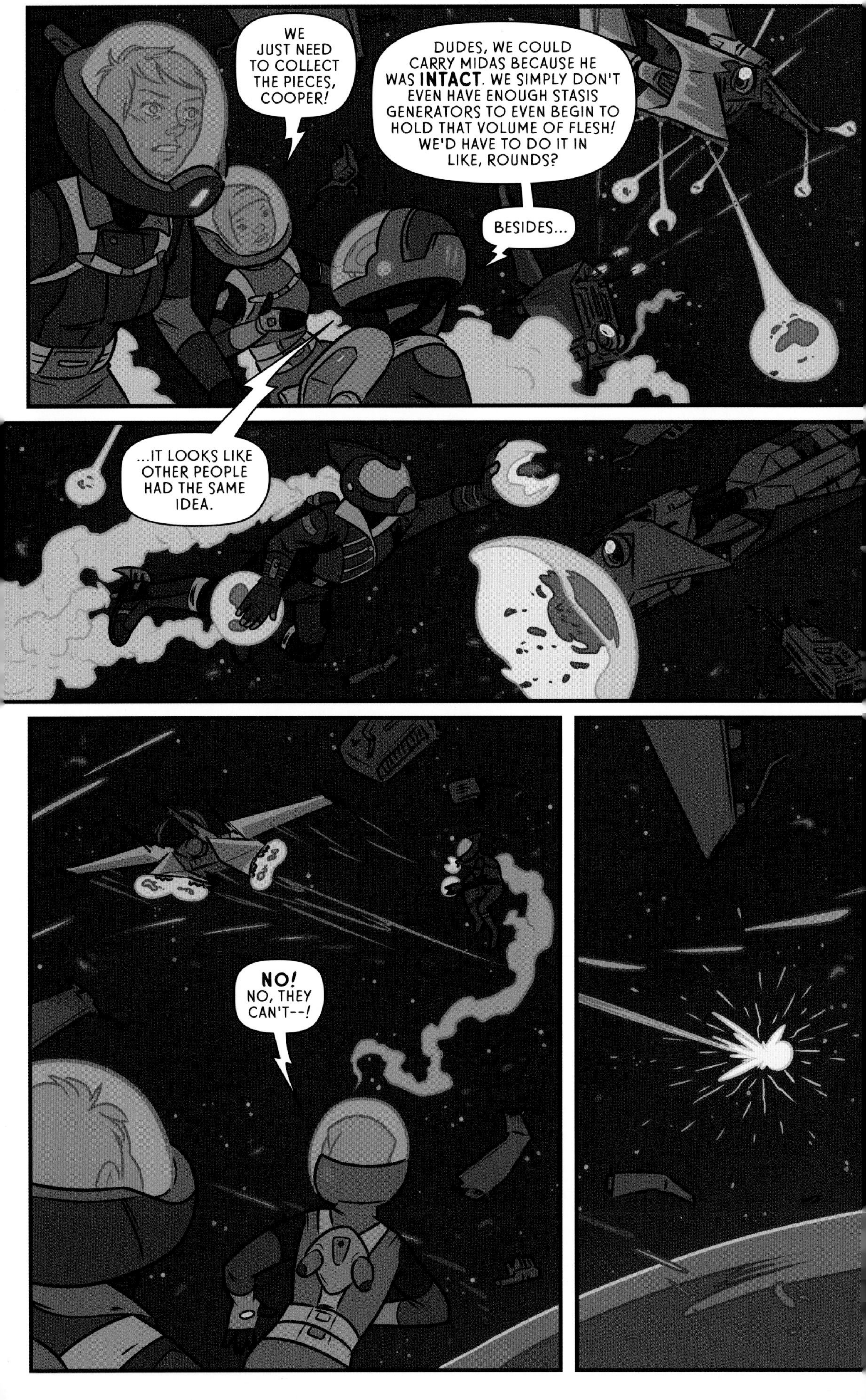
WE JUST NEED TO COLLECT THE PIECES, COOPER!
DUDES, WE COULD CARRY MIDAS BECAUSE HE WAS **INTACT**. WE SIMPLY DON'T EVEN HAVE ENOUGH STASIS GENERATORS TO EVEN BEGIN TO HOLD THAT VOLUME OF FLESH! WE'D HAVE TO DO IT IN LIKE, ROUNDS?
BESIDES...
...IT LOOKS LIKE OTHER PEOPLE HAD THE SAME IDEA.
NO! NO, THEY CAN'T--!

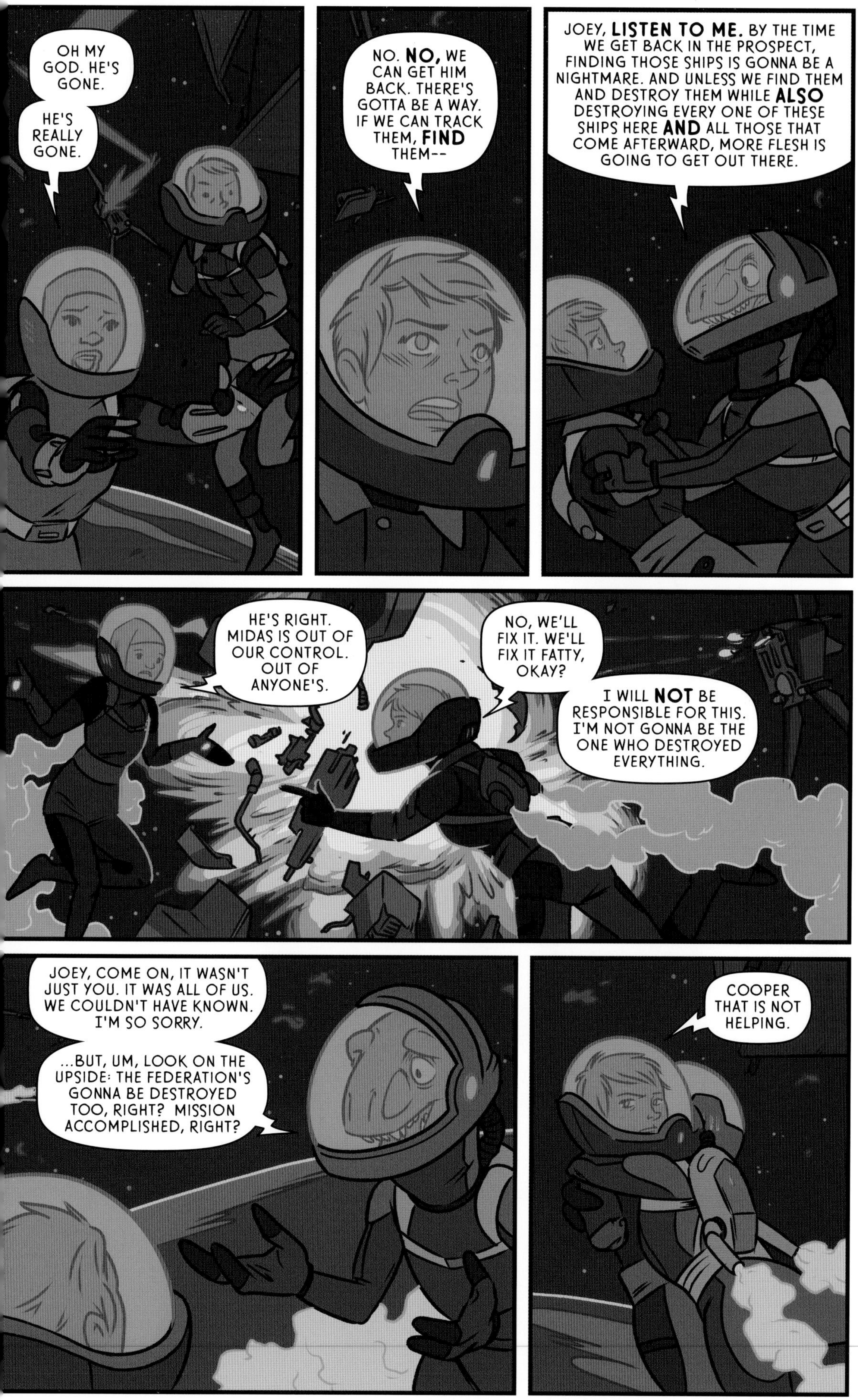
OH MY GOD. HE'S GONE.
HE'S REALLY GONE.
NO. **NO,** WE CAN GET HIM BACK. THERE'S GOTTA BE A WAY. IF WE CAN TRACK THEM, **FIND** THEM--
JOEY, **LISTEN TO ME.** BY THE TIME WE GET BACK IN THE PROSPECT, FINDING THOSE SHIPS IS GONNA BE A NIGHTMARE. AND UNLESS WE FIND THEM AND DESTROY THEM WHILE **ALSO** DESTROYING EVERY ONE OF THESE SHIPS HERE **AND** ALL THOSE THAT COME AFTERWARD, MORE FLESH IS GOING TO GET OUT THERE.
HE'S RIGHT. MIDAS IS OUT OF OUR CONTROL. OUT OF ANYONE'S.
NO, WE'LL FIX IT. WE'LL FIX IT FATTY, OKAY?
I WILL **NOT** BE RESPONSIBLE FOR THIS. I'M NOT GONNA BE THE ONE WHO DESTROYED EVERYTHING.
JOEY, COME ON, IT WASN'T JUST YOU. IT WAS ALL OF US. WE COULDN'T HAVE KNOWN. I'M SO SORRY.
...BUT, UM, LOOK ON THE UPSIDE: THE FEDERATION'S GONNA BE DESTROYED TOO, RIGHT? MISSION ACCOMPLISHED, RIGHT?
COOPER THAT IS NOT HELPING.

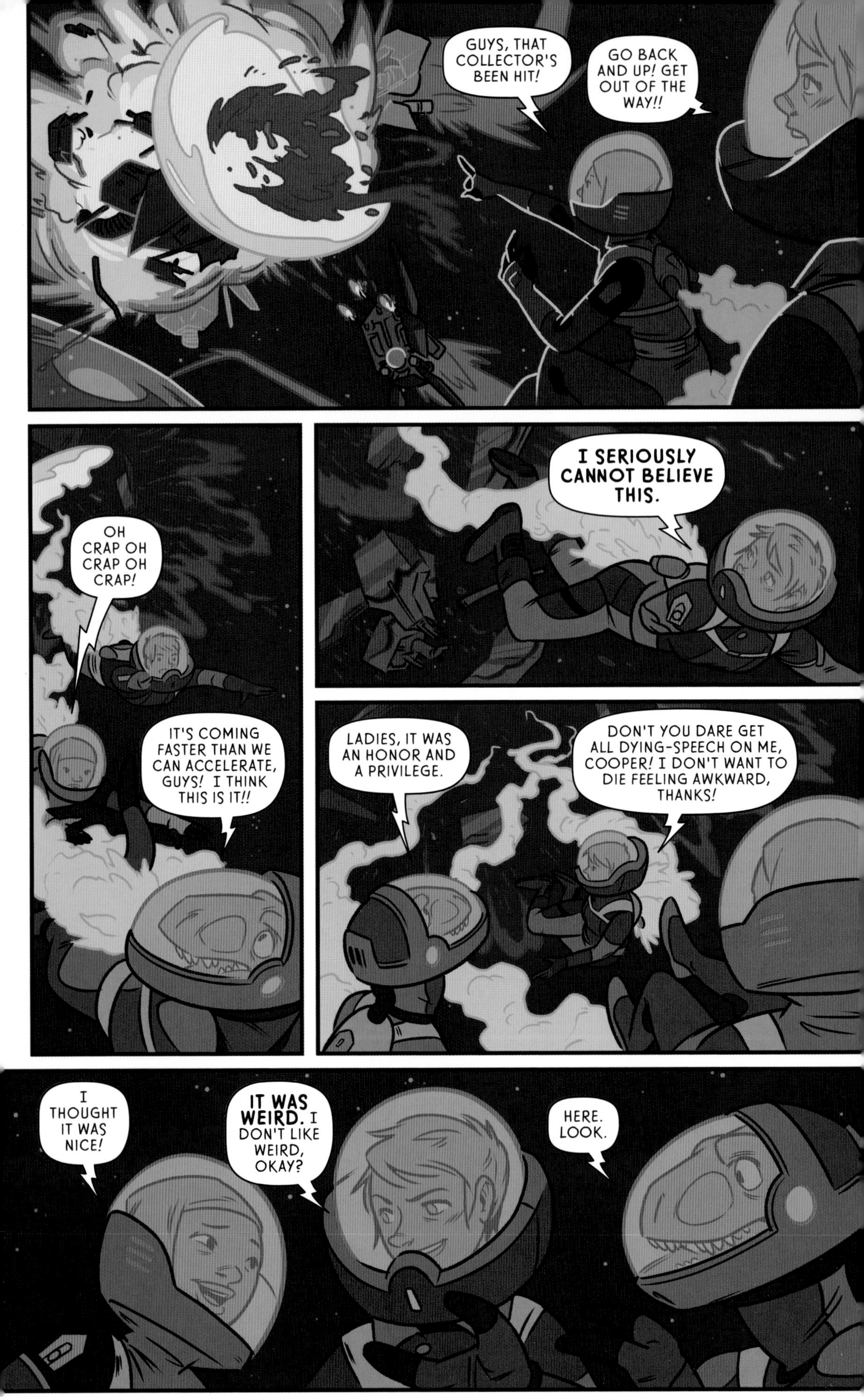
GUYS, THAT COLLECTOR'S BEEN HIT!
GO BACK AND UP! GET OUT OF THE WAY!!
OH CRAP OH CRAP OH CRAP!
I SERIOUSLY CANNOT BELIEVE THIS.
IT'S COMING FASTER THAN WE CAN ACCELERATE, GUYS! I THINK THIS IS IT!!
LADIES, IT WAS AN HONOR AND A PRIVILEGE.
DON'T YOU DARE GET ALL DYING-SPEECH ON ME, COOPER! I DON'T WANT TO DIE FEELING AWKWARD, THANKS!
I THOUGHT IT WAS NICE!
IT WAS WEIRD. I DON'T LIKE WEIRD, OKAY?
HERE. LOOK.

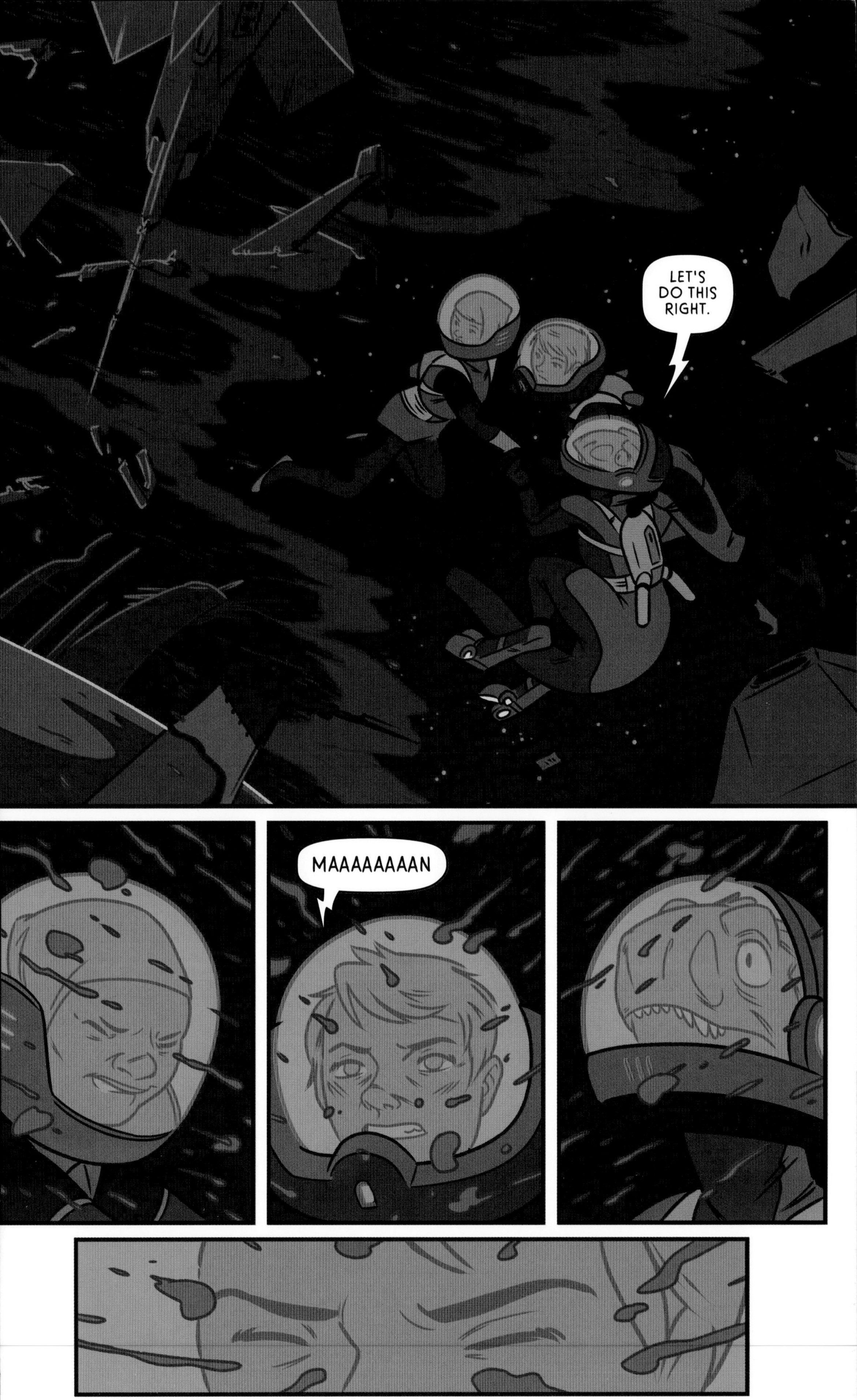
LET'S DO THIS RIGHT.
MAAAAAAAAN

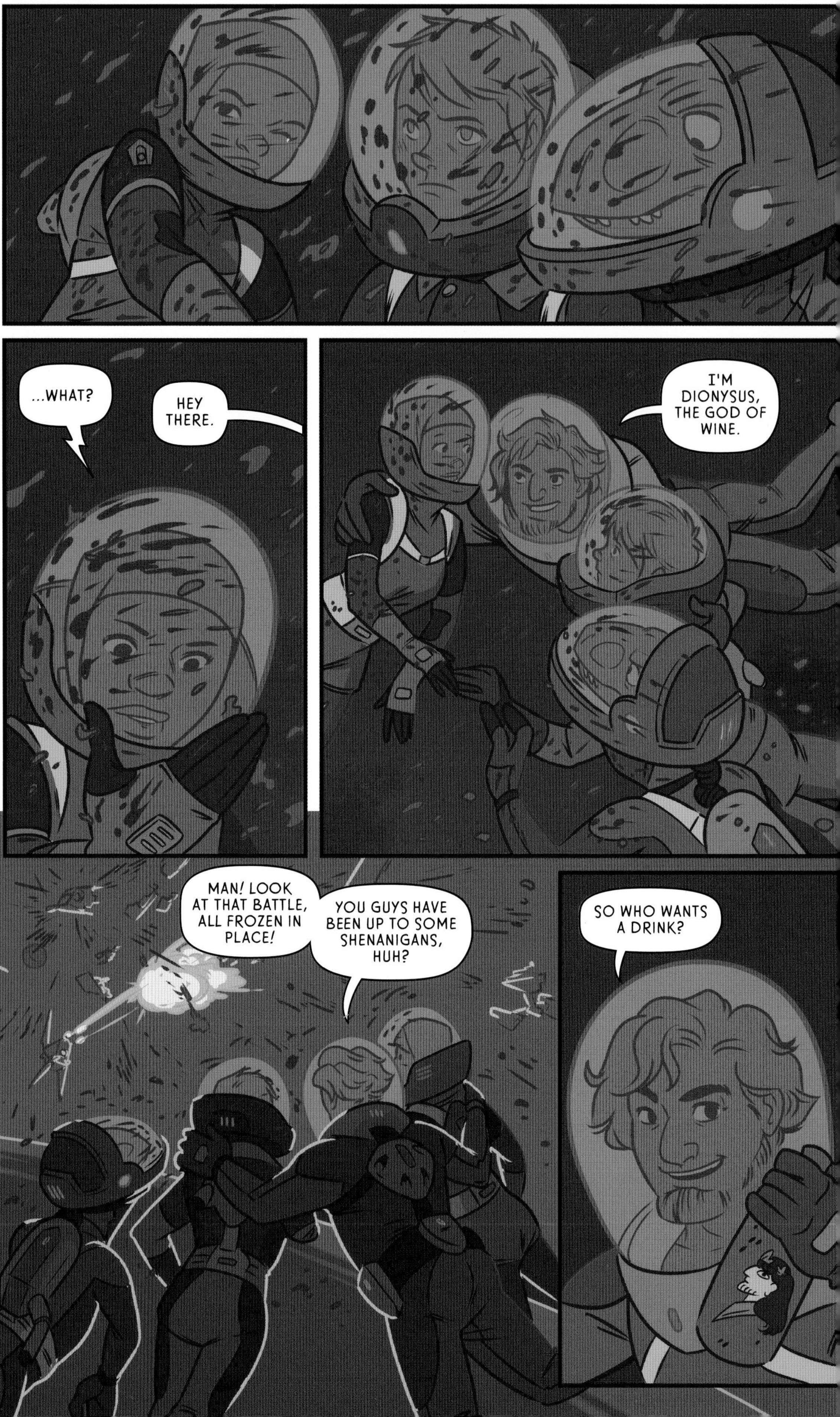
...WHAT?
HEY THERE.
I'M DIONYSUS, THE GOD OF WINE.
MAN! LOOK AT THAT BATTLE, ALL FROZEN IN PLACE!
YOU GUYS HAVE BEEN UP TO SOME SHENANIGANS, HUH?
SO WHO WANTS A DRINK?

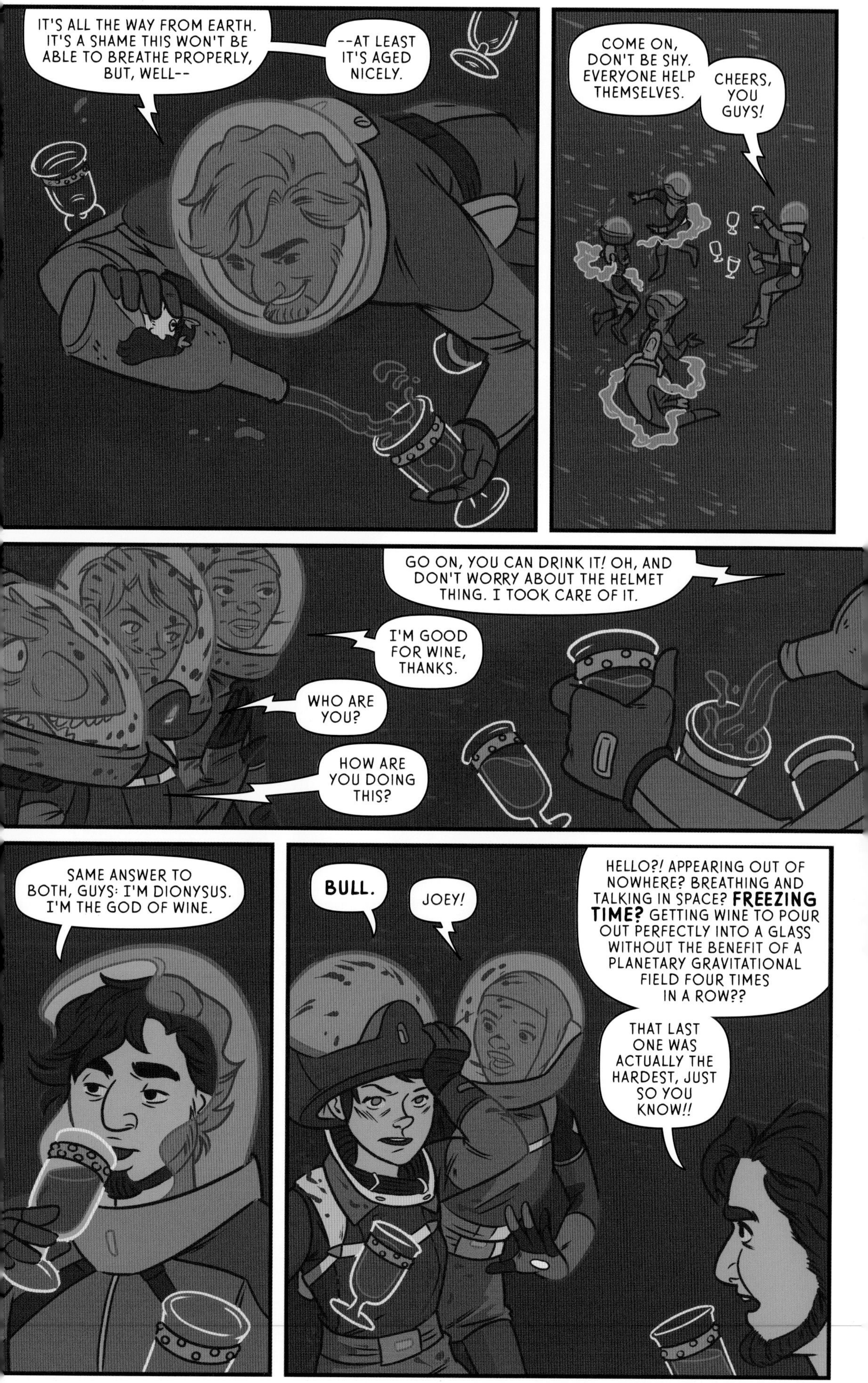

IT'S ALL THE WAY FROM EARTH. IT'S A SHAME THIS WON'T BE ABLE TO BREATHE PROPERLY, BUT, WELL--
--AT LEAST IT'S AGED NICELY.
COME ON, DON'T BE SHY. EVERYONE HELP THEMSELVES.
CHEERS, YOU GUYS!
GO ON, YOU CAN DRINK IT! OH, AND DON'T WORRY ABOUT THE HELMET THING. I TOOK CARE OF IT.
I'M GOOD FOR WINE, THANKS.
WHO ARE YOU?
HOW ARE YOU DOING THIS?
SAME ANSWER TO BOTH, GUYS: I'M DIONYSUS. I'M THE GOD OF WINE.
BULL.
JOEY!
HELLO?! APPEARING OUT OF NOWHERE? BREATHING AND TALKING IN SPACE? **FREEZING TIME?** GETTING WINE TO POUR OUT PERFECTLY INTO A GLASS WITHOUT THE BENEFIT OF A PLANETARY GRAVITATIONAL FIELD FOUR TIMES IN A ROW??
THAT LAST ONE WAS ACTUALLY THE HARDEST, JUST SO YOU KNOW!!

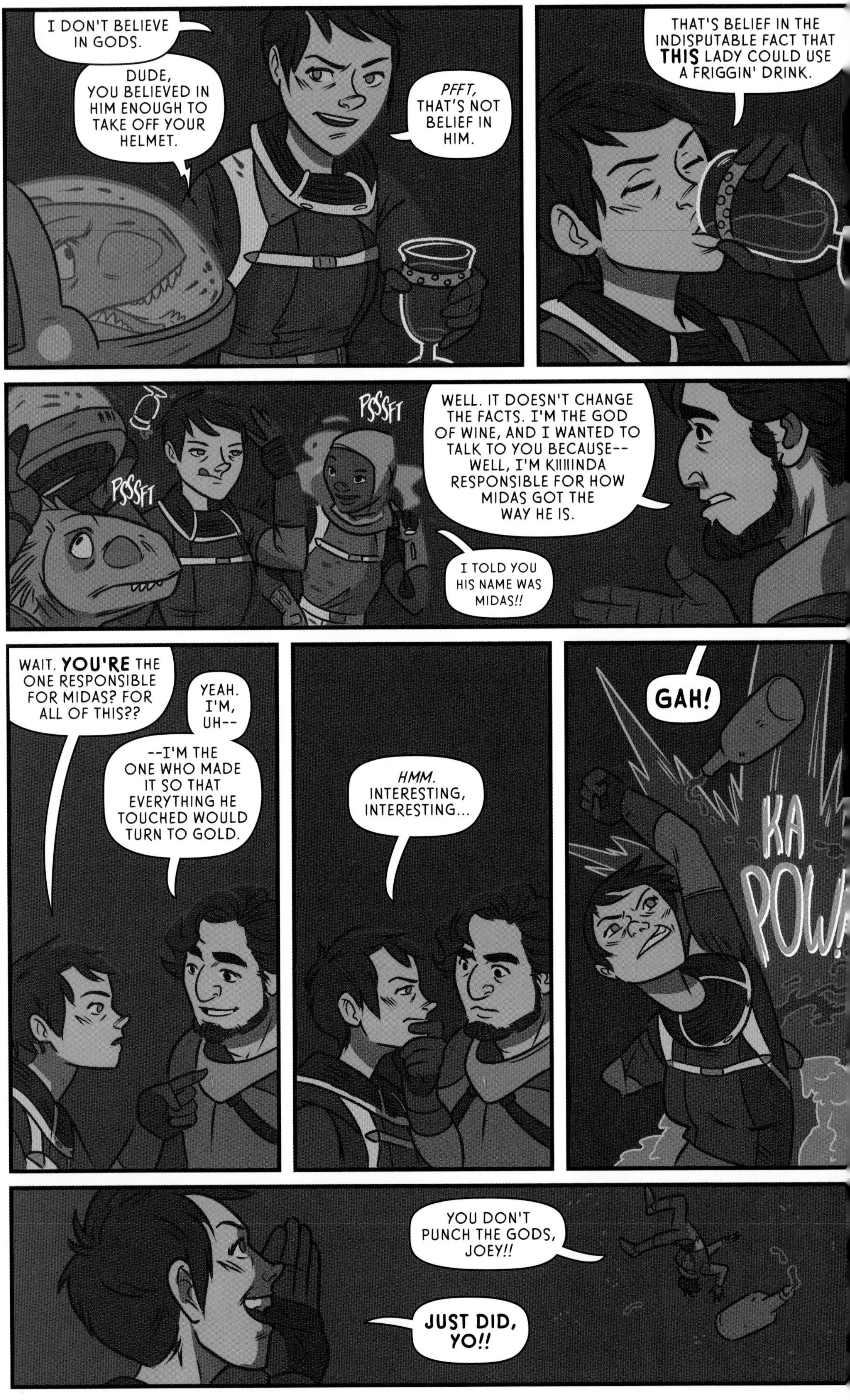
I DON'T BELIEVE IN GODS.
DUDE, YOU BELIEVED IN HIM ENOUGH TO TAKE OFF YOUR HELMET.
PFFT, THAT'S NOT BELIEF IN HIM.
THAT'S BELIEF IN THE INDISPUTABLE FACT THAT THIS LADY COULD USE A FRIGGIN' DRINK.
PSSSFT
PSSSFT
WELL. IT DOESN'T CHANGE THE FACTS. I'M THE GOD OF WINE, AND I WANTED TO TALK TO YOU BECAUSE-- WELL, I'M KIIIIINDA RESPONSIBLE FOR HOW MIDAS GOT THE WAY HE IS.
I TOLD YOU HIS NAME WAS MIDAS!!
WAIT. YOU'RE THE ONE RESPONSIBLE FOR MIDAS? FOR ALL OF THIS??
YEAH. I'M, UH--
--I'M THE ONE WHO MADE IT SO THAT EVERYTHING HE TOUCHED WOULD TURN TO GOLD.
HMM. INTERESTING, INTERESTING...
GAH!
KA POW!
YOU DON'T PUNCH THE GODS, JOEY!!
JUST DID, YO!!

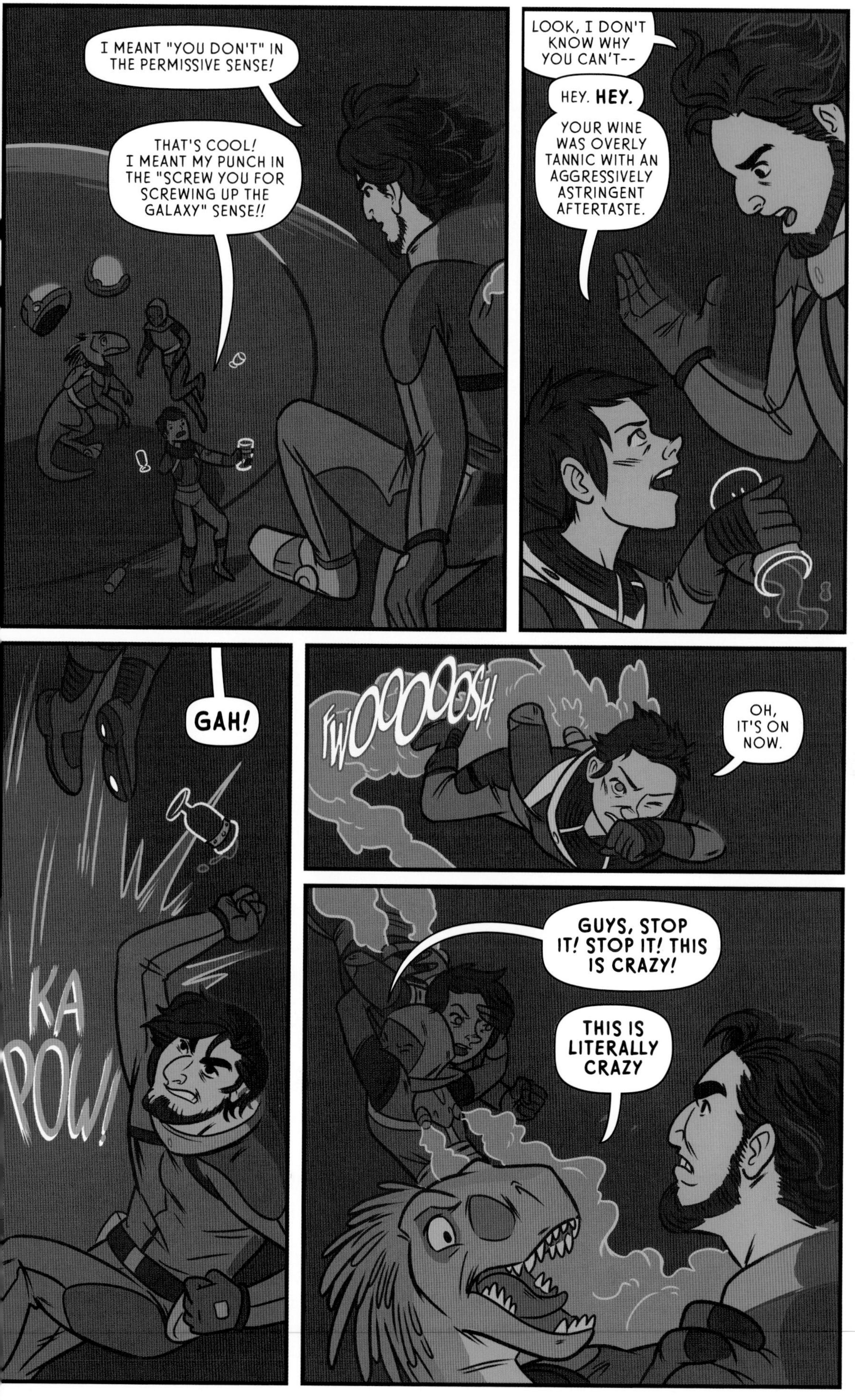

I MEANT "YOU DON'T" IN THE PERMISSIVE SENSE!
THAT'S COOL! I MEANT MY PUNCH IN THE "SCREW YOU FOR SCREWING UP THE GALAXY" SENSE!!
LOOK, I DON'T KNOW WHY YOU CAN'T--
HEY. HEY.
YOUR WINE WAS OVERLY TANNIC WITH AN AGGRESSIVELY ASTRINGENT AFTERTASTE.
GAH!
KA POW!
FWOOOOOOSH
OH, IT'S ON NOW.
GUYS, STOP IT! STOP IT! THIS IS CRAZY!
THIS IS LITERALLY CRAZY

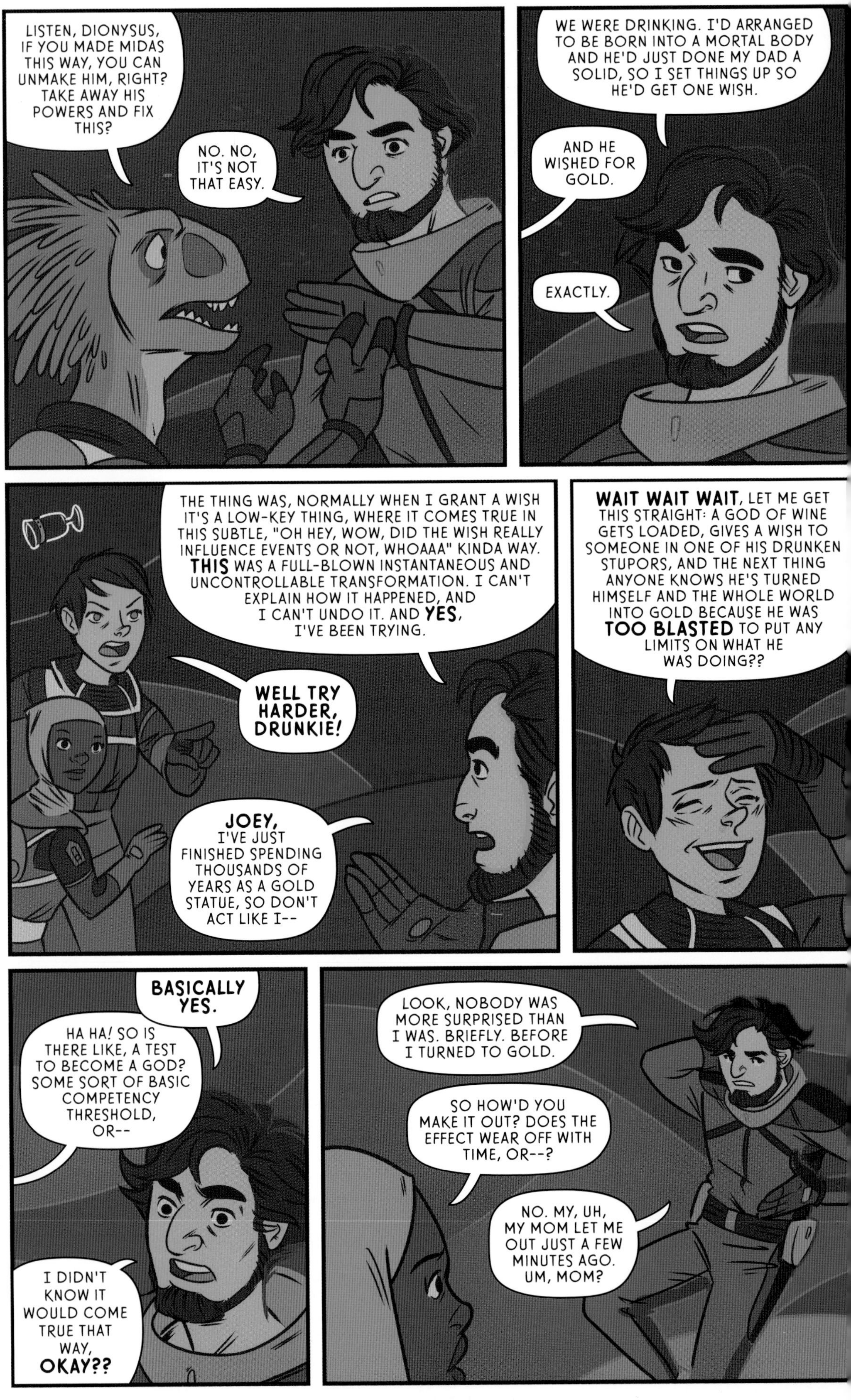
LISTEN, DIONYSUS, IF YOU MADE MIDAS THIS WAY, YOU CAN UNMAKE HIM, RIGHT? TAKE AWAY HIS POWERS AND FIX THIS?
NO. NO, IT'S NOT THAT EASY.
WE WERE DRINKING. I'D ARRANGED TO BE BORN INTO A MORTAL BODY AND HE'D JUST DONE MY DAD A SOLID, SO I SET THINGS UP SO HE'D GET ONE WISH.
AND HE WISHED FOR GOLD.
EXACTLY.
THE THING WAS, NORMALLY WHEN I GRANT A WISH IT'S A LOW-KEY THING, WHERE IT COMES TRUE IN THIS SUBTLE, "OH HEY, WOW, DID THE WISH REALLY INFLUENCE EVENTS OR NOT, WHOAAA" KINDA WAY. **THIS** WAS A FULL-BLOWN INSTANTANEOUS AND UNCONTROLLABLE TRANSFORMATION. I CAN'T EXPLAIN HOW IT HAPPENED, AND I CAN'T UNDO IT. AND **YES**, I'VE BEEN TRYING.
WELL TRY HARDER, DRUNKIE!
JOEY, I'VE JUST FINISHED SPENDING THOUSANDS OF YEARS AS A GOLD STATUE, SO DON'T ACT LIKE I--
WAIT WAIT WAIT, LET ME GET THIS STRAIGHT: A GOD OF WINE GETS LOADED, GIVES A WISH TO SOMEONE IN ONE OF HIS DRUNKEN STUPORS, AND THE NEXT THING ANYONE KNOWS HE'S TURNED HIMSELF AND THE WHOLE WORLD INTO GOLD BECAUSE HE WAS **TOO BLASTED** TO PUT ANY LIMITS ON WHAT HE WAS DOING??
BASICALLY YES.
HA HA! SO IS THERE LIKE, A TEST TO BECOME A GOD? SOME SORT OF BASIC COMPETENCY THRESHOLD, OR--
I DIDN'T KNOW IT WOULD COME TRUE THAT WAY, **OKAY??**
LOOK, NOBODY WAS MORE SURPRISED THAN I WAS. BRIEFLY. BEFORE I TURNED TO GOLD.
SO HOW'D YOU MAKE IT OUT? DOES THE EFFECT WEAR OFF WITH TIME, OR--?
NO. MY, UH, MY MOM LET ME OUT JUST A FEW MINUTES AGO. UM, MOM?

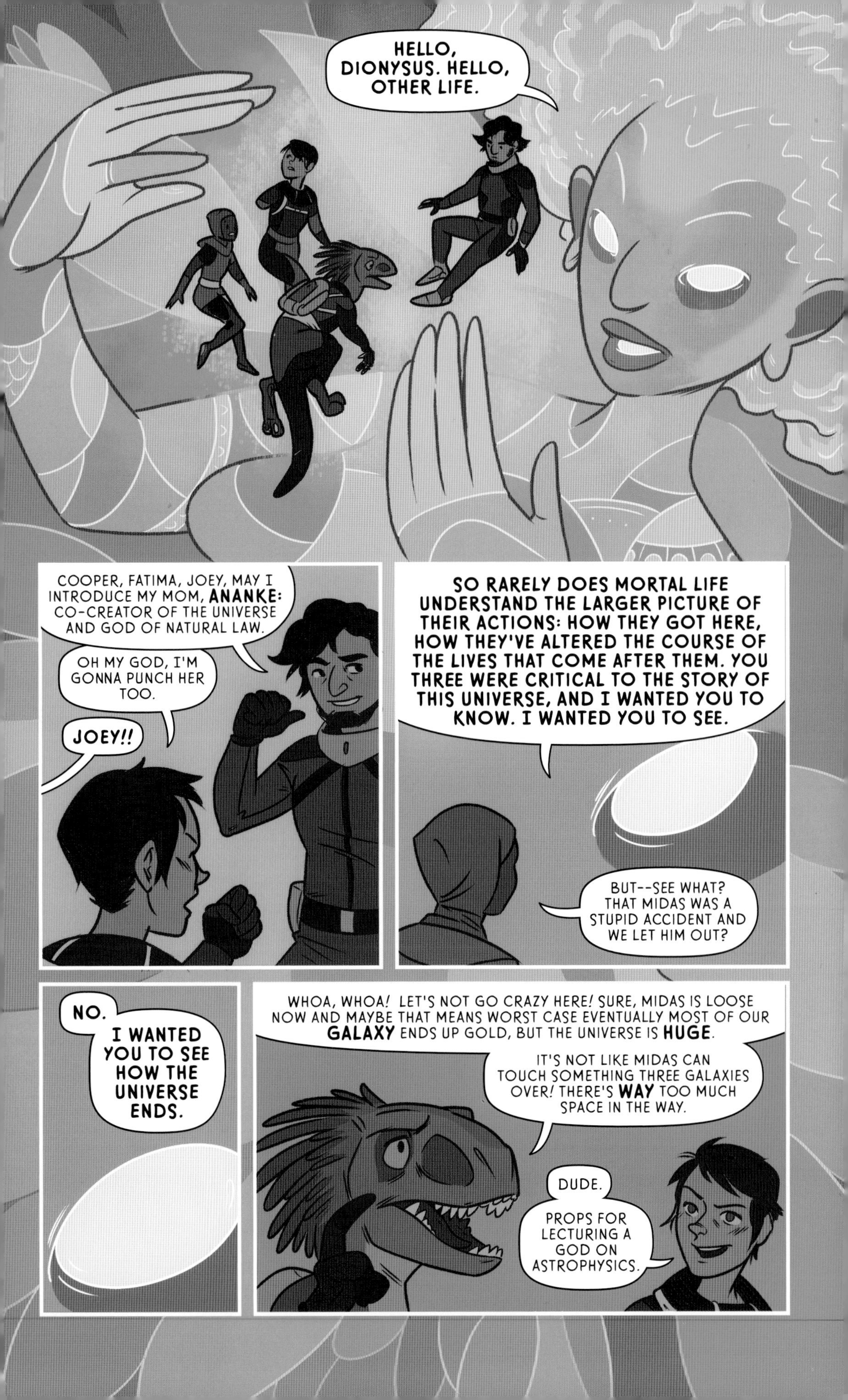
HELLO, DIONYSUS. HELLO, OTHER LIFE.
COOPER, FATIMA, JOEY, MAY I INTRODUCE MY MOM, ANANKE: CO-CREATOR OF THE UNIVERSE AND GOD OF NATURAL LAW.
OH MY GOD, I'M GONNA PUNCH HER TOO.
JOEY!!
SO RARELY DOES MORTAL LIFE UNDERSTAND THE LARGER PICTURE OF THEIR ACTIONS: HOW THEY GOT HERE, HOW THEY'VE ALTERED THE COURSE OF THE LIVES THAT COME AFTER THEM. YOU THREE WERE CRITICAL TO THE STORY OF THIS UNIVERSE, AND I WANTED YOU TO KNOW. I WANTED YOU TO SEE.
BUT--SEE WHAT? THAT MIDAS WAS A STUPID ACCIDENT AND WE LET HIM OUT?
NO.
I WANTED YOU TO SEE HOW THE UNIVERSE ENDS.
WHOA, WHOA! LET'S NOT GO CRAZY HERE! SURE, MIDAS IS LOOSE NOW AND MAYBE THAT MEANS WORST CASE EVENTUALLY MOST OF OUR GALAXY ENDS UP GOLD, BUT THE UNIVERSE IS HUGE.
IT'S NOT LIKE MIDAS CAN TOUCH SOMETHING THREE GALAXIES OVER! THERE'S WAY TOO MUCH SPACE IN THE WAY.
DUDE.
PROPS FOR LECTURING A GOD ON ASTROPHYSICS.

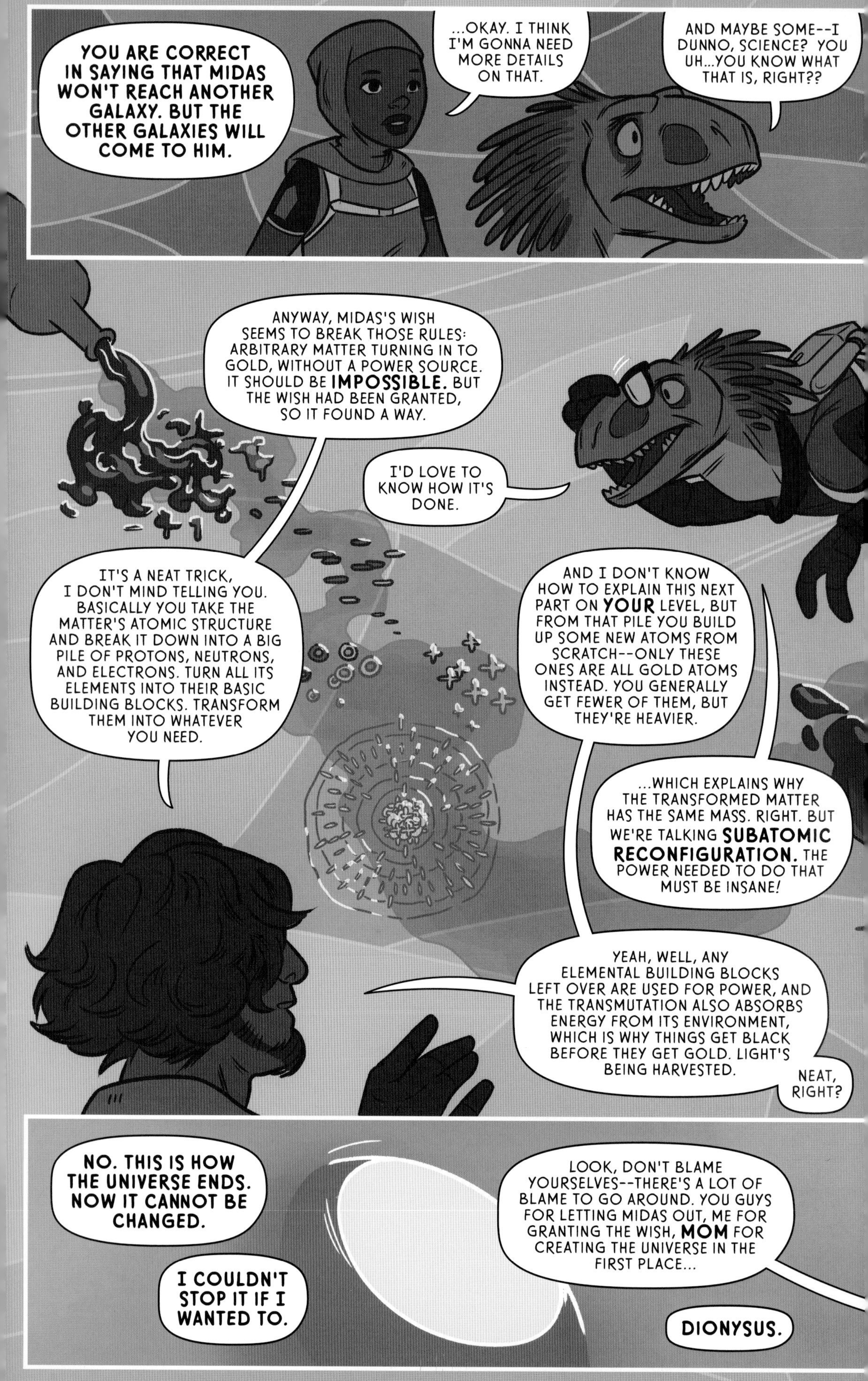
YOU ARE CORRECT IN SAYING THAT MIDAS WON'T REACH ANOTHER GALAXY. BUT THE OTHER GALAXIES WILL COME TO HIM.
...OKAY. I THINK I'M GONNA NEED MORE DETAILS ON THAT.
AND MAYBE SOME--I DUNNO, SCIENCE? YOU UH...YOU KNOW WHAT THAT IS, RIGHT??
ANYWAY, MIDAS'S WISH SEEMS TO BREAK THOSE RULES: ARBITRARY MATTER TURNING IN TO GOLD, WITHOUT A POWER SOURCE. IT SHOULD BE **IMPOSSIBLE.** BUT THE WISH HAD BEEN GRANTED, SO IT FOUND A WAY.
I'D LOVE TO KNOW HOW IT'S DONE.
IT'S A NEAT TRICK, I DON'T MIND TELLING YOU. BASICALLY YOU TAKE THE MATTER'S ATOMIC STRUCTURE AND BREAK IT DOWN INTO A BIG PILE OF PROTONS, NEUTRONS, AND ELECTRONS. TURN ALL ITS ELEMENTS INTO THEIR BASIC BUILDING BLOCKS. TRANSFORM THEM INTO WHATEVER YOU NEED.
AND I DON'T KNOW HOW TO EXPLAIN THIS NEXT PART ON **YOUR** LEVEL, BUT FROM THAT PILE YOU BUILD UP SOME NEW ATOMS FROM SCRATCH--ONLY THESE ONES ARE ALL GOLD ATOMS INSTEAD. YOU GENERALLY GET FEWER OF THEM, BUT THEY'RE HEAVIER.
...WHICH EXPLAINS WHY THE TRANSFORMED MATTER HAS THE SAME MASS. RIGHT. BUT WE'RE TALKING **SUBATOMIC RECONFIGURATION.** THE POWER NEEDED TO DO THAT MUST BE INSANE!
YEAH, WELL, ANY ELEMENTAL BUILDING BLOCKS LEFT OVER ARE USED FOR POWER, AND THE TRANSMUTATION ALSO ABSORBS ENERGY FROM ITS ENVIRONMENT, WHICH IS WHY THINGS GET BLACK BEFORE THEY GET GOLD. LIGHT'S BEING HARVESTED.
NEAT, RIGHT?
NO. THIS IS HOW THE UNIVERSE ENDS. NOW IT CANNOT BE CHANGED.
I COULDN'T STOP IT IF I WANTED TO.
LOOK, DON'T BLAME YOURSELVES--THERE'S A LOT OF BLAME TO GO AROUND. YOU GUYS FOR LETTING MIDAS OUT, ME FOR GRANTING THE WISH, **MOM** FOR CREATING THE UNIVERSE IN THE FIRST PLACE...
DIONYSUS.

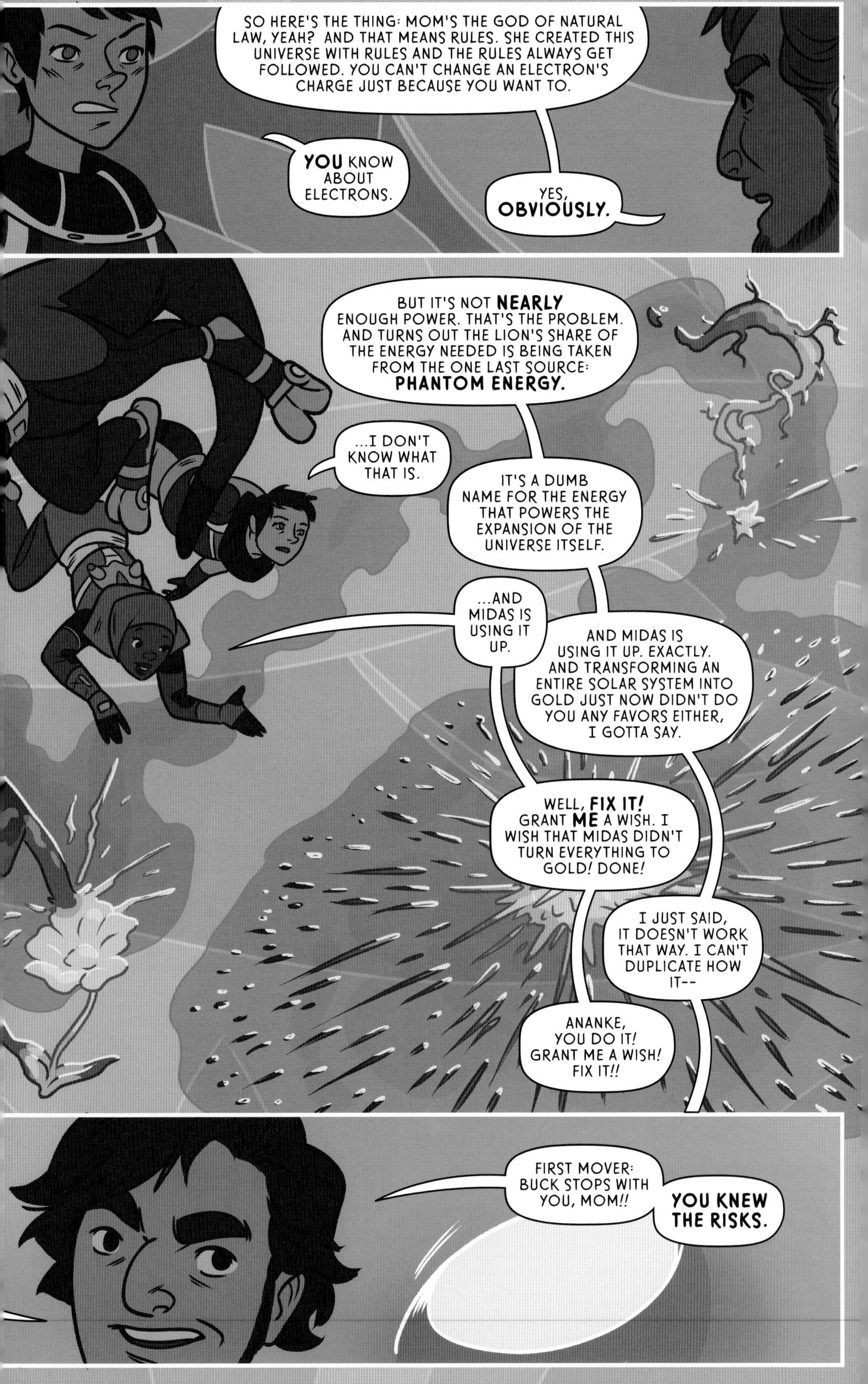
SO HERE'S THE THING: MOM'S THE GOD OF NATURAL LAW, YEAH? AND THAT MEANS RULES. SHE CREATED THIS UNIVERSE WITH RULES AND THE RULES ALWAYS GET FOLLOWED. YOU CAN'T CHANGE AN ELECTRON'S CHARGE JUST BECAUSE YOU WANT TO.
YOU KNOW ABOUT ELECTRONS.
YES, OBVIOUSLY.
BUT IT'S NOT NEARLY ENOUGH POWER. THAT'S THE PROBLEM. AND TURNS OUT THE LION'S SHARE OF THE ENERGY NEEDED IS BEING TAKEN FROM THE ONE LAST SOURCE: PHANTOM ENERGY.
...I DON'T KNOW WHAT THAT IS.
IT'S A DUMB NAME FOR THE ENERGY THAT POWERS THE EXPANSION OF THE UNIVERSE ITSELF.
...AND MIDAS IS USING IT UP.
AND MIDAS IS USING IT UP. EXACTLY. AND TRANSFORMING AN ENTIRE SOLAR SYSTEM INTO GOLD JUST NOW DIDN'T DO YOU ANY FAVORS EITHER, I GOTTA SAY.
WELL, FIX IT! GRANT ME A WISH. I WISH THAT MIDAS DIDN'T TURN EVERYTHING TO GOLD! DONE!
I JUST SAID, IT DOESN'T WORK THAT WAY. I CAN'T DUPLICATE HOW IT--
ANANKE, YOU DO IT! GRANT ME A WISH! FIX IT!!
FIRST MOVER: BUCK STOPS WITH YOU, MOM!!
YOU KNEW THE RISKS.

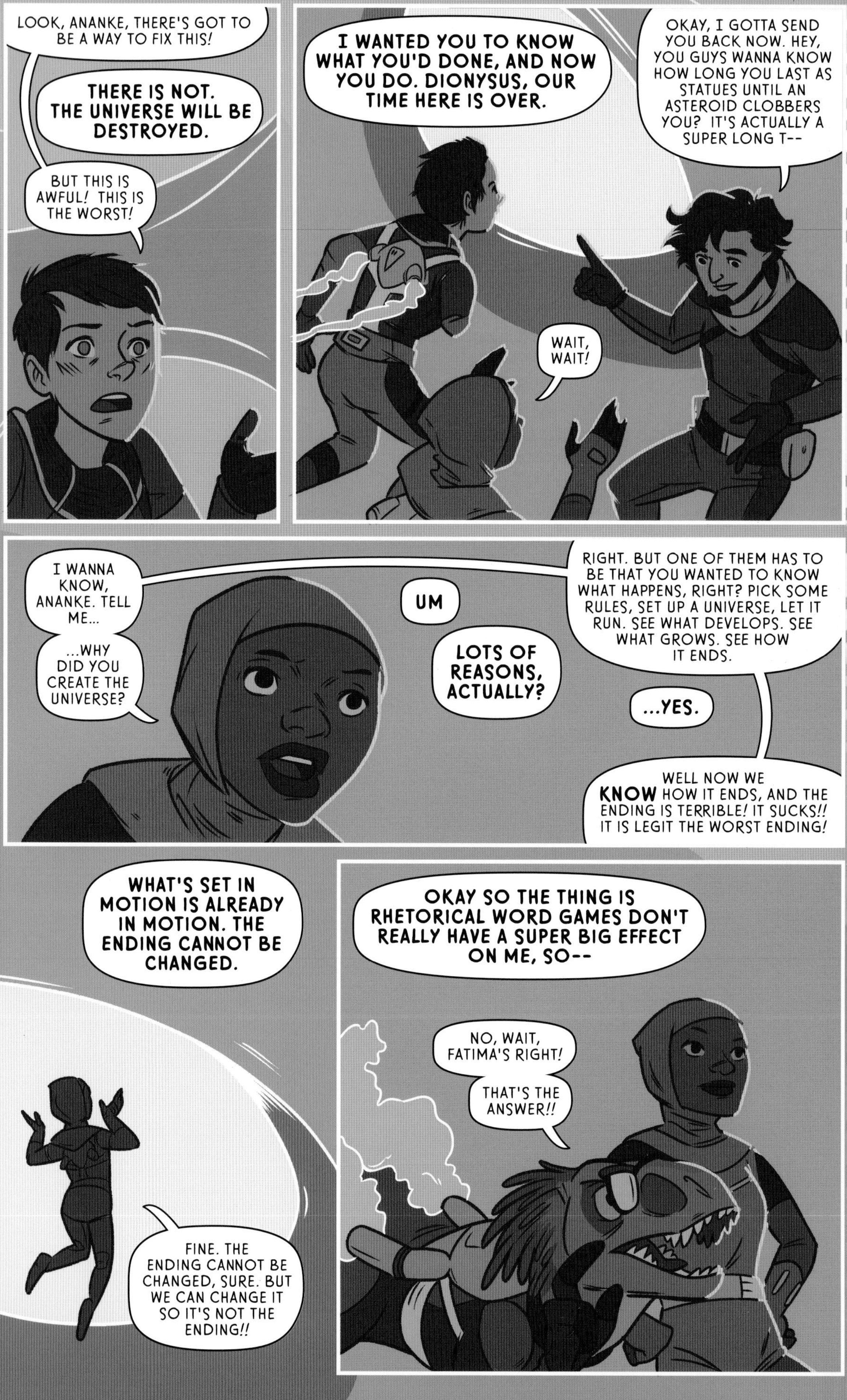
LOOK, ANANKE, THERE'S GOT TO BE A WAY TO FIX THIS!
THERE IS NOT. THE UNIVERSE WILL BE DESTROYED.
BUT THIS IS AWFUL! THIS IS THE WORST!
I WANTED YOU TO KNOW WHAT YOU'D DONE, AND NOW YOU DO. DIONYSUS, OUR TIME HERE IS OVER.
OKAY, I GOTTA SEND YOU BACK NOW. HEY, YOU GUYS WANNA KNOW HOW LONG YOU LAST AS STATUES UNTIL AN ASTEROID CLOBBERS YOU? IT'S ACTUALLY A SUPER LONG T--
WAIT, WAIT!
I WANNA KNOW, ANANKE. TELL ME...
...WHY DID YOU CREATE THE UNIVERSE?
UM
LOTS OF REASONS, ACTUALLY?
RIGHT. BUT ONE OF THEM HAS TO BE THAT YOU WANTED TO KNOW WHAT HAPPENS, RIGHT? PICK SOME RULES, SET UP A UNIVERSE, LET IT RUN. SEE WHAT DEVELOPS. SEE WHAT GROWS. SEE HOW IT ENDS.
...YES.
WELL NOW WE KNOW HOW IT ENDS, AND THE ENDING IS TERRIBLE! IT SUCKS!! IT IS LEGIT THE WORST ENDING!
WHAT'S SET IN MOTION IS ALREADY IN MOTION. THE ENDING CANNOT BE CHANGED.
FINE. THE ENDING CANNOT BE CHANGED, SURE. BUT WE CAN CHANGE IT SO IT'S NOT THE ENDING!!
OKAY SO THE THING IS RHETORICAL WORD GAMES DON'T REALLY HAVE A SUPER BIG EFFECT ON ME, SO--
NO, WAIT, FATIMA'S RIGHT!
THAT'S THE ANSWER!!

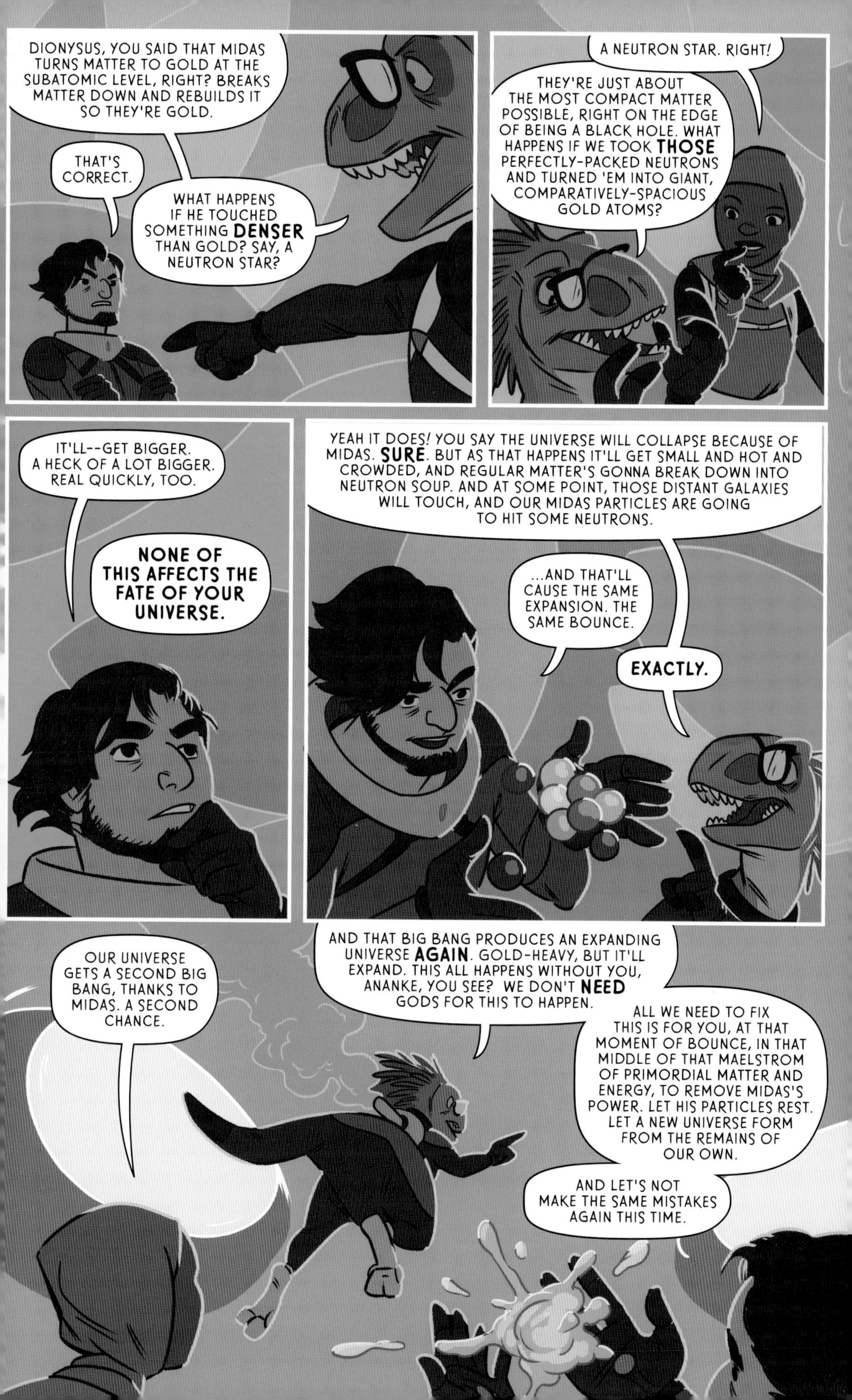
DIONYSUS, YOU SAID THAT MIDAS TURNS MATTER TO GOLD AT THE SUBATOMIC LEVEL, RIGHT? BREAKS MATTER DOWN AND REBUILDS IT SO THEY'RE GOLD.
THAT'S CORRECT.
WHAT HAPPENS IF HE TOUCHED SOMETHING DENSER THAN GOLD? SAY, A NEUTRON STAR?
A NEUTRON STAR. RIGHT!
THEY'RE JUST ABOUT THE MOST COMPACT MATTER POSSIBLE, RIGHT ON THE EDGE OF BEING A BLACK HOLE. WHAT HAPPENS IF WE TOOK THOSE PERFECTLY-PACKED NEUTRONS AND TURNED 'EM INTO GIANT, COMPARATIVELY-SPACIOUS GOLD ATOMS?
IT'LL--GET BIGGER. A HECK OF A LOT BIGGER. REAL QUICKLY, TOO.
NONE OF THIS AFFECTS THE FATE OF YOUR UNIVERSE.
YEAH IT DOES! YOU SAY THE UNIVERSE WILL COLLAPSE BECAUSE OF MIDAS. SURE. BUT AS THAT HAPPENS IT'LL GET SMALL AND HOT AND CROWDED, AND REGULAR MATTER'S GONNA BREAK DOWN INTO NEUTRON SOUP. AND AT SOME POINT, THOSE DISTANT GALAXIES WILL TOUCH, AND OUR MIDAS PARTICLES ARE GOING TO HIT SOME NEUTRONS.
...AND THAT'LL CAUSE THE SAME EXPANSION. THE SAME BOUNCE.
EXACTLY.
OUR UNIVERSE GETS A SECOND BIG BANG, THANKS TO MIDAS. A SECOND CHANCE.
AND THAT BIG BANG PRODUCES AN EXPANDING UNIVERSE AGAIN. GOLD-HEAVY, BUT IT'LL EXPAND. THIS ALL HAPPENS WITHOUT YOU, ANANKE, YOU SEE? WE DON'T NEED GODS FOR THIS TO HAPPEN.
ALL WE NEED TO FIX THIS IS FOR YOU, AT THAT MOMENT OF BOUNCE, IN THAT MIDDLE OF THAT MAELSTROM OF PRIMORDIAL MATTER AND ENERGY, TO REMOVE MIDAS'S POWER. LET HIS PARTICLES REST. LET A NEW UNIVERSE FORM FROM THE REMAINS OF OUR OWN.
AND LET'S NOT MAKE THE SAME MISTAKES AGAIN THIS TIME.

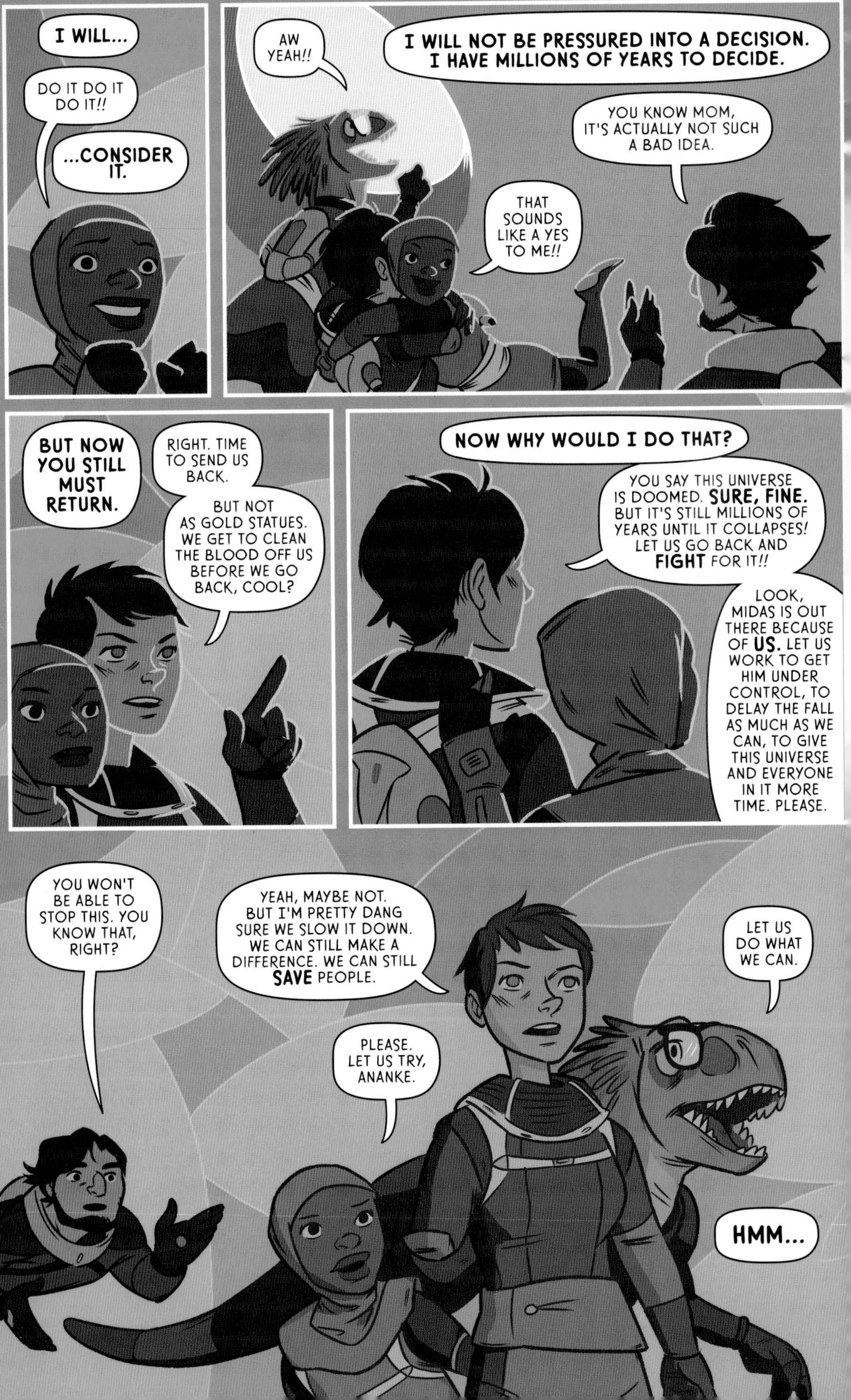
I WILL...
DO IT DO IT DO IT!!
...CONSIDER IT.
AW YEAH!!
I WILL NOT BE PRESSURED INTO A DECISION. I HAVE MILLIONS OF YEARS TO DECIDE.
YOU KNOW MOM, IT'S ACTUALLY NOT SUCH A BAD IDEA.
THAT SOUNDS LIKE A YES TO ME!!
BUT NOW YOU STILL MUST RETURN.
RIGHT. TIME TO SEND US BACK.
BUT NOT AS GOLD STATUES. WE GET TO CLEAN THE BLOOD OFF US BEFORE WE GO BACK, COOL?
NOW WHY WOULD I DO THAT?
YOU SAY THIS UNIVERSE IS DOOMED. SURE, FINE. BUT IT'S STILL MILLIONS OF YEARS UNTIL IT COLLAPSES! LET US GO BACK AND FIGHT FOR IT!!
LOOK, MIDAS IS OUT THERE BECAUSE OF US. LET US WORK TO GET HIM UNDER CONTROL, TO DELAY THE FALL AS MUCH AS WE CAN, TO GIVE THIS UNIVERSE AND EVERYONE IN IT MORE TIME. PLEASE.
YOU WON'T BE ABLE TO STOP THIS. YOU KNOW THAT, RIGHT?
YEAH, MAYBE NOT. BUT I'M PRETTY DANG SURE WE SLOW IT DOWN. WE CAN STILL MAKE A DIFFERENCE. WE CAN STILL SAVE PEOPLE.
LET US DO WHAT WE CAN.
PLEASE. LET US TRY, ANANKE.
HMM...

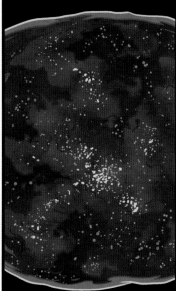
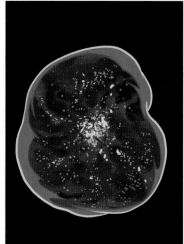
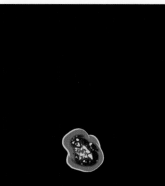
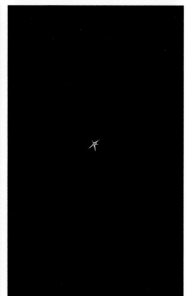

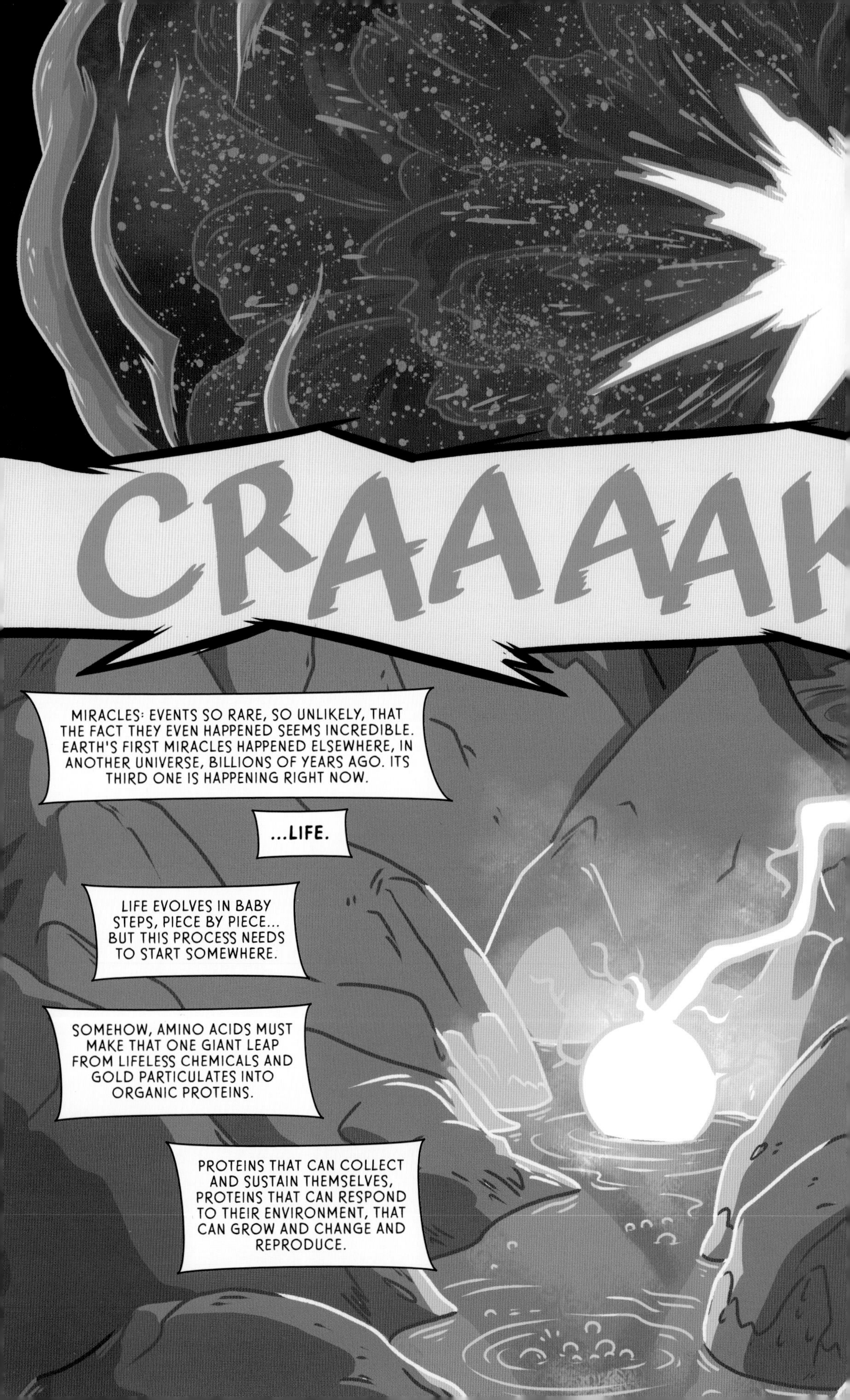
CRAAAK
MIRACLES: EVENTS SO RARE, SO UNLIKELY, THAT THE FACT THEY EVEN HAPPENED SEEMS INCREDIBLE. EARTH'S FIRST MIRACLES HAPPENED ELSEWHERE, IN ANOTHER UNIVERSE, BILLIONS OF YEARS AGO. ITS THIRD ONE IS HAPPENING RIGHT NOW.
...LIFE.
LIFE EVOLVES IN BABY STEPS, PIECE BY PIECE... BUT THIS PROCESS NEEDS TO START SOMEWHERE.
SOMEHOW, AMINO ACIDS MUST MAKE THAT ONE GIANT LEAP FROM LIFELESS CHEMICALS AND GOLD PARTICULATES INTO ORGANIC PROTEINS.
PROTEINS THAT CAN COLLECT AND SUSTAIN THEMSELVES, PROTEINS THAT CAN RESPOND TO THEIR ENVIRONMENT, THAT CAN GROW AND CHANGE AND REPRODUCE.

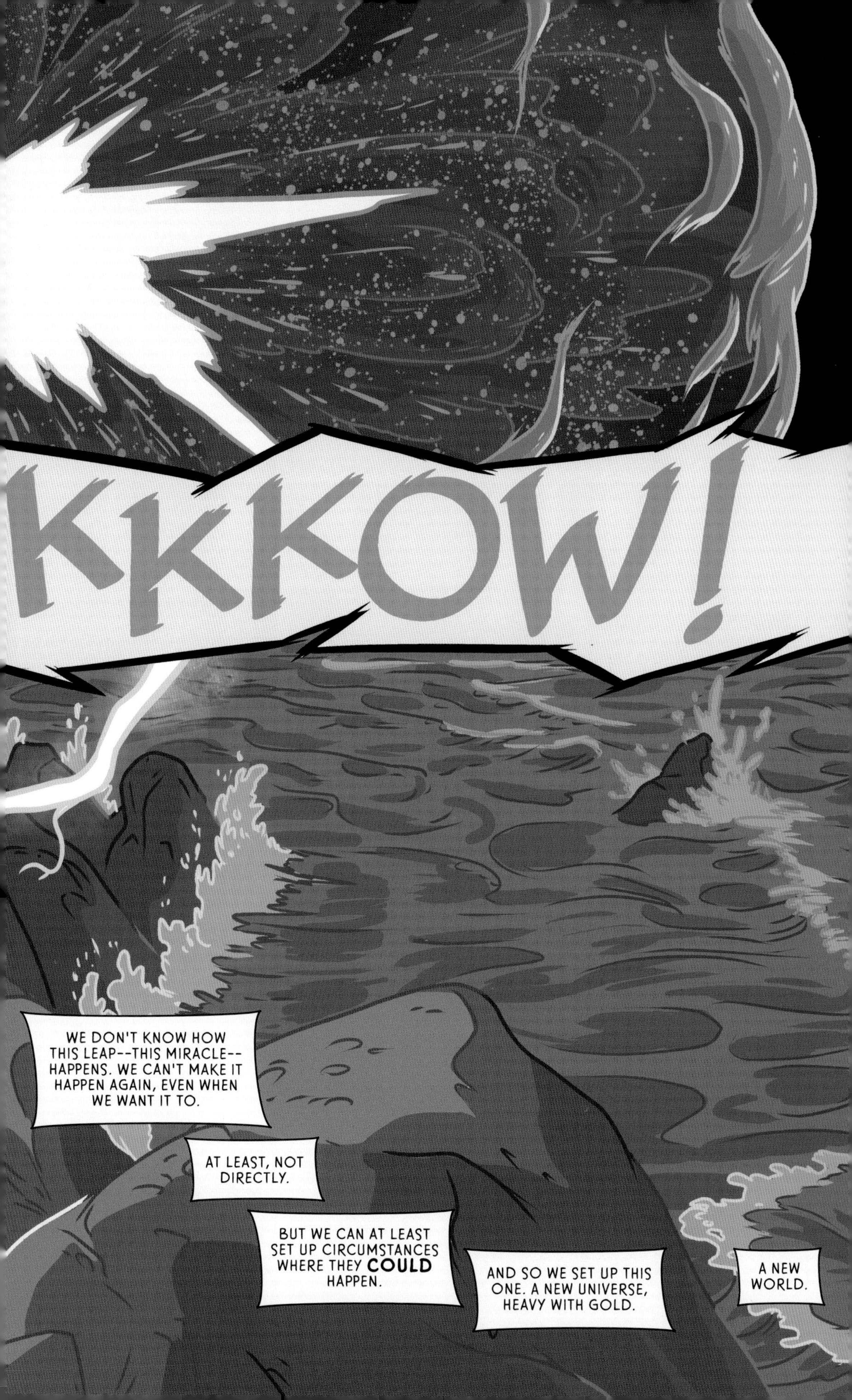
KKKOW!
WE DON'T KNOW HOW THIS LEAP--THIS MIRACLE--HAPPENS. WE CAN'T MAKE IT HAPPEN AGAIN, EVEN WHEN WE WANT IT TO.
AT LEAST, NOT DIRECTLY.
BUT WE CAN AT LEAST SET UP CIRCUMSTANCES WHERE THEY COULD HAPPEN.
AND SO WE SET UP THIS ONE. A NEW UNIVERSE, HEAVY WITH GOLD.
A NEW WORLD.

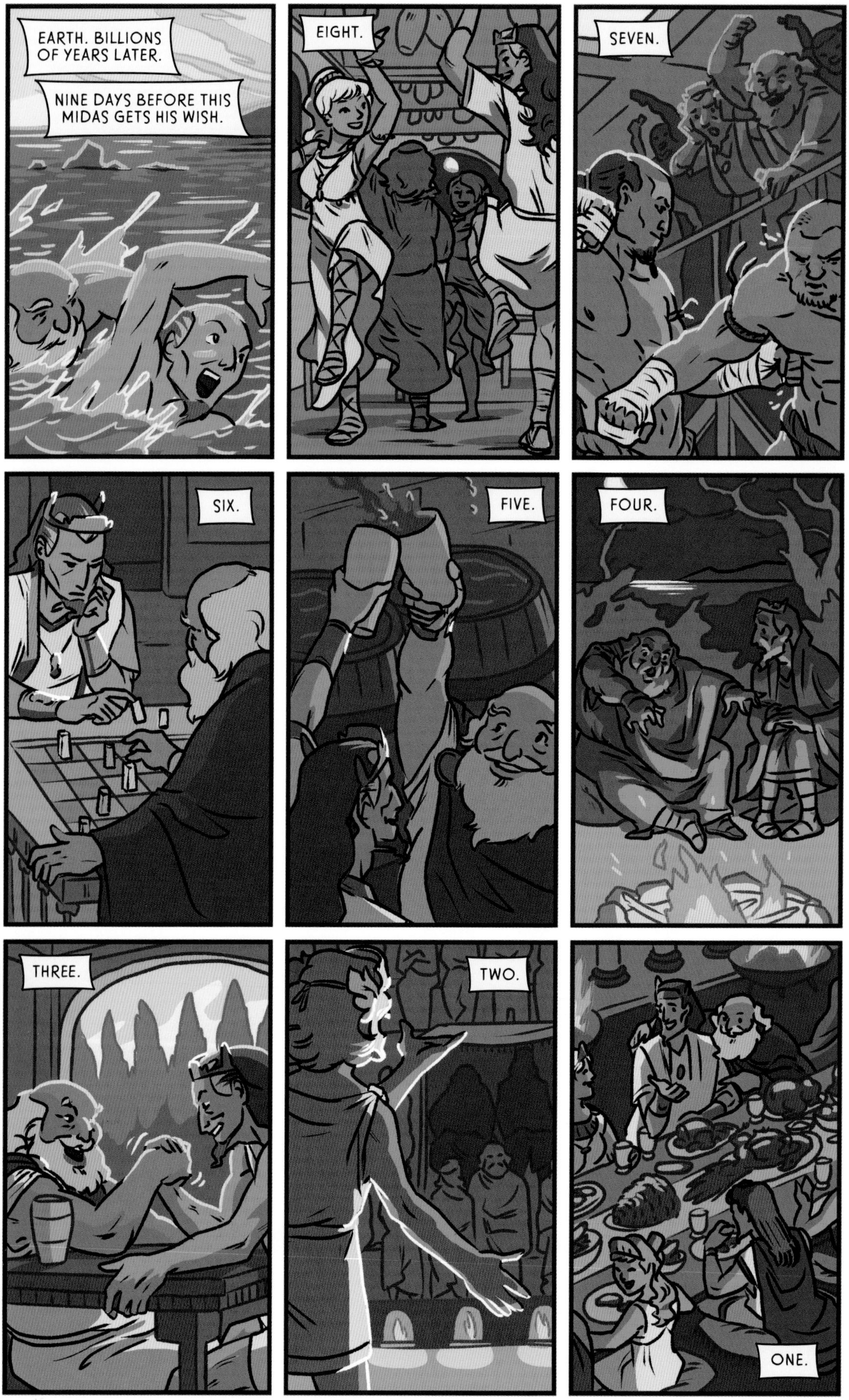
EARTH. BILLIONS OF YEARS LATER.
NINE DAYS BEFORE THIS MIDAS GETS HIS WISH.
EIGHT.
SEVEN.
SIX.
FIVE.
FOUR.
THREE.
TWO.
ONE.

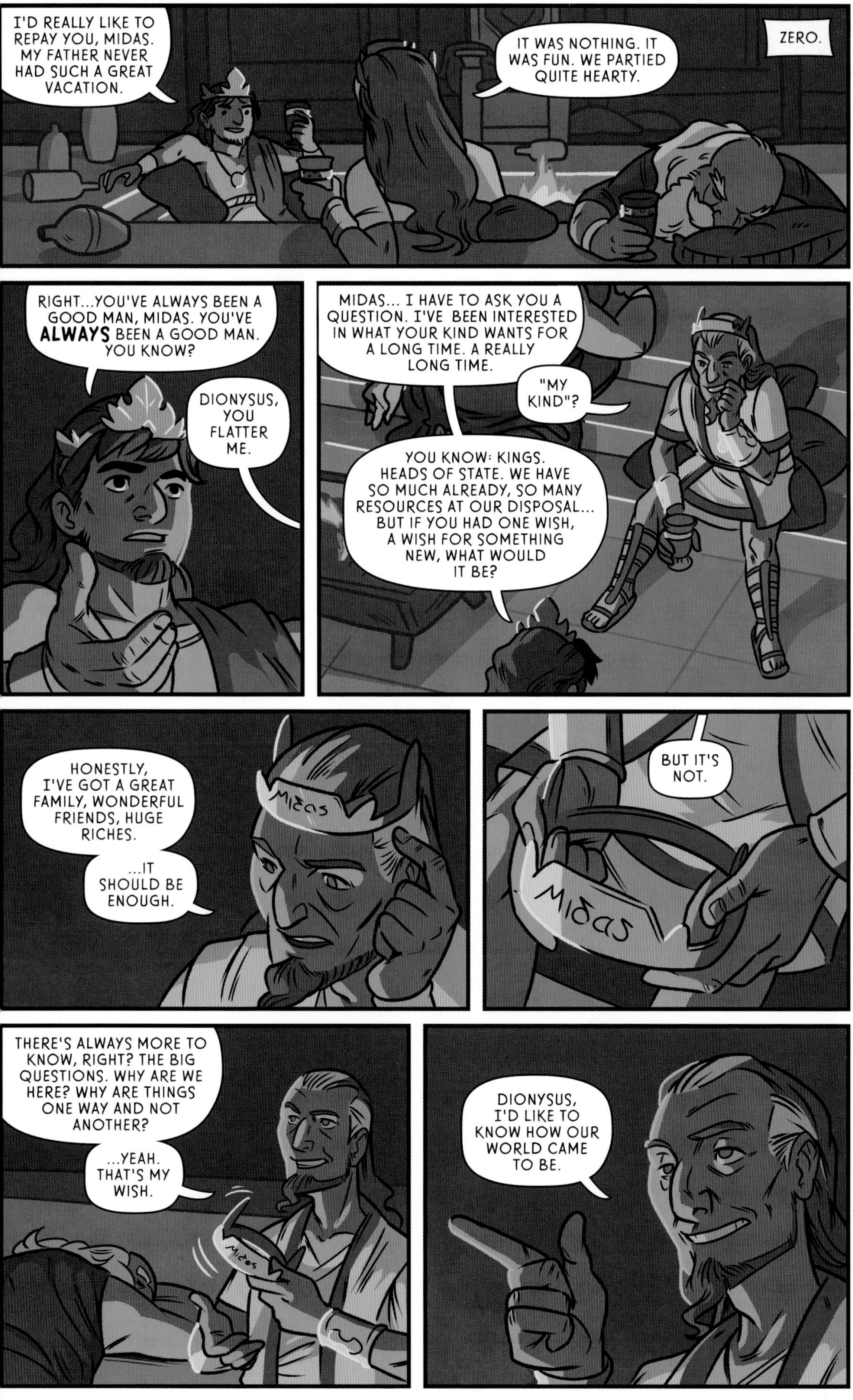
I'D REALLY LIKE TO REPAY YOU, MIDAS. MY FATHER NEVER HAD SUCH A GREAT VACATION.
IT WAS NOTHING. IT WAS FUN. WE PARTIED QUITE HEARTY.
ZERO.
RIGHT...YOU'VE ALWAYS BEEN A GOOD MAN, MIDAS. YOU'VE **ALWAYS** BEEN A GOOD MAN. YOU KNOW?
DIONYSUS, YOU FLATTER ME.
MIDAS... I HAVE TO ASK YOU A QUESTION. I'VE BEEN INTERESTED IN WHAT YOUR KIND WANTS FOR A LONG TIME. A REALLY LONG TIME.
"MY KIND"?
YOU KNOW: KINGS. HEADS OF STATE. WE HAVE SO MUCH ALREADY, SO MANY RESOURCES AT OUR DISPOSAL... BUT IF YOU HAD ONE WISH, A WISH FOR SOMETHING NEW, WHAT WOULD IT BE?
HONESTLY, I'VE GOT A GREAT FAMILY, WONDERFUL FRIENDS, HUGE RICHES.
...IT SHOULD BE ENOUGH.
MIDAS
BUT IT'S NOT.
MIDAS
THERE'S ALWAYS MORE TO KNOW, RIGHT? THE BIG QUESTIONS. WHY ARE WE HERE? WHY ARE THINGS ONE WAY AND NOT ANOTHER?
...YEAH. THAT'S MY WISH.
MIDAS
DIONYSUS, I'D LIKE TO KNOW HOW OUR WORLD CAME TO BE.

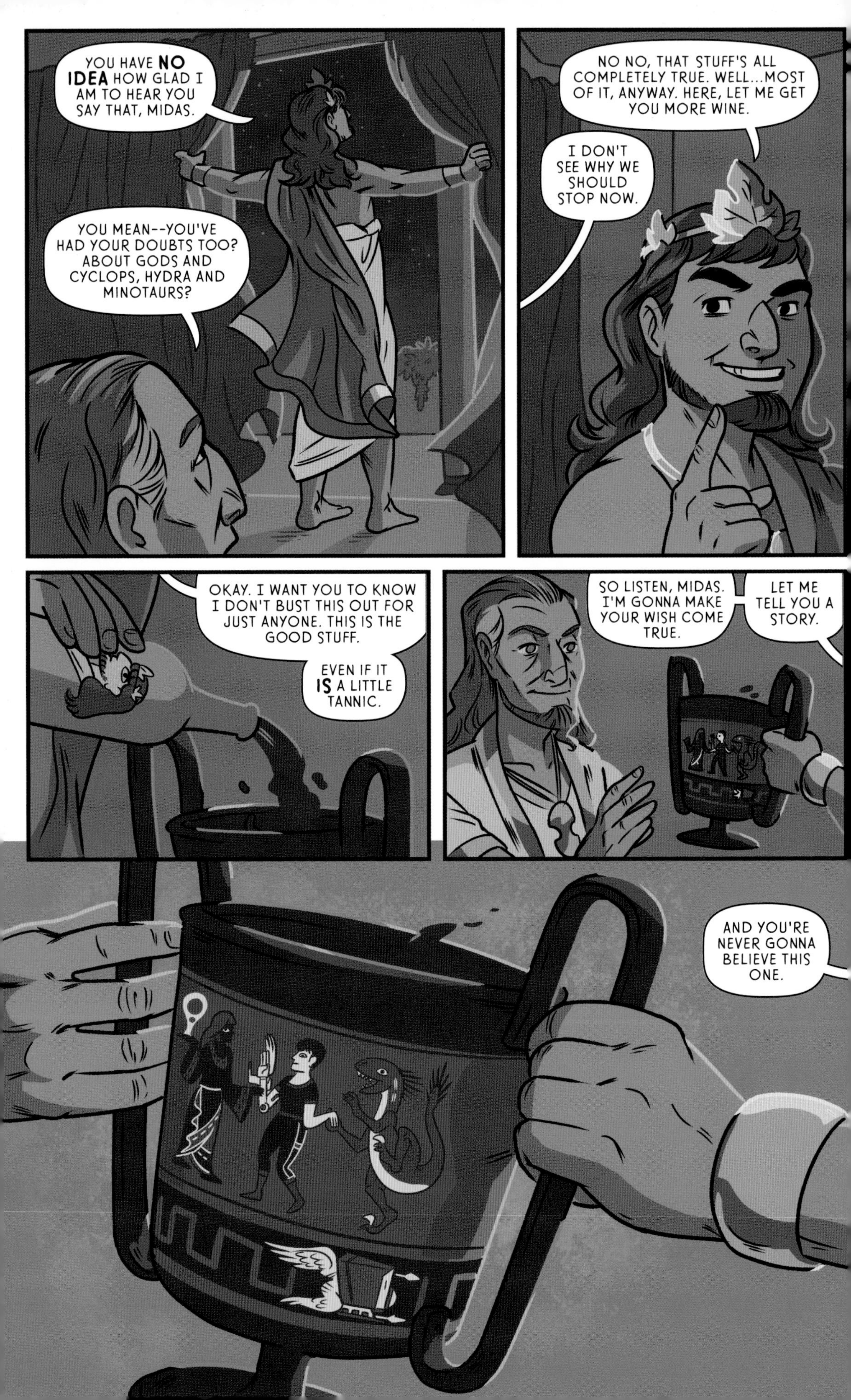
YOU HAVE **NO IDEA** HOW GLAD I AM TO HEAR YOU SAY THAT, MIDAS.
YOU MEAN--YOU'VE HAD YOUR DOUBTS TOO? ABOUT GODS AND CYCLOPS, HYDRA AND MINOTAURS?
NO NO, THAT STUFF'S ALL COMPLETELY TRUE. WELL...MOST OF IT, ANYWAY. HERE, LET ME GET YOU MORE WINE.
I DON'T SEE WHY WE SHOULD STOP NOW.
OKAY. I WANT YOU TO KNOW I DON'T BUST THIS OUT FOR JUST ANYONE. THIS IS THE GOOD STUFF.
EVEN IF IT **IS** A LITTLE TANNIC.
SO LISTEN, MIDAS. I'M GONNA MAKE YOUR WISH COME TRUE.
LET ME TELL YOU A STORY.
AND YOU'RE NEVER GONNA BELIEVE THIS ONE.

"MAN! YOU GUYS HAVE BEEN UP TO SOME **SHENANIGANS,** HUH?"

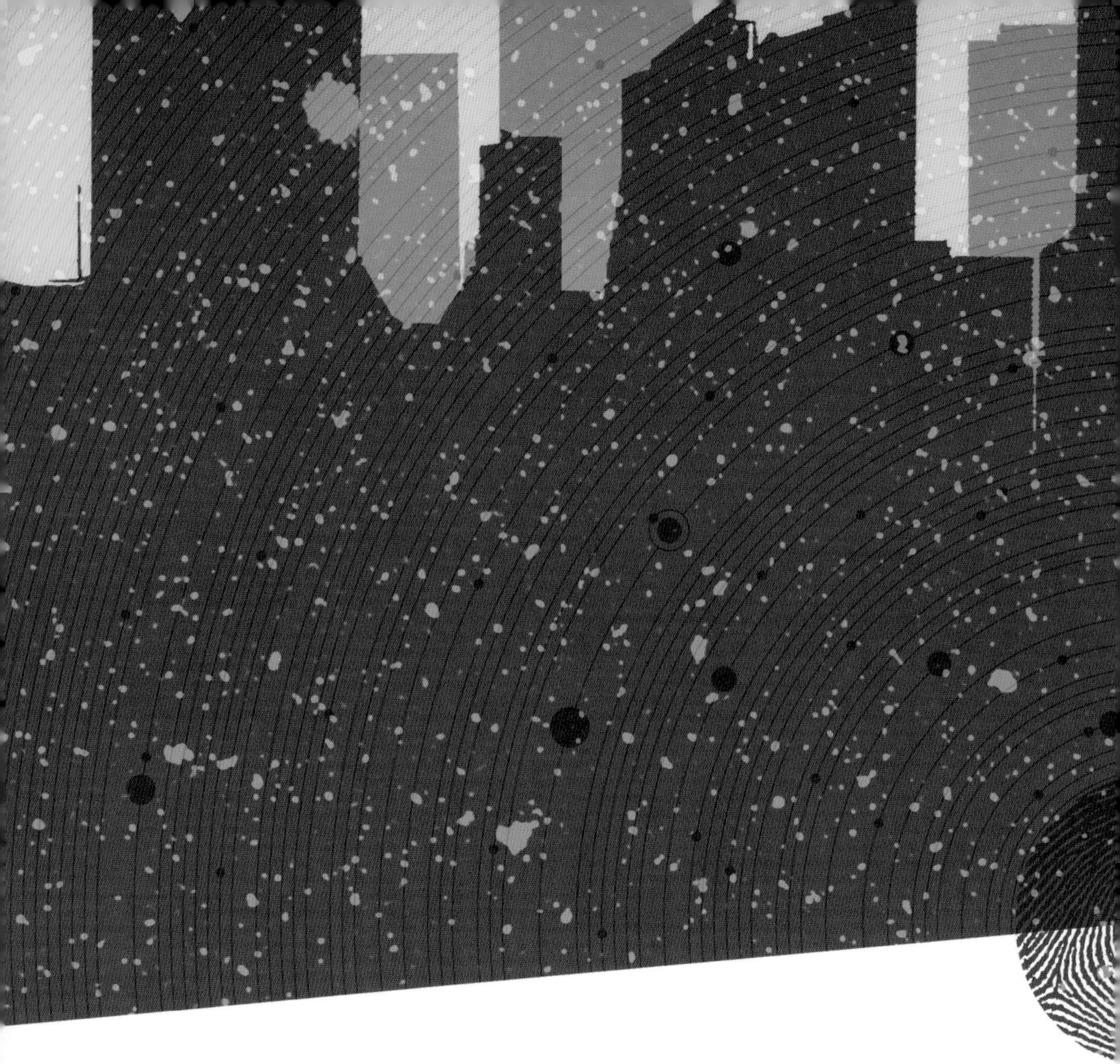

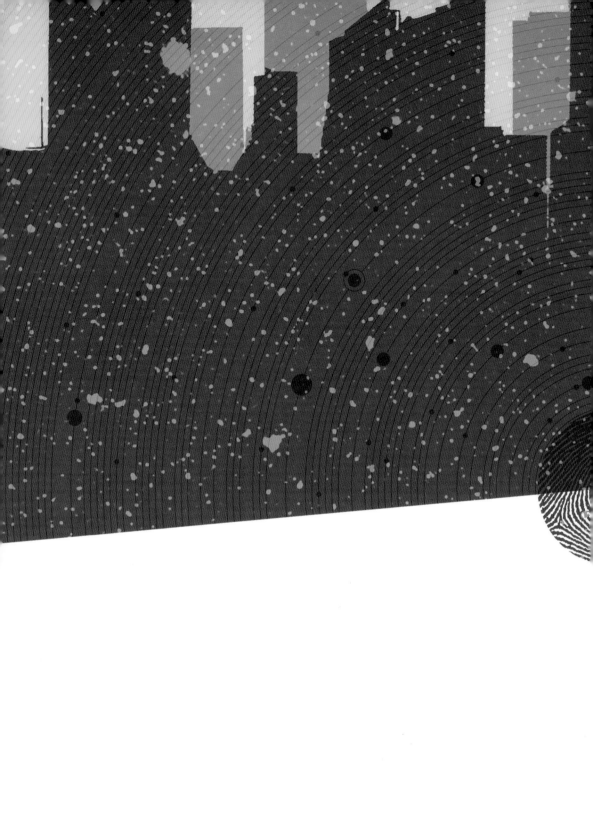

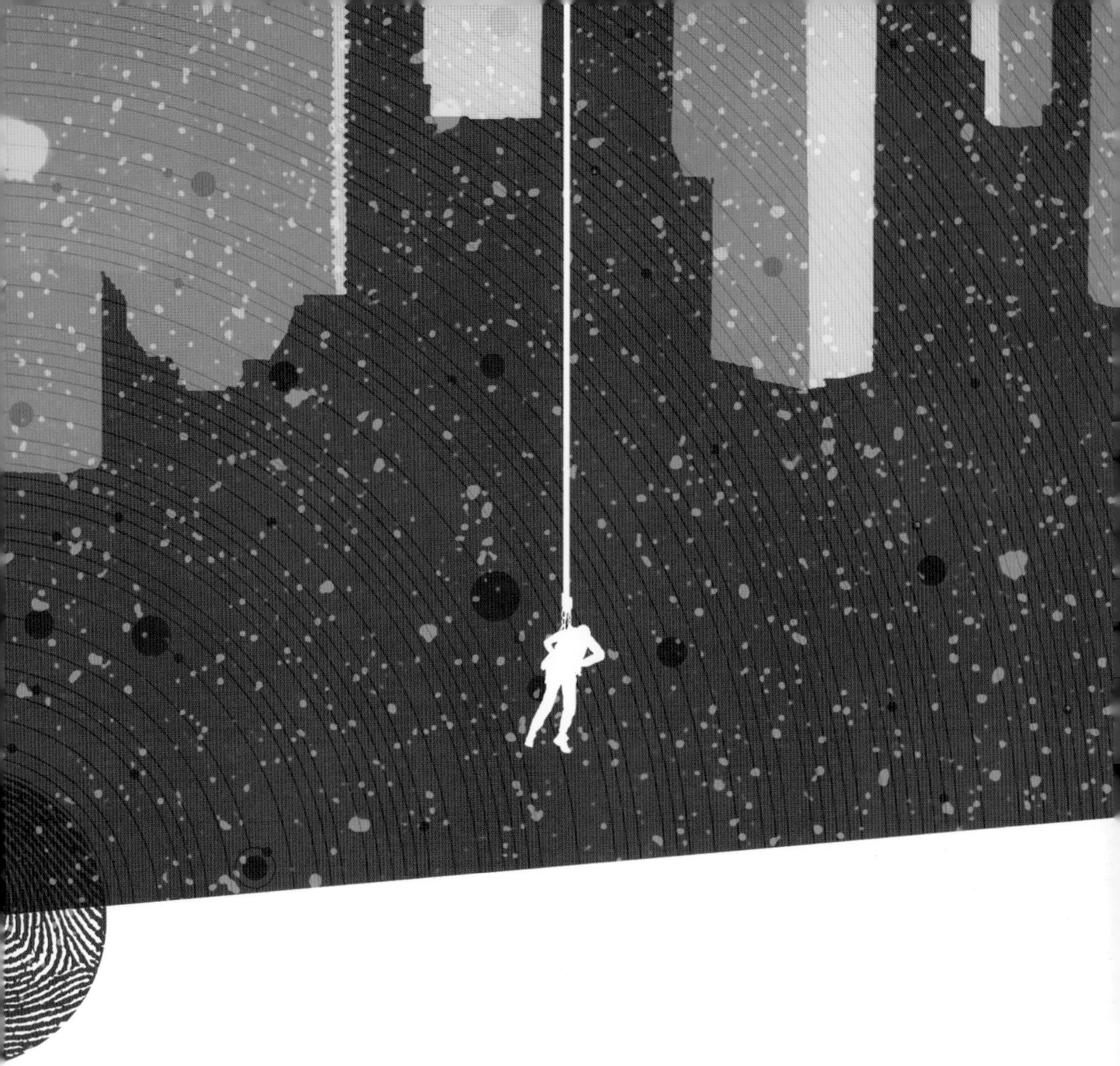

COVER
GALLERY

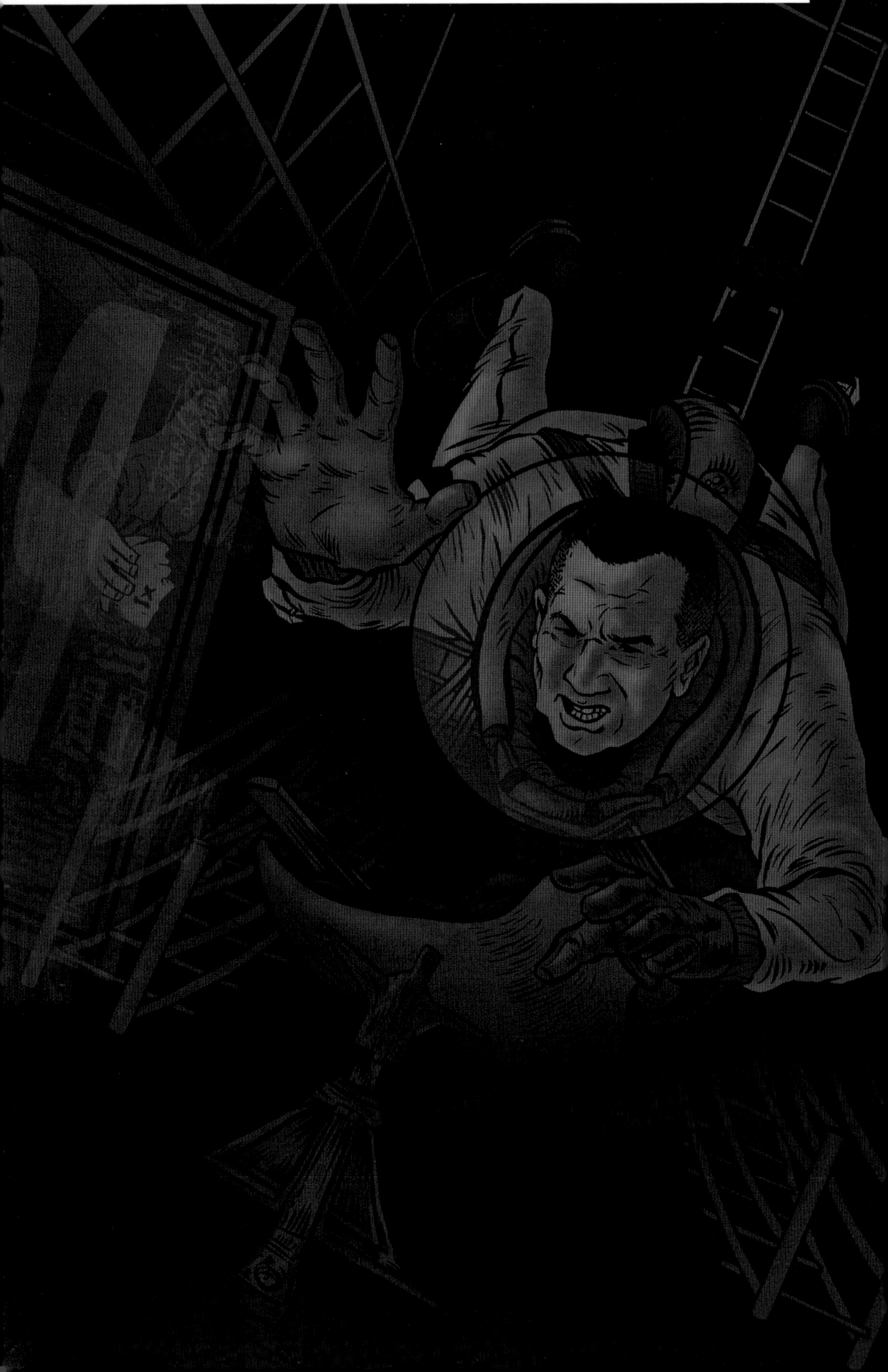

ISSUE FIVE VARIANT **EMILY CARROLL**

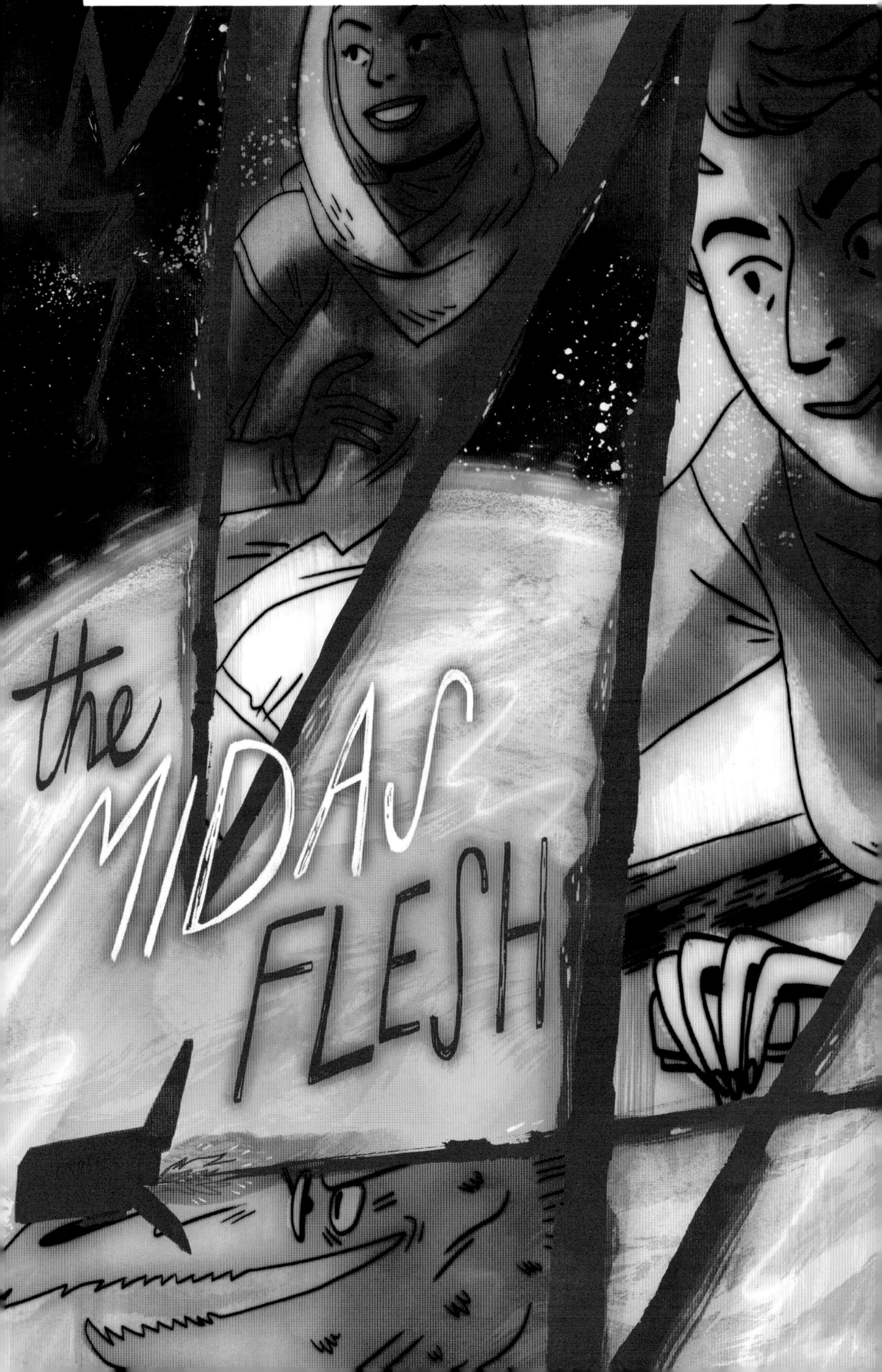
the MIDAS FLESH

ISSUE SIX **JOHN KEOGH**

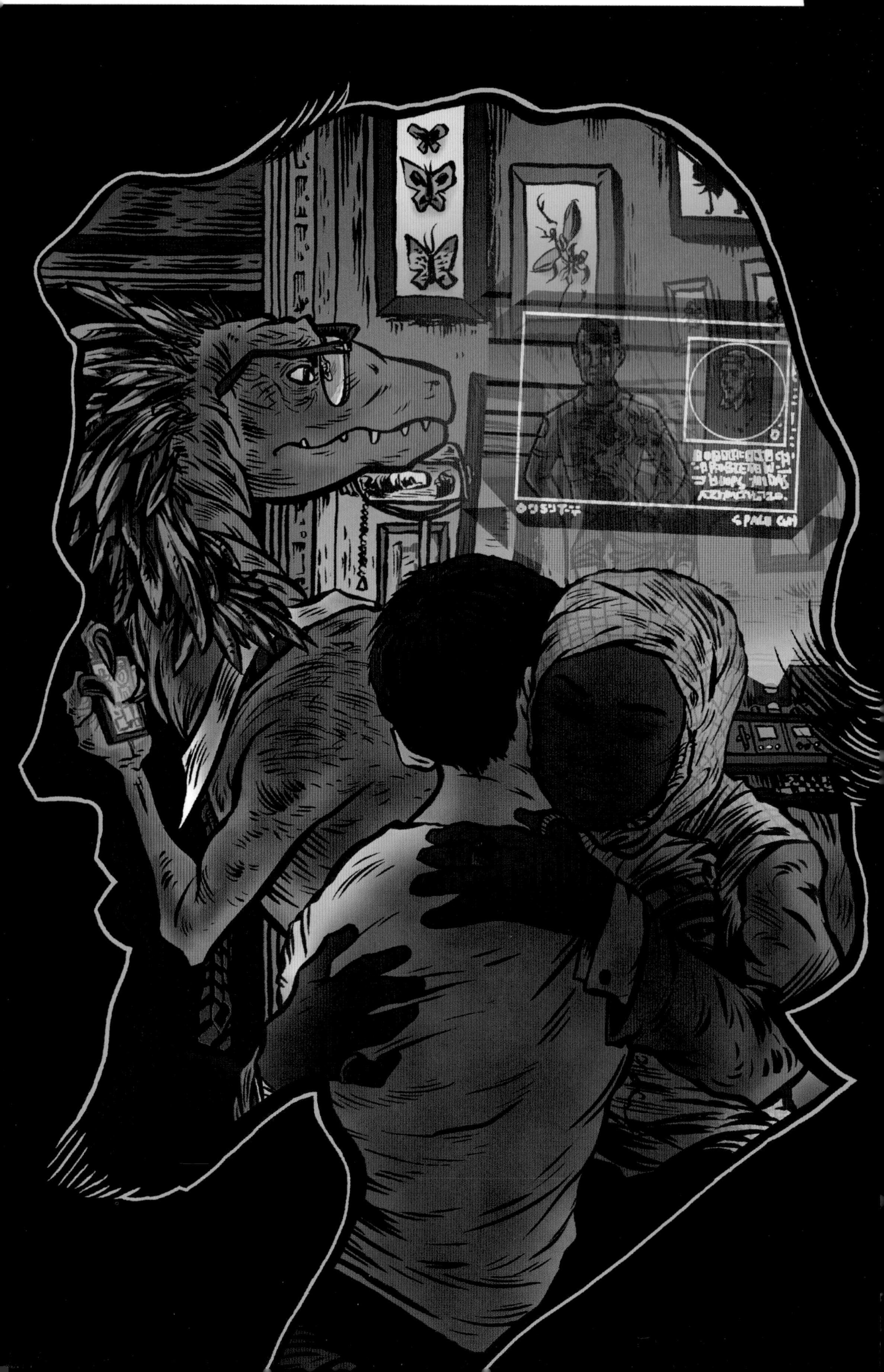

ISSUE SIX VARIANT **DAVID MALKI**

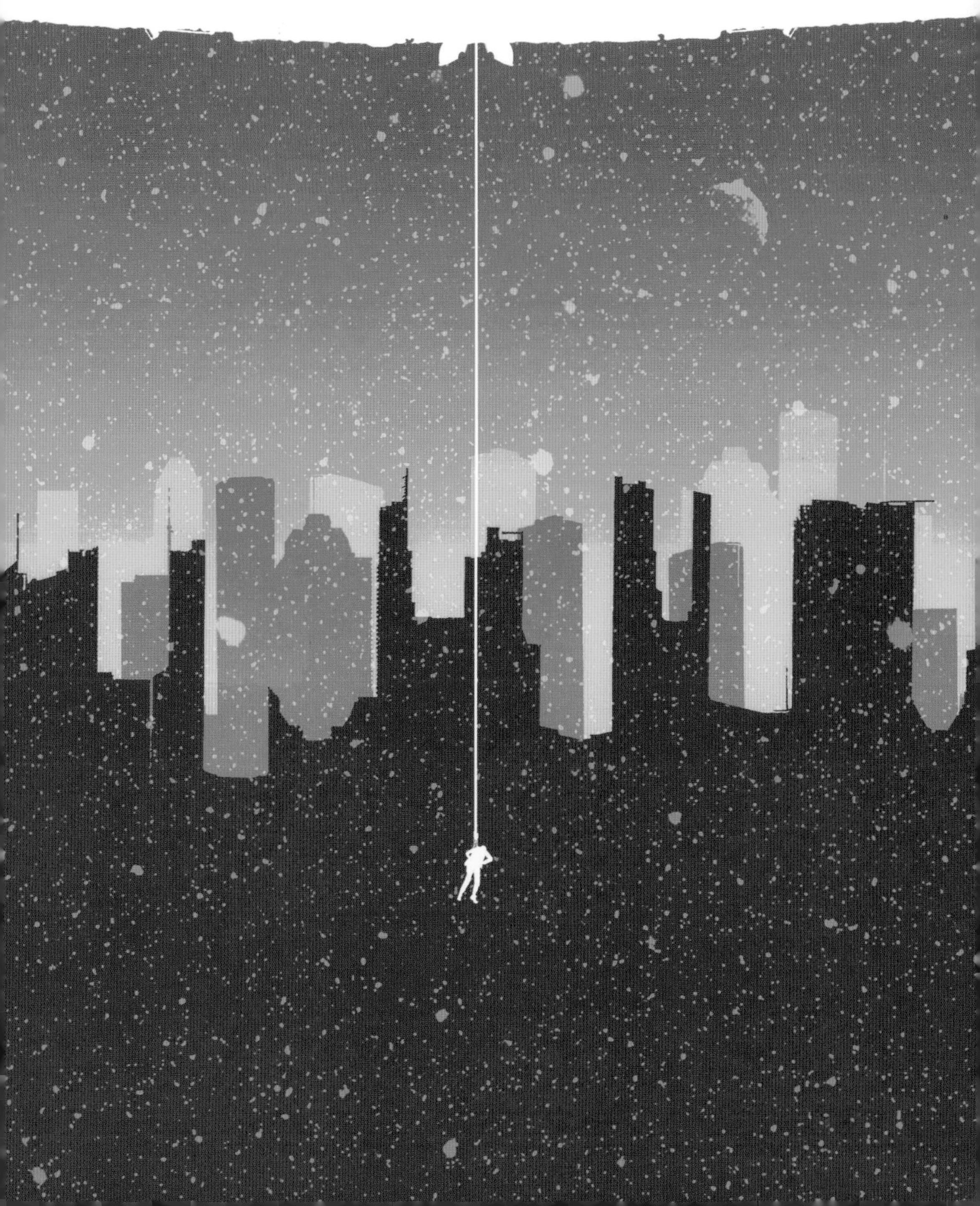

ISSUE SEVEN **JOHN KEOGH**

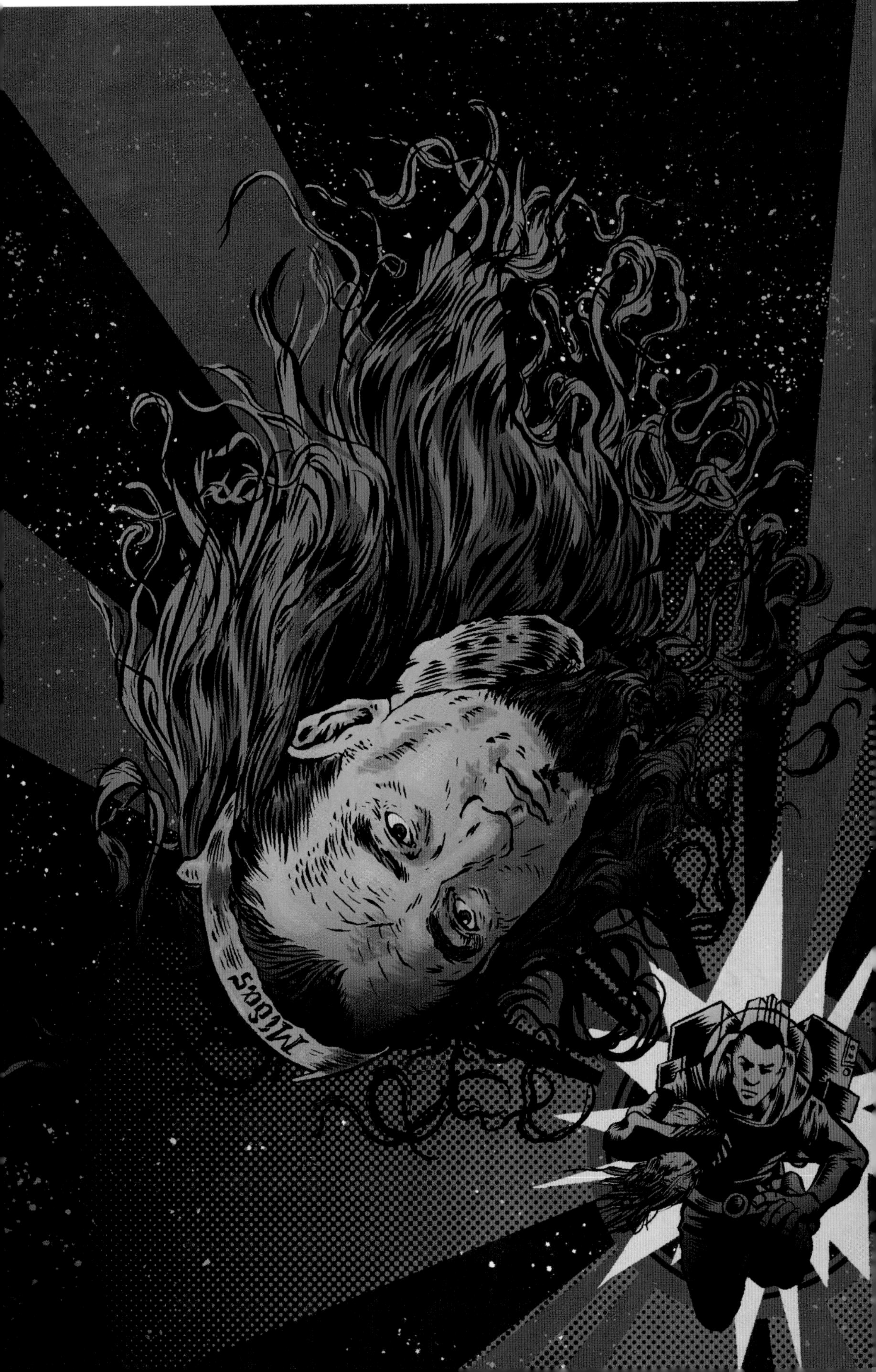

ISSUE SEVEN VARIANT **DAVID HELLMAN**

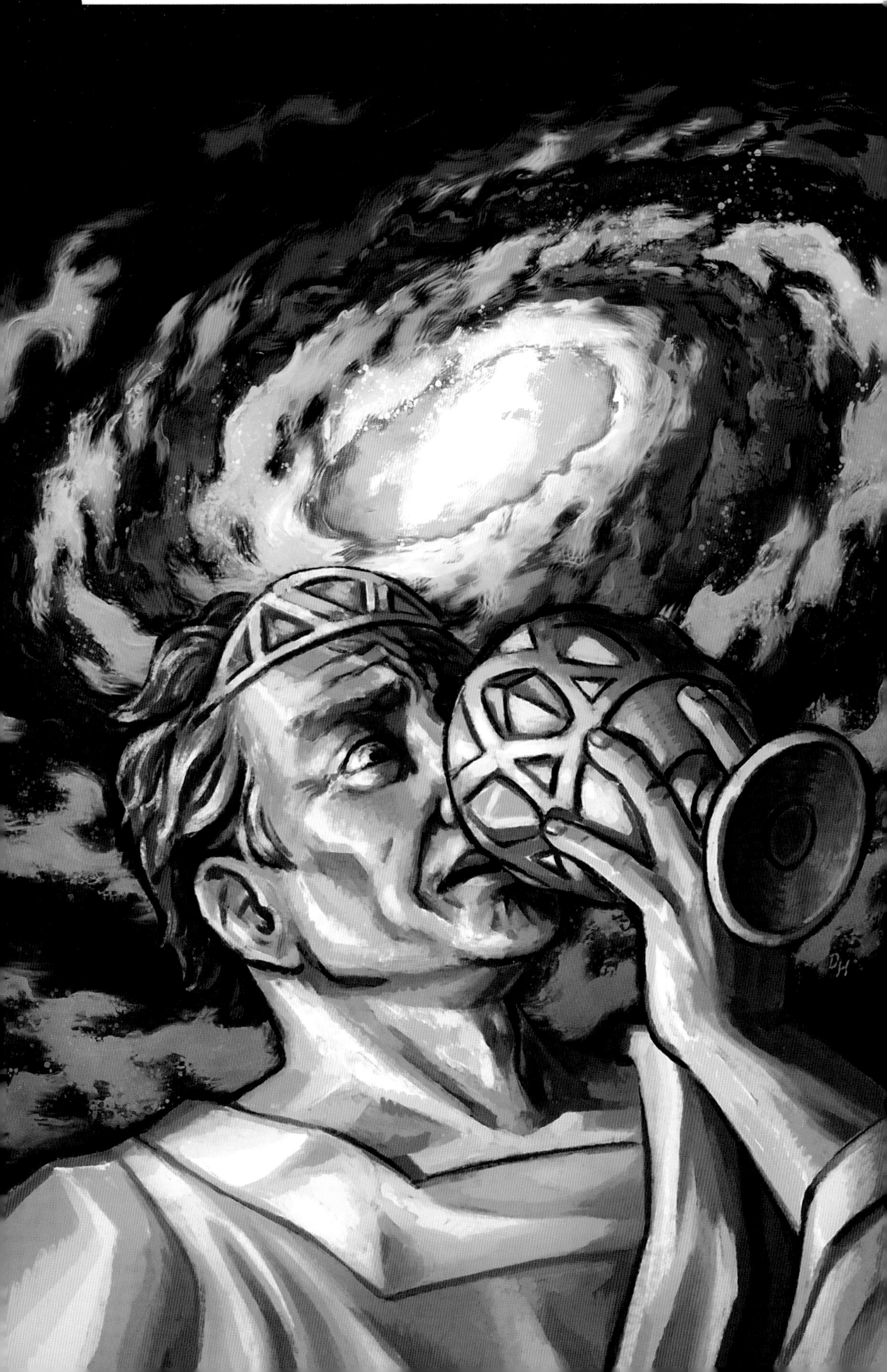
DH

ISSUE EIGHT **JOHN KEOGH**

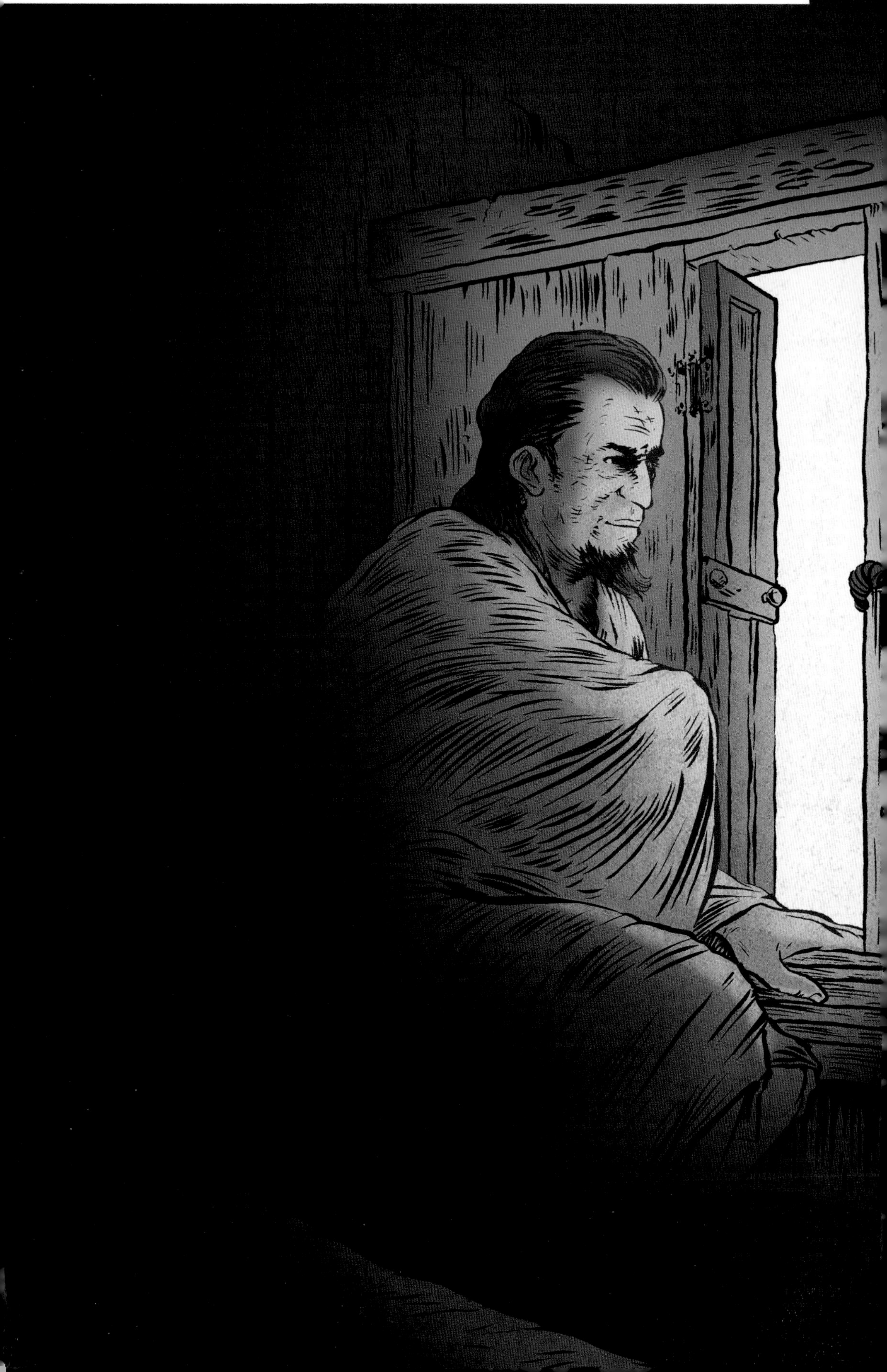

ISSUE EIGHT VARIANT **ANDREW HUSSIE & JOHN KEOGH**

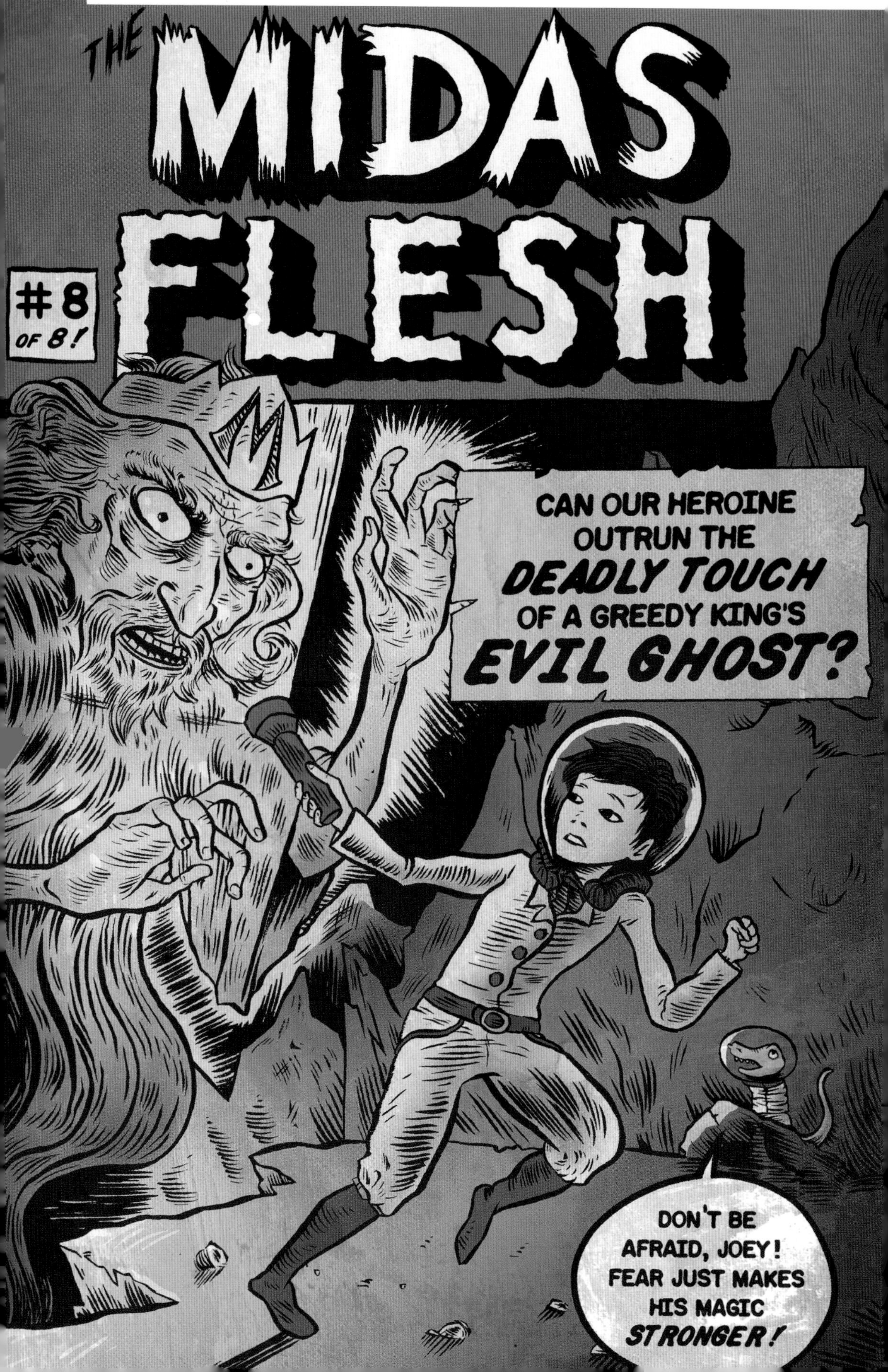
THE MIDAS FLESH
#8 OF 8!
CAN OUR HEROINE OUTRUN THE DEADLY TOUCH OF A GREEDY KING'S EVIL GHOST?
DON'T BE AFRAID, JOEY! FEAR JUST MAKES HIS MAGIC STRONGER!